FACTS

1989

A Concise Record of the Arab-Israeli Conflict

by Leonard J. Davis
editors Eric Rozenman
Jeff Rubin

Near East Report

Washington, D.C.

Distributed by the Dorothy and Harold Greenwald
Israel Resource Center by the
Zionist Organization of America as a public service.

Additional copies of Myths and Facts 1989 can
be purchased for $3.95. Bulk orders are available
at discount rates: 10-50 copies at $3.50 each;
51-100 copies at $3.00 each; more than 100 cop-
ies at $2.50 each. We will bill for postage.

Near East Report
Washington weekly on
American policy in the
Middle East

Established 1957

500 N. Capitol St., N.W.
Room 307
Washington, D.C. 20001

TABLE OF CONTENTS

Maps

Charts

Preface

This volume of *Myths and Facts* is dedicated to the memory of Isaiah L. "Si" Kenen, founder and first editor of *Near East Report* and of *Myths and Facts*. By training, Si Kenen was a lawyer, but he chose to work as a journalist, and indeed was one of the organizers of The Newspaper Guild. When he founded the American Israel Public Affairs Committee and *Near East Report* in the 1950's, he never deserted his training or first profession. He remained passionately devoted to justice and to the truth. *Myths and Facts* is the result.

Those who worked with Si Kenen saw another profession: he was a teacher. Weekly, as his young staff filed their articles for *Near East Report*, he would invite us to his desk as he edited, carved and sculpted the paragraphs that went into each edition. Throughout the process, he patiently explained and taught, willing to listen if we argued for the survival of a bon mot or a favorite phrase.

Since Si Kenen's first editions of *Myths and Facts*, other editors have continued to mold the publication from a 28-page booklet to its present form. This edition's editors, Eric Rozenman and Jeff Rubin, were confronted with some of the most difficult propaganda claims, and for their efforts I give them my thanks.

For their past contributions, I wish to acknowledge previous editors, Sheila F. Segal, Wolf Blitzer, Alan Tigay, Moshe Decter, and M. J. Rosenberg. This new edition still contains large segments written by Aaron David Rosenbaum, and I thank him for his contribution. Over the years, the research and data collection have been carried out by able research assistants, Minette Perler Warnick, Harriet P. Leon, Robin Schwartz, Cheryl Kritz, Frandee Wolf, Susan Werman, Nancy Shekter, Todd Winer and Mimi Birke. I would like to thank Carmella Baccari, Joan Dine, Todd Warnick, and especially Shellie Davis, for their assistance. Special thanks go to Esther Chesney, who helped produce the first volume of *Myths and Facts* and has contributed to every subsequent edition.

In an early edition of *Myths and Facts*, Si Kenen warned: "Ever since the State of Israel was established in 1948, the Arab states have waged war against her on four fronts: military, diplomatic, economic and propaganda. Punctuating the gunfire, there has been a never-ending propaganda fusillade to capture world opinion and to isolate Israel."

The battle continues.

Leonard J. Davis

1

The Right To Exist

MYTH

"Israel is an artificial entity created by the United Nations and has no right to exist."

FACT

For years much anti-Israel rhetoric invariably has begun by claiming that Israel has no right to exist as a sovereign Jewish state.

Israel, in fact, has a continuous history more ancient than that of most other nations. Its international "birth certificate" was validated by the promise of the Bible; uninterrupted Jewish settlement from the time of Joshua onward; the British Balfour Declaration of 1917; the League of Nations Mandate, which incorporated the Balfour Declaration; the UN partition resolution of 1947; Israel's admission to the UN in 1949; the recognition of Israel by most other states; and, most of all, the society created by Israel's people in decades of thriving, dynamic national existence.

Abba Eban on the right to exist:

"Nobody does Israel any service by proclaiming its 'right to exist.'

"Israel's right to exist, like that of the United States, Saudi Arabia and 152 other states, is axiomatic and unreserved. Israel's legitimacy is not suspended in midair awaiting acknowledgement. . . .

"There is certainly no other state, big or small, young or old, that would consider mere recognition of its 'right to exist' a favor, or a negotiable concession. . . ."

—*The New York Times*, November 15, 1981

The Jewish people have maintained ties to their historic homeland for more than 3,700 years. A national language and a distinct civilization have been maintained. The re-

1

turn to Israel has continued throughout the centuries, and 78 years of nation-building, beginning in 1870, culminated with the reestablishment of a Jewish state.

MYTH

"Zionism is racism."

FACT

Zionism is the national liberation movement of the Jewish people. It is a modern realization of a 1,900-year-old dream to rebuild Israel after the destruction by Rome of the Second Temple in 70 C.E. and expulsion of many of the Jews. History has demonstrated the need to ensure Jewish security through a national homeland. Zionism recognizes that Jewishness is defined by shared religion, culture, and history. More than 3.6 million Jews of all colors and from more than 100 countries are represented in Israel's population. Over 700,000 Moslem and Christian Arabs, Druze, Baha'is, Circassians and other ethnic groups also are citizens of Israel.

Many Christians have traditionally supported the goals and ideals of Zionism. Israel's open and democratic character and its scrupulous protection of the religious and political rights of Christians and Moslems rebut the charge of exclusivity.

The rights of every religious community are guaranteed by Israeli law. In contrast, nearly every Arab state proclaims Islam as the state religion, and minority groups are harassed or oppressed.

Although Israel's Law of Return grants immediate citizenship to all Jews requesting it, Israeli citizenship laws for non-Jews are more liberal than those of the United States and most other Western states. The Arab states define citizenship strictly by native parentage. It is almost impossible to become a naturalized citizen in many Arab states, especially Algeria, Saudi Arabia and the Gulf sheikdoms. Many other Arab states have laws that facilitate the naturalization of foreign Arabs with the specific exception of Palestinian Arabs.

The covert rescue of more than 8,000 black Ethiopian Jews—facing oppression and famine—by Israel between Nov. 1984 and March 1985 in "Operation Moses" demonstrated conclusively the absence of racial considerations in Zionist ideology. More than 15,000 Ethiopian Jews now live in Israel, out of a remaining Ethiopian Jewish population of approximately 25,000. After their traumatic escape and sometimes difficult absorption, these members of "Beta-Israel"—the House of Israel, as they refer to themselves—are home.

MYTH

"The Zionists could have chosen another country besides Palestine."

FACT

In the late nineteenth century, the rise of religious and racist anti-Semitism led to a resurgence of pogroms in Russia and Eastern Europe, shattering promises of equality and tolerance. This stimulated Jewish immigration to Palestine from Europe.

At the same time, there was a parallel wave of Jewish immigration to Palestine from Yemen, Morocco, Iraq and Turkey. These Jews were unaware of Theodor Herzl's political Zionism or of European pogroms. They were motivated by the centuries-old religious dream of the "Return to Zion" and a fear of Arab intolerance. Upon hearing that the gates of Palestine were open, they braved the hardship of travel and went to the "Land of Israel".

In 1897, Jewish leaders formally organized the Zionist movement, calling for the restoration of the Jewish national home, where Jews could find sanctuary and self-determination and work for the renascence of their civilization and culture.

The Zionist ideal of a return to Israel has profound religious roots. Many Jewish prayers speak of Jerusalem, Zion and the Land of Israel. The injunction not to forget Jerusalem is a major tenet of Judaism. Jewish religion, culture and history, then, require that only in the land of Israel can the Jewish commonwealth be rebuilt.

3

MYTH

"The Balfour Declaration was a British plot to stifle Arab nationalism."

FACT

Zionist leaders appealed to the Turkish government to facilitate Jewish settlement in Palestine, but in vain. During World War I, many Jews were forced to leave Palestine by the harsh Ottoman regime. In 1917, Britain issued the Balfour Declaration:

> "His Majesty's Government views with favour the establishment in Palestine of a national home for the Jewish people, and will use their best endeavours to facilitate the achievement of this object, it being clearly understood that nothing shall be done which may prejudice the civil and religious rights of existing non-Jewish communities in Palestine or the rights and political status enjoyed by Jews in any other country."

The Balfour Declaration won the approval of the United States and other Western powers. At first, there was hope that Arabs also would accept it. Emir Faisal, son of the acknowledged leader of the Arabs, Sherif Hussein, met with Dr. Chaim Weizmann and other Zionist leaders during the 1919 Paris Peace Conference. They signed an agreement which, "mindful of the racial kinship and racial bonds existing between the Arab and the Jewish people," declared that "the surest means of working out the consummation of their national aspirations is through the closest possible collaboration of the development of the Arab state and Palestine."

The agreement looked to the fulfillment of the Balfour Declaration and also called for all necessary measures ". . . to encourage and stimulate immigration of Jews into Palestine on a large scale, and as quickly as possible to settle Jewish immigrants upon the land through closer settlement and extensive cultivation of the soil."

On March 3, 1919, one day after Weizmann presented the Zionist case to the peace conference, Faisal wrote to Felix Frankfurter, a noted Harvard law professor and Zionist leader, declaring:

4

"The Arabs, especially the educated among us, look with deepest sympathy on the Zionist movement. . . . We will wish the Jews a hearty welcome home. . . . We are working together for a reformed and revised Near East and our two movements complete one another. The Jewish movement is nationalist and not imperialist. Our movement is nationalist and not imperialist. And there is room in Syria for us both. [*Under Turkish rule, Syria included part of Palestine.*] Indeed, I think that neither can be a real success without the other."

T. E. Lawrence ("Lawrence of Arabia"), the champion of Arab nationalism who had arranged the meeting, prophesied in 1920 that the success of Zionist settlement "will involve inevitably the raising of the present Arab population to their own material level, only a little after themselves in point of time, and the consequences might be of the highest importance for the future of the Arab world."

Faisal had conditioned his acceptance on the fulfillment of British wartime promises to the Arabs, who had hoped for independence in a vast part of the Ottoman empire.

But these hopes were temporarily dashed when the French took over the mandate for Syria, ejecting Faisal, who had been proclaimed king of Syria. As consolation, the British named Faisal king of Iraq. And, in a further effort to placate the Arabs, Colonial Secretary Winston Churchill cut away four-fifths of Palestine—some 35,000 square miles—creating a brand new Arab entity, Transjordan, and installed Faisal's brother, Abdullah, as emir. Britain administered Transjordan until 1946, when independence was granted. This apportionment—the first partition of Palestine and of the promised Jewish National Home—was a blow to the Zionists, but they most reluctantly accepted it, as the British simultaneously took over the League of Nations Mandate for Palestine in 1922. *(See accompanying map.)*

It should be emphasized that Arab hopes for a vast empire have since been realized. Today the Arab world includes 21 separate Arab states spanning an area of more than five million square miles with a population estimated at 188 million.

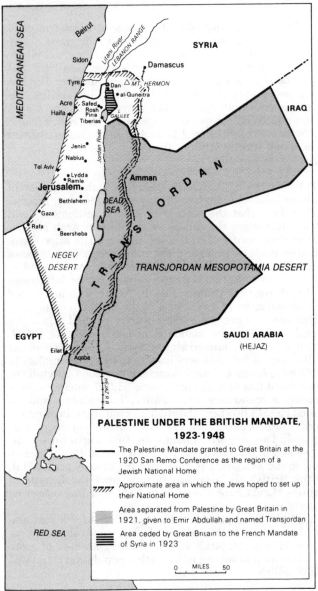

MEDITERRANEAN SEA

Beirut

SYRIA

Sidon

Litani River

LEBANON RANGE

Damascus

Tyre

MT. HERMON

Dan
al-Quneitra

Acre
Safed
Rosh
Pina
Tiberias

Haifa

L.
GALILEE

IRAQ

Jenin

Jordan River

Nablus

Tel Aviv

Lydda
Ramle

Amman

Jerusalem

DEAD
SEA

T R A N S J O R D A N

Bethlehem

Gaza

Rafa

Beersheba

NEGEV
DESERT

TRANSJORDAN MESOPOTAMIA DESERT

EGYPT

SAUDI ARABIA
(HEJAZ)

Eilat

Aqaba

HEJAZ R.R.

RED SEA

PALESTINE UNDER THE BRITISH MANDATE,
1923-1948

The Palestine Mandate granted to Great Britain at the
1920 San Remo Conference as the region of a
Jewish National Home

Approximate area in which the Jews hoped to set up
their National Home

Area separated from Palestine by Great Britain in
1921, given to Emir Abdullah and named Transjordan

Area ceded by Great Britain to the French Mandate
of Syria in 1923

0   MILES   50

Based on Howard M. Sachar, *A History of Israel*, Alfred A. Knopf, 1979.

6

MYTH

"Israel was established to serve Western imperialism and colonialism."

FACT

Israel was established by Jews—from all over the world—who began returning to their historic homeland in large numbers during the 19th century. In most instances, the British and French governments attempted to block Jewish settlement in Palestine for imperialistic reasons.

Despite their administrative obligation under the League of Nations Mandate, the British adopted a pro-Arab policy designed to prevent the establishment of the Jewish state. Britain put its military bases in the Arab states—not in the Jewish homeland.

Arabs met Jewish immigration with terrorism and violence in 1920, 1929 and throughout the 1930's. Jews sought to defend themselves but the sporadic assaults by the Arabs against Jews accomplished their objective—to intimidate the British into restricting Jewish immigration and land purchases.

British historian Paul Johnson in his 1983 book, *Modern Times*, writes: "The notion that Israel was created by imperialism is not only wrong but the reverse of the truth. Everywhere in the west the foreign offices, defense ministries and big business were against the Zionists."

MYTH

"The British helped the Jews displace the native Arab population of Palestine."

FACT

Quite the contrary. The British government drastically limited Jewish immigration into Palestine in 1921, 1929, and finally 1939. Britain severely restricted Jews from purchasing land on a large scale, even at exorbitant prices. Yet, at the same time, Arabs from Egypt and Syria freely entered the Mandate to take advantage of the higher wages and living standards generated by Jewish settlement. According to British census figures, Arab population rose by 75.2%, as compared with a 25% increase in populous Egypt. Between World War I and World War II, the Jewish population in

Palestine rose by 375,000; the non-Jewish population rose by 380,000.

Significantly, the Arab increase was largest in areas of intensive Jewish development. The Arab population increased by 216% in Haifa, 134% in Jaffa and 90% in Jerusalem. In contrast, the Arab population had much smaller increases where there was an absence of Jewish development: 42% in Nablus, 40% in Jenin, 32% in Bethlehem. (*Arab Immigration into Pre-State Israel, 1922-1931* by Fred M. Gottheil and *Palestine Royal Commission Report, 1937*, p. 279.)

The Arab immigration was undoubtedly even larger than official statistics show because these figures do not reflect the influx of Arabs who crossed into Palestine without immigration formalities. Indirect confirmation of the influx was provided by the United Nations Relief and Works Agency (UNRWA), established to assist Arabs displaced by the 1948 Arab-Israeli war. Juliana Geran Pilon, senior policy analyst at the Heritage Foundation, noted in a 1985 paper, "How UNRWA Has Failed the Palestinian Refugees," that the agency had no adequate record of the Palestinian Arab population in 1948 and found it difficult to define a refugee. "The listing of nonexistent persons and widespread duplication became routine." UNRWA ultimately defined a refugee as "a needy person whose normal residence was Palestine for a minimum of *two years* preceding the outbreak of the conflict of 1948 . . ." (emphasis added).

According to Pilon, "one reason for the very short minimal resdence requirement is that a large number of Arabs had come to Palestine only after 1934 when Jews began arriving in the area in increasing numbers." Joan Peters examined this phenomenon in *From Time Immemorial: The Origins of the Arab-Jewish Conflict Over Palestine*, Harper & Row, 1984. She showed that Jews did not displace Arabs but that Jewish settlement and subsequent economic development attracted Arab immigration.

Britain fought the drive for Jewish statehood in Palestine as a threat to its empire and its relations with the Arabs. British anti-Jewish policies climaxed in 1939 with the infamous White Paper, which ordered that future Jewish immigration be limited to 10,000 a year for five years and to an additional 25,000 refugees from Nazism—75,000 in all. Jews would be allowed to buy land in only 5% of the coun-

8

try. At the end of 10 years, there would be an independent state—an Arab state.

Thus, at a time when Jewish need was greatest, when Hitler was threatening the extermination of the Jews of Europe and when doors were closing all over the world, the British government announced a policy which all but shut Palestine's gates and which would have ended any possibility of the establishment of a Jewish state.

When British troops left Palestine on the eve of Israel's independence, they turned over strategic positions and military materiel to the Arabs.

MYTH

"Palestine was always an Arab country."

Chronology 1936-1949

1936-1939
Arab terrorism against Palestinian Jews. 517 Jews murdered.
May 17, 1939
British issue the White Paper restricting immigration and land purchase in Palestine for five years.
1939-1945
World War II. Six million Jews murdered by Nazis in Europe.
1940-1945
Palestinian Jews join allied forces to fight the Nazis; British refuse immigration to Jewish survivors from Europe.
May 1942
"Biltmore Program" calling for creation of a Jewish state adopted by American Zionist Conference in New York.
June 29, 1946
"Black Sabbath"—British invade the Jewish Agency in Jerusalem, confiscate secret documents, arrest 2,500, and hang seven members of the Irgun.
July 22, 1946
Irgun blows up the King David Hotel, site of British military headquarters, after issuing warning.
April 1947
British government turns Palestine problem over to the UN.
July 1947
British attempt to return *Exodus 1947*, a boatload of 4,500 Jewish refugees, to France. Jews are finally interned in British-occupied zone of Germany.

FACT

Even after the destruction of the Temple in Jerusalem and the beginning of the exile, Jewish life in Palestine continued and often flourished. Large Jewish communities were reestablished in Jerusalem and Tiberias by the ninth century. In the 11th century, Jewish communities grew in Rafah, Gaza, Ashkelon, Jaffa and Caesarea. Many Palestinian Jews were massacred by the Crusaders during the 12th century, but the chronicles (1167) of the famous traveller, Benjamin of Tudela, Spain, nevertheless reported Jews throughout the region.

From the 13th through 15th centuries, large numbers of rabbis and Jewish pilgrims immigrated to Jerusalem and

---

November 29, 1947

UN Special Committee on Palestine recommends partition of Palestine into two independent states: Arab and Jewish. British refuse to help implement the decision.

January 1948

First detachments from Arab Liberation Army enter Palestine from Syria and Jordan to attack Jewish villages.

April 9, 1948

To end blocade of Jerusalem and Arab attacks on Jewish convoys, Irgun and Stern groups attack Deir Yassin. Attack is condemned by Jewish Agency.

April 13, 1948

Arab massacre of Hadassah Hospital employees on their way to Mount Scopus Hospital. 78 Jews killed.

May 12, 1948

Arabs attack Kfar Etzion, 100 Jews killed.

May 14, 1948

State of Israel proclaimed. Declaration of Independence signed.

May 15, 1948

Armies of Egypt, Transjordan, Iraq, Syria, Lebanon and Saudi Arabia attack Israel. Eight months of warfare ensue.

January-July 1949

Armistice agreements signed with Egypt, Lebanon, Transjordan and Syria.

1949-1967

Jordan bars Israeli access to holy sites in East Jerusalem.

May 14, 1949

Israel admitted to the United Nations.

the Galilee. Prominent rabbis established communities in Safed, Jerusalem, and elsewhere during the next 300 years. By the early 19th century—years before the birth of the modern Zionist movement—there were many thousands of Jews living throughout Palestine. (See *The Forgotten Generations* by Dan Bahat.)

Palestine was never an exclusively Arab country, although Arabic gradually became the language of a majority of the population after the Arab invasions of the seventh century. There never was an Arab state in Palestine, and there never was a separate Palestinian Arab nation. Palestinian Arab nationalism is largely a post-World War I phenomenon, its growth accelerating mostly *after* the 1967 Six-Day War.

Palestinian Arabs never created their own self-contained unit nor any form of separate political or social identity. They were not autonomous at any time. In many respects, Palestinian Arab nationalism resembles, as Harold Fisch wrote in *The Zionist Revolution,* "a strange imitation of the doctrine of Jewish nationhood," an anti-Zionism whose original impulse was to destroy Israel, not to build a comparable state for Palestinian Arabs.

MYTH

"The West settled Jews in Palestine at the expense of the Arabs, in order to relieve its conscience over the failure of the democracies to stave off Hitler's extermination of Jews."

FACT

The 1917 Balfour Declaration and other formal and informal expressions of Western support for the Jewish state long preceded Hitler.

It was the Arabs who terrorized Jews in Palestine and who pressured the British to keep the Jews out—before the Nazis took power. And when Hitler did emerge, Arabs supported him. The leader of the long, anti-Jewish Arab campaign in Palestine was the Mufti of Jerusalem, Haj Amin el Husseini, the Islamic leader, who openly collaborated with Hitler during World War II.

"The Germans," Husseini said admiringly at a November 1943 rally in Berlin, "know how to get rid of the Jews." The Mufti sent several letters to high Nazi officials, including one to Heinrich Himmler on July 27, 1944, urging Germany "to do all that is necessary to prohibit the emigration of Jews to Palestine."

Documents presented at the 1946 Nuremberg trials testified to the Mufti's complicity.

MYTH

"Palestine was a fertile agricultural land before the Zionists arrived."

FACT

For many centuries, Palestine was a sparsely populated, poorly cultivated and widely-neglected expanse of eroded hills, sandy deserts, and malarial marshes. Its ancient irrigation systems had crumbled. Its forests were cut down.

The Report of the Palestine Royal Commission quotes an account of the Maritime Plain in 1913:

> "The road leading from Gaza to the north was only a summer track suitable for transport by camels and carts . . . no orange groves, orchards or vineyards were to be seen until one reached Yabna [Yavne] village. . . . Houses were all of mud. No windows were anywhere to be seen. . . . The ploughs used were of wood. . . . The yields were very poor. . . . The sanitary conditions in the village were horrible. Schools did not exist. . . . The western part, towards the sea, was almost a desert. . . . The villages in this area were few and thinly populated. Many ruins of villages were scattered over the area, as owing to the prevalence of malaria, many villages were deserted by their inhabitants."

Mark Twain, who visited Palestine in 1867, described it as:

"... [a] desolate country whose soil is rich enough, but is given over wholly to weeds—a silent mournful expanse. ... A desolation is here that not even imagination can grace with the pomp of life and action. ... We never saw a human being on the whole route. ... There was hardly a tree or a shrub anywhere. Even the olive and the cactus, those fast friends of a worthless soil, had almost deserted the country." *(The Innocents Abroad.)*

Lewis French, Director of Development named by the British Government, in 1931, wrote:

> "We found it inhabited by fellahin who lived in mud hovels and suffered severely from the prevalent malaria. . . . Large areas . . . were uncultivated. . . . The fellahin, if not themselves cattle thieves, were always ready to harbor these and other criminals. The individual plots . . . changed hands annually. There was little public security, and the fellahin's lot was an alternation of pillage and blackmail by their neighbors, the Bedouin."

The regeneration of Palestine, and the growth of its population, came only after Jews returned in massive numbers.

MYTH

"Jews bought land from poor Arabs at bargain prices."

FACT

At the end of World War I, some of Palestine's land was owned by absentee landlords who lived in Cairo, Damascus and Beirut. About 80% of the Palestinian Arabs were debt-ridden peasants, semi-nomads and Bedouins.

Analyses of land purchases from 1880 to 1948 show that 73% of Jewish plots were purchased from large landowners, not poor fellahin. (A. Granott, *The Land System in Palestine*, London, 1952.)

Most of the land purchased had not been cultivated previously because it was swampy, rocky, sandy or, for some other reason, regarded as uncultivable. According to the Peel Commission (1937):

> "The Arab charge that the Jews have obtained too large a proportion of good land cannot be maintained. Much of the land now carrying orange groves was sand dunes or swamp and uncultivated when it was purchased . . . there was at the time at least of the earlier sales little evidence that the owners possessed either the resources or training needed to develop the land."

Moreover, British policy encouraged Arab settlement on potentially fertile state lands and barred Jews.

The Peel Commission stated that in only three years, 1933-1935, Jews paid 4,202,180 British pounds (more than $20 million at 1936 exchange rates) to Arab landowners,

13

mostly estate-holders. Moshe Aumann, in his *Land Owner-ship in Palestine, 1880-1948*, wrote:

> "In 1944, Jews paid between $1,000 and $1,100 per acre in Palestine, mostly for arid or semi-arid land; in the same year, rich black soil in Iowa was selling for about $110 per acre (U.S. Department of Agriculture)."

MYTH

"Arabs were displaced by Jewish settlement."

FACT

British inquiries showed that these complaints were groundless. After one such investigation, the British offered new lands to allegedly displaced Arabs. Only 347 peasants, out of scores of thousands who lived undisturbed on the land, took advantage of the offer. (*Government of Palestine Memoranda*, London, 1937, Colonial No. 133, p. 37.)

In fact, when large-scale Jewish immigration began, there was a shortage of labor, and many thousands of Arabs from Transjordan, Syria and Iraq were able to get work in Palestine.

MYTH

"Most of the area of Israel was Arab owned."

FACT

According to British government statistics, prior to the establishment of the state, 8.6% of the land area now known as Israel was owned by Jews; 3.3% by Arabs who remained there; 16.5% by Arabs who left the country. More than 70% of the land was owned by the government. Under international law, ownership passed to Israel in 1948. The public lands included most of the Negev Desert—half of Palestine's post-1922 total area. (*Survey of Palestine, 1946*, British Mandate Government, p. 257.)

MYTH

"The establishment of the Jewish state violated the right of the Palestinian Arabs to self-determination."

FACT

In 1947, the UN had offered self-determination to both Arabs and Jews in western Palestine. Both had been offered their own separate state. Palestinian Arabs could have created their own state in the portion allotted to them under partition at any time. The Arabs unanimously rejected this offer, and the partition boundaries were erased by the Arab invasion. It was the Arab states—not the Jews—who destroyed the proposed Arab Palestine—as they sought to grab all the territory for themselves.

Ironically, the only group in the Middle East which actively *supported* the creation of a Palestinian Arab state was the Palestinian Jewish community, by virtue of its support for the UN partition resolution.

In the 1948 War of Independence, part of what was designated as Arab Palestine was seized by Transjordan in the east (the West Bank and east Jerusalem) and by Egypt on the southwest coast (Gaza). Israeli forces captured western Galilee, which had been used as a base by Arab irregulars. The Israelis opened a new road from the Mediterranean coast to bring food and water to beseiged Jerusalem.

MYTH

"Arabs formed a majority of the population in Palestine."

FACT

At the time of the 1947 partition resolution, the Arabs did have a majority in western Palestine as a whole. *But the Jews were in a majority in the area allotted to them by the resolution.*

However, it should be stressed that a major reason for the Arab majority was that many thousands came from neighboring Arab countries to find work, opportunity and education in the area, which was undergoing rapid development because of Zionist settlement. Prior to the mandate in 1922, Palestine's Arab population had been declining. After 1922, Arabs began to come from Syria, Iraq, Lebanon, Transjordan and Egypt. Evidence of this migration can be seen even today on the West Bank. Two of the most prominent families in the region are the Ja'abari and Masri clans.

Ja'abar is the name of a village in Iraq and *masri* is Arabic for Egyptian.

The population increase was partly attributable to better health conditions in Jewish Palestine. The recorded Moslem infant mortality rate fell from 19.6% in 1922 to 14% in 1939. During that period, the non-Jewish population in the country soared by 75.2%.

The Arabs were free to come but Jewish immigration was restricted and later denied. Jews might have become a majority in all of Palestine if they had been permitted to enter the country as the League of Nations Mandate contemplated and had they not been barred by Arab and British obstruction. Hundreds of thousands of Jews who might have found refuge in Palestine were murdered by the Nazis. Because of this catastrophe, what would have been the Jewish "majority" in Palestine never arrived.

MYTH

"Israel's extensive racism can be seen in its trade with South Africa."

FACT

Israel, like all nations, wants relations with as many countries as possible. Like the United States and scores of other countries, Israel maintains trade and diplomatic relations with South Africa. But in no way does that translate to support of the racial policies of the South African government.

Israel's President Chaim Herzog reiterated his country's early opposition to South Africa's official racial segregation policy when he told the president of Liberia in Aug. 1983, "Israel and its government have consistently condemned publicly the policy of apartheid, and I take this opportunity to express once more our abhorrence of apartheid and of any form of racism wherever it may occur."

Israel's economic trade with South Africa is minuscule in comparison to the trade between South Africa and Europe, the United States, Arab countries and even black African states. A 1987 U.S. State Department report to Congress— and analyses by the Defense Market Intelligence Survey and Stockholm International Peace Research Institute—showed that France, Great Britain and West Germany, and to a lesser extent Switzerland and the Netherlands, violated the UN arms trading embargo on South Africa. Exclusive focus on Israel for its relatively low-level trade with Pretoria reflected an anti-Israel, not anti-South Africa agenda. In 1986 and 1987, Israel's commercial ties with South Africa totalled approximately 1% of South Africa's overall trade. Imports from Pretoria by black African states were much greater. South Africa maintains commercial relations with most of the members of the Organization of African Unity. After Israel prohibited new arms sales to South Africa in 1987, a group of U.S. House leaders called on France and Italy to take the same steps to ensure compliance with the weapons embargo. In Sept. of that year the Israeli Cabinet approved broad additional sanctions on non-military trade and cultural, athletic, scientific and other ties with Pretoria.

"It is unfair to link Israel to South Africa," former U.S. Ambassador Andrew Young argued in Sept. 1979. **"If there is a link, you must compare Britain, Germany, Japan and the United States. All of them have links with South Africa. Israel becomes a too easy scapegoat for other problems we have."**

Most of South Africa's arms come from France, Italy, and Great Britain. Jordan, it has been revealed, sold tanks, surface-to-surface missiles and jeeps to South Africa in the mid-1970's. In 1980, *The Sunday Times* of London revealed that Egypt was playing a third-party role to facilitate a French sale of armored vehicles and ground-to-air missiles to South Africa. In 1979, the paper reported, Italian missile parts were shipped to South Africa via West Germany.

South Africa also maintains extensive trade ties with the Arab world. According to the Shipping Research Bureau (SRB) in Amsterdam, South Africa receives much of its oil from Arab members of OPEC. In June 1984, the Bureau, an anti-apartheid research foundation, reported South Africa received 76% of its oil shipments in 1981 and 1982 from Saudi Arabia, Oman, and the United Arab Emirates. In

Nov. 1987, a UN intergovernmental group accused Arab oil exporting nations of "frequent and regrettable violations" of UN and Arab League embargoes on petroleum shipments to South Africa. In 1986, the SRB estimated that Persian Gulf countries provided half of South Africa's crude oil needs in 1983 and 1984. The 1987 UN study noted that, despite denials, countries like Saudi Arabia, the United Arab Emirates, Oman, Egypt and Iran—faced by a glut in the market—would rather supply oil surreptitiously than comply with embargoes.

Despite recent sensationalist stories of nuclear cooperation between Israel and South Africa, no proof whatsoever has been produced to substantiate the claim. According to a United Nations study, "Implementation of the Declaration of Denuclearization of Africa," published by the Secretary General in Sept. 1980, "Until specific examples of actual nuclear exchanges or transactions can be cited as clear evidence of such cooperation, this whole question remains in a state of uncertainty . . . [and] speculation."

In 1979, a U.S. surveillance satellite detected a mysterious flash off the coast of Africa, spurring speculation that Israel or South Africa had tested a nuclear device. No nuclear fallout was detected, however, and in 1980 a White House-appointed panel of scientists concluded that the flash was "probably not" a nuclear explosion. "Sufficient internal inconsistency [exists] to cast serious doubt whether that signal originated from a nuclear explosion," the panel stated.

Israel has had a long history of friendly relations with black African countries. But in 1973, under intense pressures from the Arab world, including threats of oil-supply interruption and even of assassination, most black African states severed their ties to Israel. From 1957 until 1973, Israel trained thousands of Africans in agriculture and economics and maintains today extensive informal relations with many African states including operation of numerous agricultural, health, and economic development programs. Beginning in 1982, Zaire, Liberia, Ivory Coast, Cameroon and Togo have renewed diplomatic relations with Israel.

MYTH

"Evidence of racism in Zionism can be found in the Israel's treatment of the Black Hebrews."

FACT

The Black Hebrew Community in Israel is a religious cult located in the Negev towns of Dimona, Arad and Mitzpeh Ramon. The vast majority of the group are American-born. The group originated in Chicago, where their leader, Ben Ami Carter, claims to have received instructions from God to lead his "people" to Israel to "claim their birthright." Carter asserts that the Black Hebrews—officially called the Original African Hebrew Nation of Jerusalem—are "true" Jews, directly descended from the Patriarchs and the 10 lost tribes.

The first Black Hebrews arrived in Israel in the late 1960's after they were expelled from Liberia. The Israeli government granted them temporary visas and helped them find housing and employment pending investigation of their Jewish identities. It was subsequently determined by the religious authorities that they were not Jews.

Members of the Black Hebrew cult continued to arrive in Israel, often remaining in the country in violation of their tourist visas. Illegal immigration and high birthrates swelled the group's size to 1,300 by June 1987, outstripping the community's resources, creating overcrowded living conditions and placing a burden on the Israeli government. On several occasions, Israeli authorities enforcing visa regulations have detained or denied entry to American black tourists suspected of membership in the Black Hebrew cult.

The Black Hebrew issue has been thoroughly investigated by an Israeli Knesset committee. In 1980, the committee issued its report, which ruled out deportation of the Black Hebrews on humanitarian grounds. The report noted the group's long tenure in Israel, its determination to stay, and the fact that some cult members were "stateless persons," having renounced their U.S. citizenship. The committee recommended granting the cult its own settlement if its leadership guaranteed not to bring in any more illegal immigrants.

Another examination of the Black Hebrew cult was undertaken by a delegation of American blacks sponsored by the A. Philip Randolph Institute and the Black Americans to Support Israel Committee (BASIC). The report concluded, "From all the evidence we have heard, including that from the Black Hebrew Community, we conclude that official racism plays no part in this sensitive problem."

Since 1977, there have been numerous accounts of Federal investigations of the Black Hebrews in the United States. In 1980, Federal agents charged that members of the cult were operating a systematic fraud and theft scheme which robbed U.S. banks of over $4 million dollars. Authorities suspect that much of the stolen money was being funnelled to cult leaders in Israel.

In 1981, the U.S. Postal Inspection Service arrested several cult members in a Washington D.C. suburb and seized 63 passports, 56 driver's licenses, 180 airline tickets, 51 checkbooks and 341 birth certificates. Also seized was a document, "Business Course 101," which detailed how to defraud credit card companies and obtain false passports.

In 1982, a joint FBI-Israeli police analysis concluded that 30 of the Black Hebrews in Israel were felons wanted in the United States. At least a dozen cult members tried to obtain U.S. passports under false names during 1983, according to U.S. State Department officials.

In 1987, the U.S. Court of Appeals in Washington, D.C. overturned the conviction of nine Black Hebrews on nearly 400 separate federal racketeering verdicts, ruling that the trial judge erred in dismissing a juror who objected to the way the law was written. The nine had been found guilty of operating "an international crime ring that trafficked in millions of dollars worth of stolen airline tickets and used bogus credit cards and worthless checks to purchase hundreds of thousands of dollars of merchandise," according to news stories. One of the men involved, Warren Brown—also known as Prince Asiel—reportedly was the leader of the sect in the United States. Yet only a few months later, all nine entered surprise guilty pleas, ending one of the longest, most expensive criminal prosecutions in District history.

Also in 1987, after a series of demonstrations outside the Israeli Embassy and B'nai Brith headquarters in Washington, and disruptions of meetings of pro-Israel organizations, Carter himself said the group would "permanently cease dissemination of all literature, statements, and articles that may be seen as anti-Semitic or anti-Zionist." And it was revealed that summer that the Israeli Ministry of Labor and Social Affairs operated a hot lunch program for 450 Black Hebrew children, most of whom seemed malnourished and vulnerable to disease as a result of the sect's dietary and medical practices.

2

Partition

MYTH

"The United Nations unjustly partitioned Palestine."

FACT

As World War II came to an end the extent of the catastrophe that had befallen the Jewish people became known. There were demands everywhere for swift action to rehabilitate and resettle those who had survived the Holocaust through the establishment of a Jewish state.

The British tried but failed to work out an agreement acceptable to both Arabs and Jews. They turned the problem over to the UN early in 1947.

The UN sent an 11-nation special commission (UNSCOP) to Palestine to investigate. None of the Great Powers was on that body.

UNSCOP found two peoples, Arabs and Jews, both claiming all the country. To satisfy the national aspirations of both peoples, UNSCOP proposed termination of the British Mandate and partition of the area into an Arab state and a Jewish state. The Jewish state was already in existence in all but name. Eager for independence, the Jews of Palestine were ready to accept a compromise—partition. But the Arabs boycotted UNSCOP.

Seven nations—Canada, Czechoslovakia, Guatemala, The Netherlands, Peru, Sweden and Uruguay—recommended partition: the establishment of two separate states, Jewish and Arab, to be joined by economic union, with a Jerusalem enclave. Three nations—India, Iran and Yugoslavia—recommended a unitary state with Arab and Jewish provinces. Australia abstained.

Arab diplomats proclaimed three "no's": no partition, no further Jewish immigration, and no Jewish state.

The *ad hoc* committee of the UN General Assembly rejected the Arab demand for a unitary Arab state, 29-12, with 14 abstentions and two absentees. World opinion strongly favored the UN partition resolution and it was adopted by a vote of 33-13, with 10 abstentions, on Nov. 29, 1947.

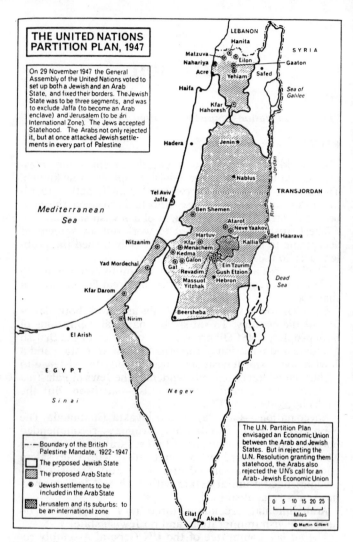

THE UNITED NATIONS PARTITION PLAN, 1947

On 29 November 1947 the General Assembly of the United Nations voted to set up both a Jewish and an Arab State, and fixed their borders. The Jewish State was to be three segments, and was to exclude Jaffa (to become an Arab enclave) and Jerusalem (to be an International Zone). The Jews accepted Statehood. The Arabs not only rejected it, but at once attacked Jewish settlements in every part of Palestine

The U.N. Partition Plan envisaged an Economic Union between the Arab and Jewish States. But in rejecting the U.N. Resolution granting them statehood, the Arabs also rejected the UN's call for an Arab-Jewish Economic Union

— · — Boundary of the British Palestine Mandate, 1922 - 1947

☐ The proposed Jewish State

▨ The proposed Arab State

◉ Jewish settlements to be included in the Arab State

▨ Jerusalem and its suburbs: to be an international zone

0 5 10 15 20 25
Miles

© Martin Gilbert

Martin Gilbert, *The Arab-Israeli Conflict Its History in Maps,* Weidenfeld and Nicolson, London, 1967.

MYTH

"The United Nations had no right to declare a Jewish state."

FACT

Under the Lausanne agreement of 1923, Turkey surrendered all claims to Palestine to the Mandatory power, Britain. The UN, as successor to the League of Nations and as the recognized power responsible for mandates, had a legal right to recommend partition when Britain asked for a recommendation in 1947.

MYTH

"Israel usurped all of Palestine in 1948."

FACT

Nearly 80% of what was the historic land of Palestine and the Jewish National Home, as defined by the League of Nations, was severed by the British in 1922 and allocated to what later became Transjordan. Jewish settlement there was barred. Britain's precipitous decision to grant Transjordan independence in 1946 did not change the Palestinian Arab nature of the majority of Transjordan's population or erase the extensive links between Transjordanian Palestine and the land west of the Jordan River.

Transjordan's independence did force an artificial redefinition of "Palestine," however, restricting it to 20% of the original Palestine Mandate. The UN partitioned this *remaining* land into two states. With Jordan's annexation of the West Bank in 1950, Palestinian Arabs (under an Arab monarchy, the Hashemites) controlled about 80% of the territory of the Mandate, while the Palestinian Jewish state held a bare 17.5% (Gaza was the remainder).

3

The War of 1948

MYTH

"Israel was the aggressor in 1948."

FACT

Throughout the 1947 UN debate, the Palestine Arab Higher Committee threatened war, while spokesmen for the Jewish Agency appealed for peace.

Jamal Husseini, the committee's spokesman, told the UN on Nov. 24, 1947: "The partition line proposed shall be nothing but a line of fire and blood."

Five days later the UN voted for the partition, and the Arabs began their war to prevent implementation of the UN resolution. Roads were mined, settlements isolated, convoys ambushed. By the end of the first week, scores of Jews had been killed.

Later, apartments in Jerusalem were blown up and more than 50 men, women and children were killed. Thirty-five Hebrew University students were massacred on a road near Jerusalem. The Jewish Agency was bombed and there were heavy casualties. A convoy was attacked on the road to the Hadassah Hospital on Mount Scopus; 78 Jewish doctors, nurses and scientists were murdered.

Trygve Lie, who was the UN Secretary General, wrote in his book, *In The Cause of Peace:*

"From the first week of December 1947, disorder in Palestine had begun to mount. The Arabs repeatedly had asserted that they would resist partition by force. They seemed to be determined to drive that point home by assaults upon the Jewish community in Palestine."

In Jan. 1948, the first detachments of the "Arab Liberation Army" entered Palestine from Syria and Jordan to attack Jewish villages.

The UN blamed the Arabs for the war. The UN Palestine Commission was blocked both by Arab opposition and British refusal to cooperate. It never went to Palestine to implement the resolution, but reported to the UN Security Council, on Feb. 16, 1948:

"Powerful Arab interests, both inside and outside Palestine, are defying the resolution of the General Assembly and are engaged in a deliberate effort to alter by force the settlement envisaged therein."

The Arabs never disclaimed responsibility. They claimed credit. Jamal Husseini told the UN Security Council on April 16, 1948:

"The representative of the Jewish Agency told us yesterday that they were not the attackers, that the Arabs had begun the fighting. We did not deny this. We told the whole world that we were going to fight."

The UN Security Council yielded to armed defiance and failed to carry out the partition resolution. The United States proposed a temporary trusteeship over Palestine, pending further negotiations. The General Assembly held a special session, but the U.S. proposal was not adopted. The UN decided to send a mediator.

The partition resolution was never suspended or rescinded. It remained in effect, and the Jewish state in Palestine, Israel, was born on May 14, as the British finally left the country. Because of the Arab rejection, the Palestinian Arab state was aborted. Six Arab armies (Egypt, Syria, Transjordan, Saudi Arabia, Lebanon and Iraq) immediately invaded Israel, expecting to sweep the Israelis into the sea.

On May 15, Azzam Pasha, Secretary General of the Arab League, said in Cairo: "This will be a war of extermination and a momentous massacre which will be spoken of like the Mongolian massacres and the Crusades."

MYTH

"Only the United States supported Israel in its war of independence."

FACT

The United States, the Soviet Union, and most other

states recognized Israel and indicted the Arabs. The United States urged a resolution charging the Arabs with a breach of the peace.

Soviet delegate Tarasenko told the Security Council on May 20, 1948:

> "We are concerned with the plain fact that a number of Palestine's neighbor states have sent their troops into Palestine. Our knowledge of that fact is not based on rumors, or on newspaper reports, but on official documents signed by the governments of those states informing the Security Council that their troops have entered Palestine. I refer, in particular, to the documents signed and sent by the governments of Egypt and Transjordan. . . .
>
> "I should like to point out in passing that none of the states whose troops have entered Palestine can claim that Palestine forms part of its territory."

Soviet Delegate Andrei Gromyko told the Security Council, May 29, 1948;

> "This is not the first time that the Arab states, which organized the invasion of Palestine, have ignored a decision of the Security Council or of the General Assembly. The USSR delegation deems it essential that the council should state its opinion more clearly and more firmly with regard to this attitude of the Arab states toward decisions of the Security Council."

Fighting ended after the Security Council threatened on July 15 to cite the Arab governments for aggression under the charter.

The Arab war to destroy Israel failed. Indeed, as a result of their aggression, the Arabs wound up with less territory than they would have had if they had accepted the partition resolution.

The Israelis suffered enormous casualties. The 650,000 Jews of 1948 Israel counted 6,000 dead, almost 1% of their population.

MYTH

"Arab troops entered Palestine only after Israel was established."

26

FACT

The Security Council debates contradict this. In graphic testimony the British Commander of Jordan's Arab Legion, Sir John Bagot Glubb, relates (*A Soldier with the Arabs*):

"Ever since January 1948, the Arabs had been endeavoring to cut the main road from Tel Aviv to Jerusalem and thereby isolate the Jewish inhabitants of the Holy City.

"Early in January, the first detachments of the Arab Liberation Army began to infiltrate into Palestine from Syria. Some came through Jordan and even through Amman. . . . They were in reality to strike the first blow in the ruin of the Arabs of Palestine. . . . The Liberation Army attempted an attack of a Jewish colony in the Jordan Valley (Feb. 15) . . . a frontal attack which ended in fiasco."

The attempt to starve Jewish Jerusalem was only one factor which led to conflict and ultimate Arab defeat. The other, according to Glubb, was that "The Arab League, under Egyptian leadership, decided to call upon its members to attack the Jews."

"The Arab governments were largely responsible for the ruin of the Palestine Arabs," Glubb added. "By raising the hopes of the latter, they made them intransigent."

MYTH

"Israel was created through terrorism. Its methods and leaders were no different than those of the Palestine Liberation Organization today."

FACT

Terrorism—assaults and bombings of civilian populations—was neither the policy nor the practice of the Haganah (the defense force of the emerging Jewish nation) and the Jewish Agency (the Palestinian Jews' governing authority). Following World War II, the Haganah, focusing on rescuing the remnants of Europe's Jews and protecting the Jews of Palestine, resorted to attacks on British *military* installations and on Arab *military* targets.

There existed several smaller splinter groups of Jewish forces which were independent of the Jewish Agency and Haganah. One of these groups, the Irgun, surrounded an

Arab village, met with armed resistance and killed Arab civilians. This was at Deir Yassin, which was a major stronghold in the Arab blockade of Jerusalem and which housed Arab soldiers.

"In his book *The Revolt*, [Menachem] Begin says that Deir Yassin was 'an important link in the chain of Arab positions enclosing Jerusalem from the West' and that its capture was a part of a strategy, agreed with Hagana, for keeping open the lines of communication between Jerusalem and the rest of the Yishuv. There seems no reason to doubt those particular statements."

—Conor Cruise O'Brien, *The Siege: The Saga of Israel and Zionism*

But Deir Yassin stands as an isolated incident, and unlike the PLO's proud claims of responsibility which followed the scores of PLO attacks against civilians, the Jewish leadership of Palestine roundly denounced and condemned the killings.

Like the Haganah, the Irgun fought against British rule of the Jewish homeland and struck at military targets. Most Palestinian Jewish forces sought to minimize civilian casualties by giving advance warning—often at the risk of their own soldiers.

MYTH

"The Irgun bombed the King David Hotel as part of a terror campaign against civilians."

FACT

The King David Hotel was the site of the British military command and the British Criminal Investigation Division. Two events led the Irgun commanders to choose the British military headquarters as a legitimate target.

On June 29, 1946, British troops invaded the Jewish Agency in Jerusalem and confiscated large quantities of documents. Simultaneously, over 2,500 Jewish leaders from all over Palestine were placed under arrest. Not only were the documents of crucial importance to the Jewish liberation movement, but papers on Jewish agents in Arab countries were also confiscated, endangering vital intelligence activities. The information was taken to the King David Hotel.

One week later, Palestinian Jewish anger against the British and their blockade of Palestine grew. Word arrived of the massacre of 40 Jews in a pogrom in Poland; 40 Jews who might have been saved had the doors to Palestine been opened for the survivors of Hitler's concentration camps.

On July 22, the Irgun planted bombs in the basement of the hotel. Several calls were placed warning the British to evacuate. They refused, and 91 British, Arabs and Jews were killed in the blast. For decades the British denied that they had been warned.

In 1979, however, a member of the British parliament introduced evidence that the Irgun had indeed issued the warning. He offered the testimony of a British officer who heard other officers in the Kind David Hotel bar joking about a Zionist threat to the headquarters. The officer who overheard the conversation immediately left the hotel and survived.

The activities of the Irgun were thus quite different from the patterns of Arafat and the PLO who attack civilians, almost exclusively, and without prior warning.

4

The 1949 Armistice Agreements and The 1956 Sinai War

MYTH

"Israel blocked peace in 1949, following the signing of the armistice agreements."

FACT

In the fall of 1948, the UN Security Council called on Israel and the Arab states to negotiate armistice agreements.

Egypt agreed, but only after the fighting had brought the Israelis to El Arish in the Sinai Peninsula. At that time the British were ready to defend the Egyptians under an Anglo-Egyptian treaty. But, rather than accept the humiliation of British assistance, the Egyptians preferred to meet the Israelis at Rhodes.

UN mediator Ralph Bunche brought them together at the conference table and later was honored with a Nobel prize. He warned that any delegation that walked out of the negotiations would be blamed for their breakdown. By the summer of 1949, armistice agreements had been negotiated between Israel and four of the Arab states—Egypt, Jordan, Lebanon and Syria. Bunche succeeded at Rhodes because he insisted on direct talks between Israel and the Arab states—one at a time.

Meanwhile, on Dec. 11, 1948, the General Assembly adopted a resolution calling on the parties to negotiate peace and creating a Palestine Conciliation Commission (PCC), which consisted of the United States, France and Turkey. All Arab delegations voted against it. The PCC failed at Lausanne because it permitted the four Arab states to come together and to refuse to talk with the Israelis directly.

After 1949, the Arabs demanded that Israel accept the borders of the 1947 resolution before they would negotiate an end to the war they had initiated.

The purpose of this debating maneuver was to portray the Arabs as the defenders of the UN and its resolutions, and to cast Israel as its violator, although the opposite had been the case.

This attempt flouted equity's requirements that petitioners come to court with clean hands. The Arab states saw no incongruity in filing a claim for what they might have had if they had not chosen war as their instrument of policy.

They offered a novel concept which they were to use in later wars: the doctrine of the limited-liability war. Under this theory, an aggressor may reject a compromise settlement and gamble on war to win everything in the comfortable knowledge that, even if he fails, he may insist on reinstating the original compromise and claim rights under it.

MYTH

"Israel was unjustified in attacking Egypt in 1956 and should be considered the aggressor."

FACT

Continued Arab aggression was the prime cause of the 1956 conflict.

Because it claimed to be in a state of belligerence with Israel, Egypt closed the Suez Canal to Israeli shipping. On Aug. 9, 1949, the UN Mixed Armistice Commission upheld Israel's complaint that Egypt was illegally blocking the canal. On Sept. 1, 1951, the Security Council ruled that Egypt could not remain in a state of belligerence and ordered Egypt to open the canal to Israeli shipping.

But Egypt refused to comply. In addition to closing the canal, Egypt installed artillery at Sharm el-Sheikh, and barred Israeli shipping through the Strait of Tiran.

Egypt stimulated and directed *fedayeen* (terrorist) border raids deep into the heart of Israeli territory, inflicting many civilian casualties.

Article III, paragraph 2, of the armistice contained a pro-

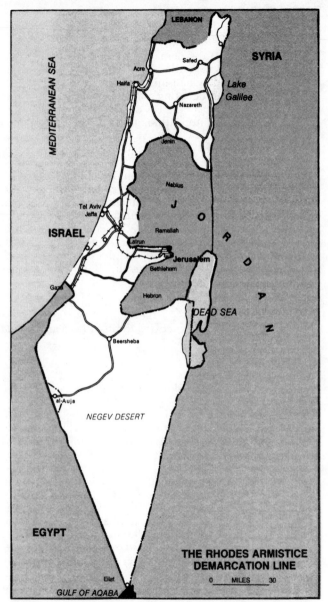

Based on Howard M. Sachar, *A History of Israel*, Alfred A. Knopf, 1979.

vision that no "paramilitary forces of either Party, including non-regular forces, shall commit any warlike or hostile act against the military or para-military forces of the other Party, or against civilians in territory under the control of that Party."

And paragraph 3 of that article stated that "no warlike act or act of hostility shall be conducted from territory controlled by one of the Parties to this Agreement against the other Party."

Ambassador Abba Eban's statement to the UN Security Council on Oct. 30, 1956, set forth the record of Egypt's continued policy of belligerency:

> "During the six years during which this belligerency has operated in violation of the Armistice Agreement there have occurred 1,843 cases of armed robbery and theft, 1,339 cases of armed clashes with Egyptian armed forces, 435 cases of incursion from Egyptian controlled territory, 172 cases of sabotage perpetrated by Egyptian military units and *fedayeen* in Israel. As a result of these actions of Egyptian hostility within Israel, 364 Israelis were wounded and 101 killed. In 1956 alone, as a result of this aspect of Egyptian aggression, 28 Israelis were killed and 127 wounded. . . ."

In 1955, Egypt began to import arms from the Soviet bloc. In 1956, Nasser nationalized the Suez Canal. The UN was unable to curb Egypt or to enforce its decision. In Oct. 1956, Nasser entered into an alliance with Jordan and stepped up *fedayeen* attacks on Israel. Israel then moved against Egypt, capturing Gaza and Sinai. She had the support of Britain and France.

Political analyst Walter Lippmann wrote at that time:

"To ignore the Egyptian raids and to treat Israel as if it were the aggressor and Egypt as if it were the innocent victim . . . was a grave mistake in policy, indefensible in principle and in fact entirely unrealistic and impracticable."

But the United States joined with the Soviet Union in a

campaign to force Israel to withdraw. There was widespread criticism of the United States because it did not, at the very least, require Egypt to renounce belligerence and to enter into peace negotiations. And Egypt soon violated its undertaking to keep the canal open for all.

The United States pressed Israel to withdraw from the Sinai in 1957 without securing any concessions for peace from Egypt. The seeds of the 1967 war thus were sown.

5

The 1967 Six-Day War

MYTH

"Israel's military strike was unprovoked."

MYTH

Israel's strike on June 5, 1967, was an inevitable response to Egypt's threatened attack. On May 22, 1967, Egypt announced a blockade of the Gulf of Aqaba, cutting off the Israeli port of Eilat. This was a violation of international agreements and an act of war by any standard. But the blockade was only one part of a buildup against Israel that had gone on for more than a year.

President Nasser had abandoned his drive for Arab unity because he wanted to organize a new radical coalition. Frustrated in his Yemen war, and provoked by a worsening economic situation, Nasser made a bitter speech in Feb. 1966, lashing out at the United States, Saudi Arabia, and Israel. He charged that Western-oriented states were forging an Islamic grouping to overthrow him.

The same week a leftist military clique affiliated with the Ba'ath Party seized power in Syria and opened a new campaign of terrorism against Israel.

"**The internal upheavals in Syria meanwhile brought to the fore extreme elements in the Ba'ath party, and the Syrians continued to send saboteurs to Israel through Jordan and Lebanon.**"

The Arab-Israeli Wars, by Chaim Herzog

The Soviets encouraged and exploited these developments. They gave new military and economic aid to the Syrians, who were in a strategic position to damage Western oil interests in Iraq, to endanger pro-Western King Hussein of Jordan, and to harass the Israelis.

The Kremlin continued to bolster Nasser with military, diplomatic and economic aid as Nasser sought to consolidate his own power and Soviet influence in Yemen and Aden (now North Yemen and South Yemen, respectively), and to subvert King Faisal in Saudi Arabia.

The Russians sought a rapprochement between Ba'athists and Nasserites, and Soviet warships sailed into the Mediterranean to shadow the U.S. Sixth Fleet.

Arab terrorist attacks grew more frequent. In 1965 there were 35 raids against Israel. In 1966 there were 41. In the first four months of 1967, there were 37. In addition, the Syrian army shelled Israeli villages from the Golan Heights.

Israel complained to the Security Council, but the Soviets protected the Syrians with their veto.

From that time on, there was no stopping the extremists. The Syrians were demanding all-out war against Israel.

Early in April the Syrians opened fire on Israeli tractors on the shore of the Sea of Galilee with machine guns, tanks and heavy mortars. Israeli planes rose to down six Syrian MiG's. Syria complained that the Egyptians had failed to come to its aid.

MYTH

"Nasser had the right to close the Strait of Tiran to Israeli shipping."

FACT

Egypt had recognized the international character of the Strait of Tiran as far back as Jan. 28, 1950, when it sent a note to the American Embassy in Cairo saying it had no intention of interfering in any way with peaceful shipping:

> "It goes without saying that this passage [through the Strait of Tiran] will remain free as in the past in conformity with international practice and with the recognized principle of international law."

In 1957, 17 maritime powers declared at the UN that Israel had a right to transit the strait. Moreover, the Convention on the Territorial Sea and Contiguous Zone, adopted by the UN Conference on the Law of the Sea on April 27, 1958, by a 62 to one vote (nine abstentions) and effective from Sept. 10, 1964, stipulated:

> "There shall be no suspension of the innocent passage of foreign ships through straits which are used for international navigation between one part of the high seas and another part of the high seas or the territorial sea of a foreign state."

Clearly, the closure of the Strait of Tiran was the *casus belli* in 1967. Any Israeli reaction thereafter was a *response* to this Egyptian first strike. President Lyndon Johnson on June 19 declared:

> "If a single act of folly was more responsible for this explosion than any other it was the arbitrary and dangerous announced decision that the Strait of Tiran would be closed. The right of innocent maritime passage must be preserved for all nations."

MYTH

"Israel committed premeditated aggression against her neighbors, catching them utterly surprised and unprepared."

FACT

On May 15, the anniversary of Israel's independence, Egyptian forces rolled into Sinai. On May 17, Cairo Radio's *Voice of the Arabs* proclaimed: "All Egypt is now prepared to plunge into total war which will put an end to Israel."

Nasser's troops occupied Sharm el-Sheikh. He insisted that UN Secretary General U Thant withdraw UN troops, and the Secretary General yielded, opening the way for an Egyptian military takeover of the Tiran Strait.

On May 18, the *Voice of the Arabs* announced:

> "As of today, there no longer exists an international emergency force to protect Israel. We shall exercise patience no more. We shall not complain any more to the UN about Israel. The sole method we shall apply against Israel is a total war which will result in the extermination of Zionist existence."

An enthusiastic echo was heard in Syria:

> "Our forces are now entirely ready not only to repulse the aggression, but to initiate the act of liberation itself, and to explode the Zionist presence in the Arab home-

land. The Syrian army, with its finger on the trigger, is united.... I, as a military man, believe that the time has come to enter into the battle of liberation." (Defense Minister Hafez Assad, later Syria's President, May 20, 1967.)

The Israelis protested the UN withdrawal. When Israel withdrew her troops from Sinai in 1957 it was on the assumption the UN emergency force would be stationed in Gaza and at Sharm el-Sheikh to prevent terrorism and to keep the Strait of Tiran open to Israeli shipping.

At this critical moment, the suggestion was made that UN emergency forces be moved over to the Israeli side of the frontier. But this would have served no purpose since UN troops would have been a long way from Sharm el-Sheikh.

U Thant flew to Cairo to ask for a breathing spell, but Nasser anticipated him with his declaration closing the strait to Israeli shipping.

Nasser knew that these drastic and provocative acts would make war "almost certain." That is what he told Field Marshal Abdul Hakim Amer (who allegedly committed suicide in Sept. 1967), according to testimony in the March 1968 trials in Cairo. And he proclaimed it to the world on May 22, when he told the Egyptian army:

"The Israeli flag shall not go through the Gulf of Aqaba.

"How to use the Star of David . . . " (Iraqi daily "Al-Manar", June 8, 1967)

Our sovereignty over the entrance to the Gulf cannot be disputed. If Israel wishes to threaten war, we tell her 'You are welcome.' "

MYTH

"Egypt never intended to go to war in June 1967."

FACT

The words of the Arab leaders, combined with their actions, clearly demonstrate that the Arab states were intent on an assault on Israel which would destroy the Jewish state. Statements by Nasser during the crisis, made this clear:

- "Our basic objective will be the destruction of Israel. The Arab people want to fight." (May 27)
- "The meaning of Sharm el-Sheikh is a confrontation with Israel. Adopting this measure obligates us to be ready to embark on a general war with Israel." (May 27)
- "We will not accept any . . . coexistence with Israel. . . Today the issue is not the establishment of peace between the Arab states and Israel. . . . The war with Israel is in effect since 1948." (May 28)
- "The armies of Egypt, Jordan, Syria and Lebanon are poised on the borders of Israel . . . to face the challenge, while standing behind us are the armies of Iraq, Algeria, Kuwait, Sudan and the whole Arab nation. This act will astound the world. Today they will know that the Arabs are arranged for battle, the critical hour has arrived. We have reached the stage of serious action and not declarations." (May 30)

On May 30, Jordan's King Hussein went to Cairo and signed a five-year mutual defense pact with Egypt. Israel now had a hostile Arab alliance on three frontiers.

Hussein and Nasser agreed that an attack on one was an attack on both, and they committed themselves "to hasten to the assistance of the attacked state." They set up a defense council and a joint command.

On May 31, the authoritative Cairo daily *Al Akhbar* put it bluntly:

"Under terms of the military agreement signed with Jordan, Jordanian artillery, coordinated with the forces of Egypt and Syria, is in a position to cut Israel in two at Qalqilya, where Israeli territory between the Jordan ar-

39

mistice line and the Mediterranean Sea is only 12 kilometers wide. . . . The military encirclement of Israel by Arab forces . . . bears out Ben Gurion's fear that Israel could yet find herself in the vise of a nutcracker."

Nasser tightened the noose around Israel on June 4, when he persuaded Iraq to join the alliance.

On May 31, President Aref of Iraq declared:

"The existence of Israel is an error which must be rectified. This is our opportunity to wipe out the ignominy which has been with us since 1948. Our goal is clear—to wipe Israel off the map."

Israel faced a dual threat: It was surrounded by armies which would be able to use Soviet weapons on all frontiers (and U.S. and British weapons on one of them). Its window to the Orient, to the Indian Ocean and to the east coast of Africa was closed.

In 1957, the Eisenhower Administration had endorsed the right of "free and innocent" passage through the Strait of Tiran to Israel's key port of Eilat. Nasser announced on May 22, 1967 that "the Strait of Tiran is part of our territorial waters. No Israeli ship will ever navigate it again. We also forbid the shipment of strategic materials to Israel on non-Israeli vessels." Backed by naval forces—in the context of the expulsion of UN forces from Sinai and the deployment in their place of three Egyptian divisions and 600 tanks—"the threat to Israel was mortal," historian Howard M. Sachar wrote. The blockade was the first act of war.

MYTH

"During the 1967 War, Israel deliberately attacked an American ship, the USS Liberty, in the Mediterranean."

FACT

The attack on the *Liberty* was a tragic mistake. But it must be recalled that the incident occurred in the midst of a full-scale war.

None of Israel's accusers has been able to explain adequately why Israel would have needed or wanted to attack an American ship. Confusion in a long line of communications in a tense atmosphere on both the American and Israeli sides—a message from the Joint Chiefs of Staff for the ship to remain at least 20 miles off the Egyptian coast never arrived—is a more probable and logical explanation. Hirsh Goodman and Ze'ev Schiff, authors of "The Attack on the Liberty," *Atlantic Monthly*, Sept., 1984, noted that only the day before, Israeli pilots accidentally bombed an Israeli armor column south of Jenin on the West Bank.

As a former high-ranking Israeli naval officer, Shlomo Erell, told the *Associated Press* (June 5, 1977), "No one would ever have dreamt that an American ship would be there. Even the United States didn't know where its ship was. We were advised by the proper authorities that there was no American ship within 100 miles." Former Israeli air force chief, Mordechai Hod, told the *Associated Press* that no Israeli aircraft had been sent on reconnaisance of the ship before the attack and that the Americans must have seen low-flying Israeli aircraft on bombing missions to Egypt. He added that Israeli planes were diverted from other missions after the Israeli navy, which identified the ship as an enemy vessel, called them in to attack. An Israeli torpedo boat commander explained that "the high masts and many weird antennas showed that this was a warship ... I suspected it was a Russian intelligence ship. ..."

Former U.S. Ambassador Walworth Barbour, who served in Tel Aviv during the Six-Day War, stated in an interview that the attack was "just a mix-up."

A notorious proponent of the theory that Israel delib-

Chronology 1951-1967

September 1, 1951
UN Security Council calls on Egypt to open Suez Canal to Israeli shipping. Egypt refuses.

July 26, 1956
Nationalization of Suez Canal decreed by the Egyptian government.

October 1956
Nasser enters an alliance with Jordan and steps up fedayeen attacks on Israel.

October 29, 1956
Sinai Campaign; Joint French, British and Israeli action is taken

erately attacked the *Liberty* is Anthony Pearson, a British writer, whose propaganda was published in a book, *Conspiracy of Silence*, and in an article in *Penthouse* magazine in 1976. Pearson erroneously asserts that Israel had tampered with Egyptian-Jordanian communications during the war, leading the Egyptians to believe that the Jordanian army was making a successful attack on Hebron (a city that was in Jordanian hands at the time). Much of Pearson's "findings" are a poor rewrite of charges published by former Rep. James Rarick of Louisiana, once described by the *Almanac of American Politics* as the "most rabidly right-wing member of Congress (who) regularly inserts [into the Congressional Record] the most vitriolic kind of far-right, sometimes anti-Semitic propaganda."

The facts are as follows: On June 8, 1967, the third day of

---

to counteract increased terrorist activity, to remove Egyptian blockade of Gulf of Aqaba and reclaim Suez Canal.

November 2, 1956

Israel occupies most of Sinai Peninsula. The Suez Canal is blocked by Egypt.

January 1957

First Israeli withdrawal from Sinai.

March 4, 1957

After receiving "maximum protection" guarantees from the United States and the UN, the second Israeli withdrawal from Gaza strip and the Sinai takes place.

June 4, 1957

The Arab League announces a boycott of all firms selling vehicles, goods and services to Israel.

May 28, 1964

Representatives of the Arab states meet in Jerusalem to announce the creation of the PLO.

May 14, 1967

President Nasser demands the withdrawal of the UN Emergency Forces from the Sinai Peninsula. UN complies. President Nasser masses troops and tanks in the Sinai.

May 18, 1967

President Nasser announces renewed blockade of Tiran Straits.

May 30, 1967

President Nasser declares, "The armies of Egypt, Jordan, Syria and Lebanon are poised on the borders of Israel."

42

the war, Israeli planes and vessels mistook the *Liberty*, which was 14 miles off the Sinai coast, for an Egyptian vessel. They attacked, killing 34 of the *Liberty's* crew.

The misidentification of the *Liberty* as an Egyptian vessel was understandable. The ship was far from the Sixth Fleet, to which it belonged. That morning, an Egyptian vessel had fired on Israeli positions in El Arish. The *Liberty* was first reported to be cruising at 22 knots, a rate usually maintained only by warships (the speed estimate turned out to be wrong). The *Liberty's* flag, according to testimony of crew members, may not have been discernible because there was little wind and the flag was knocked down after the first assault. Also after the first assault, the *Liberty's* commander refused an Israeli request that the ship identify itself. And according to testimony of its own crew, the *Liberty* bore at least a surface resemblance to the *El Quseir*, an Egyptian ship.

In 1980, one of the ship's officers, former Lieutenant James M. Ennes, Jr. charged in his book, *Assault on the Liberty*, that Israel deliberately attacked the ship to prevent it from monitoring the intended Israeli attack on Syria. He does not, however, explain why, if the *Liberty* was monitoring the Israel-Syrian border, the boat was not situated in a northern location, or at least a more central location, rather than off the Egyptian-Israeli border, as it was. Also, it is

---

May 30, 1967

Jordan's King Hussein signs a five year mutual defense pact with Egypt. Israel surrounded by a hostile Arab alliance.

June 5, 1967

Six Day War begins. Israel attacks airfields of Egypt, Jordan, Iraq and Syria.

June 8, 1967

Israeli planes mistake the *USS Liberty* for an Egyptian vessel and attack.

June 10, 1967

UN Security Council cease-fire demands accepted. Israel now controls Judea and Samaria, the Gaza Strip, the Sinai Peninsula and the Golan Heights.

November 22, 1967

UN Security Council adopts Resolution 242—the principles which were to guide negotiations for a settlement.

inconceivable that the Israelis, who were defending them-selves against massive Arab armies on two fronts already, would feel any need to hide their self-defense in the face of Syrian aggression.

Secretary of Defense Robert McNamara told Congress on July 26, 1967, "It was the conclusion of the investigatory body, headed by an admiral of the navy in whom we have great confidence, that the attack was not intentional." Is-rael apologized for the attack and paid nearly $13 million in reparations to the United States and to the families of the victims. The last payment was received in Dec. 1980, when the U.S. officially closed the books on the matter.

In 1987, McNamara repeated his belief that the attack was an accident, telling a caller on the Mutual Broadcasting Co.'s "Larry King Show" that he had seen nothing in the 20 years since to change his mind and that there had been no "cover-up."

6

Between The Wars
1967-1969

MYTH

"After the 1967 war, Israel refused to negotiate a settlement with the Arabs."

FACT

After its victory in the Six-Day War, Israel hoped that the Arab states would finally recognize the reality of its existence and enter into peace negotiations. Israel signalled to the Arab states its willingness to relinquish virtually all of the occupied territories in exchange for a genuine peace. In Moshe Dayan's oft-recalled phrase, Jerusalem was waiting only for a telephone call from Arab leaders to start negotiations.

But these hopes were dashed in Aug. 1967 when Arab leaders meeting in Khartoum adopted a formula of three "no's":

> "Kings and presidents have agreed to unified efforts at international and diplomatic levels to eliminate the consequences of aggression and to assure the withdrawal of the aggressor forces of Israel from Arab lands, but within the limits to which Arab states are committed: *no* peace with Israel, *no* negotiations with Israel, *no* recognition of Israel and maintenance of the rights of Palestinian people in their nation."

As former Major-General, now President, Chaim Herzog has written, "Israel's belief that the war had come to an end and that peace would now reign along the borders was soon dispelled. Three weeks after the conclusion of hostilities, the first major incident occurred on the Suez Canal."

MYTH

"Israel refused to implement Security Council Resolution 242, adopted in November 1967."

FACT

On Nov. 22, 1967, the UN Security Council adopted a resolution establishing the principles which were to guide the negotiations for a settlement. Both Arabs and Israelis contend that they have accepted this resolution. But there has always been sharp disagreement over its real meaning.

The Arabs point to the statement of principles calling for Israeli withdrawal but are quick to ignore the other principles which call for the "acknowledgement of the sovereignty, territorial integrity and political independence of every State in the area and their right to live in peace within secure and recognized boundaries."

Indeed, Arab states, with the obvious exception of Egypt, have gone so far as to demand Israeli withdrawal *prior* to negotiations. However, the resolution makes no such requirement. [Texts of UN Resolutions 242 and 338 appear in the appendix.]

Security Council Resolution 338, which was passed at the conclusion of the 1973 Yom Kippur War, establishes that the guidelines of Resolution 242 must be implemented through negotiations.

MYTH

"Resolution 242 called upon Israel to withdraw from all territories captured in June 1967."

FACT

There is disagreement over what Resolution 242's statement of principles means. Arabs argue that Israel must withdraw from *all* territories. Israel and the United States disagree, pointing to the fact that the Security Council voted on the English text of the resolution which deliberately avoided the use of the words *all* or *the*. Similarly, the Council did not use the French text so that it could avoid using the words *les* or *des*.

Arthur J. Goldberg, the American ambassador who led the delegation to the UN in 1967, submitted on May 8, 1973, an authoritative interpretation of the meaning of Resolution 242. Explaining that the resolution is not self-implementing and that its goal is an accepted and agreed-upon settlement, Goldberg rejected the interpretation that the resolution calls for complete Israeli withdrawal.

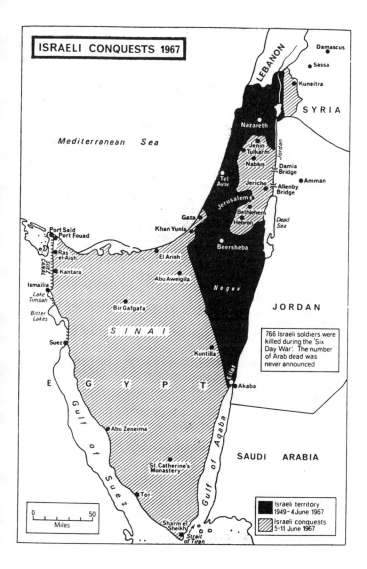

ISRAELI CONQUESTS 1967

766 Israeli soldiers were killed during the 'Six Day War'. The number of Arab dead was never announced

■ Israeli territory 1949 – 4 June 1967
▨ Israeli conquests 5-11 June 1967

Martin Gilbert, *The Arab-Israeli Conflict Its History in Maps*, Weidenfeld and Nicolson, London, 1967.

47

He wrote:

"Resolution 242 does not explicitly require that Israel withdraw to the lines occupied by it before the outbreak of the war. The Arab states urged such language; the Soviet Union . . . proposed this at the Security Council, and Yugoslavia and some other nations at the Special Session of the General Assembly. But such withdrawal language did not receive the requisite support either in the Security Council or in the Assembly.

"Resolution 242 simply endorses the principle of withdrawal of Israel's armed forces from territories occupied in the recent conflict, and interrelates this with the principle that every state in the area is entitled to live in peace within secure and recognized boundaries.

"The notable omissions—which were not accidental—in regard to withdrawal are the words *the* or *all* and *the June 5, 1967 lines.* In other words, there is lacking a declaration requiring Israel to withdraw from *the* or *all* the territories occupied by it on and after *June 5, 1967.* Rather, the resolution speaks of withdrawal from occupied territories without defining the extent of withdrawal. And the notable presence of the words 'secure and recognized boundaries,' by implication, contemplates that the parties could make territorial adjustments in their peace settlement encompassing less than a complete withdrawal of Israeli forces from occupied territories, inasmuch as Israel's prior frontiers had proved to be notably insecure."

Lord Caradon, who served as Britain's Ambassador to the United Nations during debate on Resolution 242, was asked by the Beirut *Daily Star* on June 12, 1974 why the resolution did not specify exactly what territories Israel should withdraw from. He replied, "It would have been wrong to demand that Israel return to its positions of June 4, 1967 because those positions were undesirable and artificial. After all, they were just the places where the soldiers of each side happened to be on the day the fighting stopped in 1948. They were just armistice lines. That's why we didn't demand that the Israelis return to them, and I think we were right not to. . . ."

Former Under Secretary of State for Political Affairs Eugene Rostow, who played a major role in the formulation and implementation of U.S. policy between 1966 and 1969, wrote in a letter to *The New York Times* on Nov. 25, 1973:

"Legally, Israel is in those areas as the occupying power under the authority of Security Council resolutions, which forbid the use of force to disturb Israel's possession until the parties make peace. The [Arab] armed attack of October 6, [1973] was therefore the most obvious violation of the Charter since North Korea invaded South Korea, also to reclaim national territory."

Referring to "rather surprising interviews" Hussein gave to the *New York Times* and *Washington Post* in March 1984, Ambassador Goldberg refuted the King's claim that American administrations repeatedly had assured him that Washington would ensure Israel's withdrawal from the West Bank, "presumably to be done in advance, or in lieu of, any direct negotiations between King Hussein and his Israeli counterparts." Writing in the May 28, 1984 *Jerusalem Post*, Goldberg added that "the statement in Secretary [of State] Henry Kissinger's memoirs that I assured King Hussein that we would compel Israel's withdrawal to the pre-June 5, 1967 border except for minor border rectifications, is inaccurate and unsupported by the contemporaneous records of the Department of State.

"Moreover, State Department archives reveal a realistic understanding by King Hussein of our position. King Hussein is reported to have frankly stated that having lost the war, he recognized the necessity for being flexible, both with respect to the West Bank and Jerusalem . . . . Instead of impugning the good faith of the United States and making the fallacious charge that our country has been and is at fault for not bringing Israel to heel, the counsel of wisdom for King Hussein would have been—and still remains—to honor his commitments in accepting security Council Resolutions 242 and 338 and go to the bargaining table with Israel to seek an agreed settlement.

"No one can say with certainty what would emerge from such negotiations, except to point out that the bargaining at Camp David between the parties produced results that were not anticipated by any expert at the time."

Rostow, in a column in the April 27, 1988 *Wall Street Journal*, reiterated that Resolutions 242 and 338 [adopted after the 1973 Yom Kippur War to implement 242] remain relevant. Regarding the territorial aspects of peace-making, Rostow, then a visiting professor at the U.S. National Defense University, noted "242 establishes three principles . . . : 1) Israel can occupy and administer the territories it occupied during the Six-Day War until the Arabs make peace, 2) When peace agreements are reached, they should delineate 'secure and recognized' boundaries to which Israel would withdraw, 3) Those boundaries could differ from the Armistice Demarcation Lines of 1949."

In rebutting charges of Israeli intransigence, Rostow emphasized that "To make sense of the prolonged conflict over Israel's right to exist requires the West to accept an unpalatable fact: Most Arabs believe what they frequently say—that they will destroy Israel as the Turks destroyed the Crusader Kingdom, even if it takes them a century. Unless the Arabs can be induced to compromise, and accept the repeated decisions of the world community as binding international law, the future of the area is grim."

And he noted that Jordan and Israel already are "the Arab and Jewish Palestinian states into which the mandated territory has been partitioned." The West Bank and Gaza Strip are only the remaining, as yet unallocated portions of the mandate—6% of the original whole.

MYTH

"UN Resolution 242 is inadequate and should be amended because it refers to the Palestinian Arab issue only as a 'refugee problem' and not as a problem of Palestinian Arab nationalism."

FACT

The drafters of UN Resolution 242 showed little interest in promoting a second Palestinian Arab state (after Jordan) in 1967—just as the Arab states had shown no interest for the previous 19 years.

The resolution drafters carefully chose the word *refugee* to indicate that there were *two* refugee problems—Arab and Jewish. About 800,000 Jews fled from Arab countries since 1940 and were never compensated for their losses.

Indeed, the World Organization of Jews From Arab Countries (WOJAC) estimates that such losses totalled several billion dollars by the early 1950's—several times those of the estimated 550,000 Arabs who actually fled what became Israel. [". . . Most reliable sources list the Arab refugee figure for 1948 as between 500,000, and 650,000. A case in point is the report of the Hon. Terence Prittie, who wrote that the *maximum* number of Arab refugees in 1948 was 590,000." Cited by Maurice Roumani in *The Case of the Jews from Arab Countries: A Neglected Issue.]*

The PLO understands the double-edged nature of 242. Not only does it not mention Palestinian Arab national rights, it does not mention a "Palestinian issue" at all. Mordechai Ben-Porat, a former Knesset member and a leader of WOJAC, noted in 1986 that "one of Arafat's deputies announced [the second reason] why they are against the resolution—because it includes Jews from Arab countries."

There is no procedure for amending United Nations resolutions, and what supporters of the PLO really seek is a new UN resolution to supersede Resolution 242.

7

The War of Attrition
1969-1970

MYTH

"Israel was responsible for the War of Attrition."

FACT

An impatient Nasser opened up a new war in April 1969 to bring pressure on the superpowers. Violating the UN cease-fire, he began artillery barrages across the Suez Canal. This was the beginning of the War of Attrition, which lasted 16 months and cost Israel more than 200 soldiers killed and a number of combat aircraft shot down, mostly by anti-aircraft guns and missiles.

The Israelis were outgunned more than 10-to-one along the canal, and their planes, used as "flying artillery," struck at targets deep inside Egypt. Cairo appealed to Moscow. As a result, Soviet pilots entered the battle with Israel over the canal in 1970. Five Soviet-piloted MiG-21's were downed in one day by Israeli jets shortly before the cease-fire.

MYTH

"Egypt terminated the 1969-70 War of Attrition and sought to reach some accommodation with Israel, only to have Israel spurn these initiatives."

FACT

In the summer of 1970, the United States persuaded the two countries to accept a cease-fire. The cease-fire was intended to lead to negotiations under UN auspices. Israel declared that it would accept the principle of withdrawal.

But on Aug. 7, in violation of the agreement, the Soviets and Egyptians planted a dense forest of sophisticated ground-to-air SAM-2 and SAM-3 missiles in the restricted 32-mile-deep zone along the west bank of the Suez Canal. This was a clear violation of the cease-fire. Plain language had been written into the agreement:

"Both sides will refrain from changing the military status quo within zones extending 50 kilometers to the east and the west of the cease-fire line. Neither side will introduce or construct any new military installations in these zones. Activities within the zones will be limited to the maintenance of existing installations at their present sites and positions and to the rotation and the supply of forces presently within the zones."

Time magazine (Sept. 14, 1970) observed that U.S. reconnaissance "showed that the 36 SAM-2 missiles sneaked into the cease-fire zone constitute only the first line of the most massive anti-aircraft system ever created."

The authoritative *Aviation Week and Space Technology* and Department of Defense satellite photos demonstrated conclusively that 63 SAM-3 and 70 improved SAM-2 sites were installed in a 78-mile band between the cities of Ismailia and Suez. Three years later these missiles gave air coverage to Egypt's surprise attack against Israel. [Israel's air force paid a heavy price in the initial days of the 1973 Yom Kippur War, according to *The Middle East Conflicts From 1945 to the Present* (Crescent Books, New York, 1983). "Of the total Israeli aircraft losses, 40% occurred in the first 48 hours of the war. These amounted to 14% of Israel Air Force's front line strength. But in this period Israel deliberately chose to sacrifice her air force in order to hold the ground, particularly in the Golan."]

Despite the Egyptian violations, the UN-sponsored talks resumed—additional evidence that Israel was anxious to make progress toward peace. But then came a diplomatic disaster. The talks were swiftly short-circuited by UN special Envoy Gunnar Jarring himself, when he accepted the Egyptian interpretation of Resolution 242 and called for Israel's total withdrawal to the pre-June 5, 1967 demarcation lines.

On that basis, Egypt expressed for the first time since 1948 its willingness "to enter into a peace agreement with Israel" in a letter to Jarring on Feb. 20, 1971. But this seeming moderation masked an unchanging Egyptian irredentism and unwillingness to enter into a real peace as evidenced in the letter's sweeping reservations and preconditions.

• In Egypt the crucial sentences about a "peace agreement with Israel" were neither published nor broadcast.

- Egypt refused to enter into direct talks with Israel.

- Israel attempted to transform the struggling Jarring mission into at least indirect talks by addressing all letters not to Jarring, but to the Egyptian government. Egypt refused to accept them.

- Just after the letter to Jarring, Anwar Sadat, Egypt's new president, addressed the Palestine National Council (PNC) meeting in Cairo. He promised support to the PLO "until victory" and asserted that Egypt would not accept Resolution 242. (*Radio Cairo*, Feb. 27, 1971).

- Five days after Sadat told Westerners that he was ready to make peace with Israel, Mohammed Heikal, editor of the semi-official *Al Ahram* wrote (Feb. 25, 1971):

> "Arab policy at this stage has but two objectives. The first, the elimination of the traces of the 1967 aggression through an Israeli withdrawal from all the territories it occupied that year. The second objective is the elimination of the traces of the 1948 aggression, by means of the elimination of the State of Israel itself. This is, however, as yet an abstract, undefined objective, and some of us have erred in commencing the latter step before the former."

MYTH

"Egypt repeatedly expressed a willingness to begin peace negotiations with Israel from 1971 to 1973. Israel's rejection of these initiatives led to the Yom Kippur War."

FACT

With the collapse of the Jarring mission, the United States undertook a new initiative. It proposed an Israeli-Egyptian interim agreement, calling for Israel's partial withdrawal from the Suez Canal and the opening of that waterway.

Israel was willing to enter into negotiations without preconditions, but Sadat imposed an impossible condition—that Israel agree, as part of an interim agreement, to withdraw ultimately to the old 1967 lines. In effect, Sadat was seeking an advance guarantee of the outcome of "negotiations," the political equivalent of "no-fault" wars of aggression.

54

8

The 1973 Yom Kippur War

MYTH

"Israel was responsible for the 1973 war."

FACT

On Oct. 6, 1973—Yom Kippur, the holiest day in the Jewish calendar—Egypt and Syria opened a coordinated surprise attack against Israel. On the Golan Heights, approximately 180 Israeli tanks faced an onslaught of 1,400 Syrian tanks. Along the Suez Canal, fewer than 500 Israeli defenders were attacked by 80,000 Egyptians.

Thrown onto the defensive during the first two days of the fighting, Israel mobilized its reserves and eventually was able to repulse the invaders and carry the war deep into Syria and Egypt. The Arab states were swiftly resupplied by sea and air from the Soviet Union, which rejected U.S. efforts to work toward an immediate cease-fire. Nine other Arab countries joined the battle. As a result, the United States belatedly began its own airlift to Israel. Two weeks later, Egypt was saved from a disastrous defeat by the UN Security Council, which had failed to act when the attack against Israel began or while the tide was in the Arabs' favor. A former aide to the UN Secretary General Kurt Waldheim recalled in 1987 that Waldheim showed no interest in initiating peace-making efforts so long as it looked like the Arabs might win. The aide, later a member of the British Parliament, said Waldheim began to act only after Israel went on the offensive. [Waldheim's service with a World War II German army unit guilty of war crimes in the Balkans was an issue in his successful 1986 campaign for the Austrian presidency.]

MYTH

"Egypt's Sadat had agreed to U.S. peace proposals and did not seek war."

FACT

In 1971, speaking on the anniversary of the 1952 revolution, President Sadat hurled a militant ultimatum at the United States and Israel. He would sacrifice one million soldiers and cancel his acceptance of UN Resolution 242 if the year ended without a decision. His threat did not materialize that year.

Throughout 1972, and for much of 1973, Sadat threatened war unless the United States accepted his interpretation of Resolution 242: total Israeli withdrawal from territories taken in 1967.

At the same time, the Egyptian leader carried on a diplomatic offensive among European and African states to win support for his cause. He appealed to the Soviets to bring pressure on the United States and to provide Egypt with more offensive weapons in order to cross the Suez Canal.

But at the time it appeared as if the Soviet Union was more interested in maintaining the appearance of *detente* with the United States than in confrontation in the Middle East. Therefore, it rejected Sadat's demands. In turn, Sadat suddenly expelled approximately 20,000 Soviet advisers from Egypt.

The United States agreed with Israel's view that there was no alternative to direct negotiations and that Egypt must eventually accept that course.

In an interview with *Newsweek* on April 9, 1973, Sadat again warned that he would renew the war. But it was the same threat he had made in 1971 and 1972, and most observers remained skeptical.

The U.S.-sponsored truce was three years old and Secretary of State Kissinger had opened a new dialogue for peace at the UN. Almost everyone was confident that a new war was remote.

On Sept. 26, Sadat reacted acidly to Kissinger's initiative. He told the Egyptian parliament:

"The United States is still under Zionist pressure and is wearing Zionist spectacles . . . [which] are closed to anything except what Israel wants. . . . The United States will have to take off those Zionist spectacles before they talk to us."

MYTH

"Egypt and Syria only wanted to liberate the occupied territories. They did not seek to threaten Israel proper."

FACT

In a Sept. 26, 1973, speech, Sadat admitted:

"If I want to reopen the canal, I do not have to ask permission of the United States or Israel. But the problem is not that of the canal. . . . There is the issue of Palestine, the issue of liberating the occupied lands."

On October 16, over *Radio Damascus*, President Assad of Syria declared:

"Our forces continue to pressure the enemy and will continue to strike at him until we recover the occupied territory, and we will then continue until all the land (Palestine) is liberated."

The day before, the Syrian government organ *Al-Thawra* insisted that the war "will end with the return of the Palestinian people to its land."

MYTH

"Israel fought only Egypt and Syria in the October war."

FACT

At least nine Arab states, and at least four non-Middle Eastern states, actively aided the Egyptian-Syrian war effort.

The least enthusiastic participant in the Oct. fighting was probably Jordan's King Hussein, who apparently had been kept uninformed of Egyptian and Syrian war plans. But Hussein did send two of his best units—the 40th and 60th Armored Brigades—to Syria. This force took positions in the southern sector, defending the main Amman-Damascus route and attacking Israeli positions along the Kuneitra-Sassa road on Oct. 16. Three Jordanian artillery batteries also participated in the attack, carried out by nearly 100 tanks.

A few months before the Yom Kippur War, Iraq transferred a squadron of Hunter jets to Egypt. During the war an Iraqi division of some 20,000 men and 320 tanks was deployed in central Golan and participated in the Oct. 16 attack against Israeli positions. Iraqi MiG's and pilots began operating over the Golan Heights as early as Oct. 8, the third day of the war. After the war Israel returned 17 Iraqi

Israeli-Syrian Cease Fire Lines, Oct. 24, 1973

Legend:
- Israeli-Syrian Demarcation Line 1949-1967
- Territory captured by Israel during the Six-Day War of June, 1967, until the Syrian attack on Oct. 6, 1973
- Syrian territory held by Israel at the cease fire of Oct. 24, 1973

soldiers captured during the fighting.

In addition to serving as financial underwriters, Saudi Arabia and Kuwait committed men to battle. A Saudi brigade of approximately 3,000 troops was dispatched to Syria, where it participated in fighting along the approaches to Damascus. While it is unclear just what role Kuwaiti troops played, postwar honors and decorations indicated combat participation. There were also reports that

58

Kuwait transferred British-made Lightning jets to Egypt during the war.

Violating a French ban on the transfer of French-made weapons, Libya's Col. Muammar Qaddafi turned over to Egypt approximately 40 Mirage III fighters, several of which were shot down on the Sinai front. Libya also sent an armored brigade to Egypt and supplied 100 tanks during the war.

Other North African countries responded to Arab and Soviet calls to aid the front-line states. Algeria sent three aircraft squadrons of fighters and bombers, an armored brigade, and 150 tanks. A Tunisian battalion-size unit was

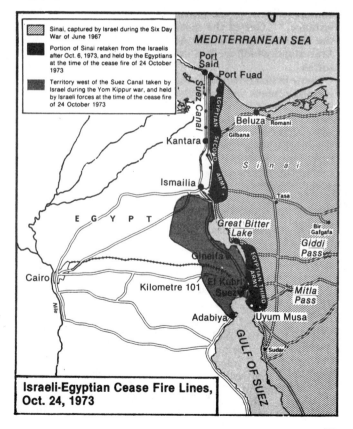

Sinai, captured by Israel during the Six Day War of June 1967

Portion of Sinai retaken from the Israelis after Oct. 6, 1973, and held by the Egyptians at the time of the cease fire of 24 October 1973

Territory west of the Suez Canal taken by Israel during the Yom Kippur war, and held by Israeli forces at the time of the cease fire of 24 October 1973

MEDITERRANEAN SEA

Port Said
Port Fuad
Suez Canal
EGYPTIAN SECOND ARMY
Beluza Romani
Gilbana
Kantara
S i n a i
Ismailia
Tasa
E G Y P T
Great Bitter Lake
Bir Gafgafa
Giddi Pass
Gineifa
EGYPTIAN THIRD ARMY
Cairo
El Kubri
Kilometre 101 Suez
Mitla Pass
Nile
Adabiya Uyum Musa
GULF OF SUEZ
Sudar

Israeli-Egyptian Cease Fire Lines, Oct. 24, 1973

stationed in the Nile Delta, Sudan stationed 3,500 troops in southern Egypt, and Morocco sent three brigades to the front lines, including 2,500 men to Syria.

Although not a participant in the Yom Kippur fighting, Lebanon opened its entire southern border, allowing Palestinian Arab terrorists to shell Israeli civilian settlements. (Terrorist organizations claim that tens of thousands of their men fought with the front-line armies.) In addition, Lebanese radar units were used by Syrian air defense forces.

President Sadat expressed his gratitude after the war. "We thank our Arab brothers," he said. "Directly after the commencement of the battle, they hastened to give us assistance. . . . One of the most magnificent achievements of the October war was the Arab solidarity and the unified Arab stand which we had not been able to achieve for centuries."

Some little-known facts that emerged from postwar intelligence reports indicate the combat roles of non-Middle East troops. According to intelligence sources (quoted in *The New York Times*, Oct. 16 and 19, 1973), 30 North Korean pilots flew base-defense missions for Egypt, and two of them were shot down. In addition, Pakistani pilots were dispatched to Egypt, while North Vietnamese SAM technicians and Cuban tank officers and artillery gunners assisted in Syria.

MYTH

"Israel mistreated Arab soldiers captured during the 1973 war."

FACT

Numerous observers reported that Israel's treatment of captured Arab soldiers was above reproach. Hugh Baker, a representative of Amnesty International, declared: "They are being treated well . . . and they seem to be getting the best medical treatment possible. The doctors are treating them as human beings." *(The Jerusalem Post*, Jan. 4, 1974.)

Soon after his release, Syrian Col. Atnon El-Kodar complained of maltreatment by Israeli doctors, charging unnecessary amputation of a leg. An American reporter, Ed deFontaine, who had met Kodar in an Israeli hospital, felt the colonel must have "had a short memory about what was done to save his life. . . . He told me that he owed his life to

[his] doctor." (*Group W. Radio,* June 11, 1974.)

On the other hand, Israeli soldiers captured by Syrian and Egyptian troops, were mistreated. Upon their surrender, dozens of Israeli POW's were murdered. Others were tortured—in violation of the Geneva Prisoners-of-War Convention.

According to a report submitted to the International Red Cross by the Israeli Government on Dec. 8, 1973, Israeli troops discovered bodies of Israeli soldiers on the Golan Heights whose hands and legs had been bound and whose eyes had been gouged. They had been executed at close range.

On the Egyptian front, according to a report submitted to the Red Cross on Dec. 9, 1973, Israeli soldiers fared no better. Surrendering soldiers were beaten, subjected to whippings, sexual attacks, burning and starvation—and many were executed.

After the war, Syria refused for months to provide lists of POW's to Israel, the Red Cross, or Secretary of State Kissinger.

Chronology 1973-1979

October 6, 1973
   Egypt and Syria launch a coordinated attack on Yom Kippur day against Israeli positions on the Golan Heights and Sinai.
October 19, 1973
   President Nixon asks Congress for $2.2 billion emergency military aid to Israel.
October 22, 1973
   UN Security Council adopts Resolution 338 calling for an immediate cease-fire, implementation of 242 and negotiations between the parties.
October 23, 1973
   Fighting resumes; UN passes Resolution 339.
October 24, 1973
   New cease-fire implemented.
October 27, 1973
   First United Nations troops arrive to police Sinai cease-fire.

On May 19, 1974, the London *Sunday Times* reported that Syrian officers had turned Israeli prisoners over to Soviet military interrogation teams. The *Times* said: "The interrogators . . . have employed medical and other techniques to break the resistance of the Israelis."

MYTH

"Israeli troops deliberately bulldozed and dynamited the entire town of Kuneitra prior to their withdrawal from the area in June 1974."

FACT

Kuneitra was severely damaged in both the 1967 and 1973 wars. In the Yom Kippur War, Kuneitra was shelled and captured by Syrian troops, retaken by Israelis, and then defended against intense Syrian counter-attacks. Tanks roamed through the town, between and through buildings. After the cease-fire, Kuneitra suffered from 81 days of artillery duels that preceded the disengagement.

November 11, 1973

Egypt and Israel sign cease-fire accord.

December 21, 1973

Geneva conference convenes. Israel, Egypt, Jordan, the United States, Soviet Union and United Nations are represented. Syria boycotts.

January 18, 1974

Egypt and Israel agree on first Sinai disengagement accord.

March 18, 1974

Arab nations agree to lift five-month oil embargo against the United States.

May 15, 1974

PLO terrorists kill 16 school children and wound 70 at a school in Maalot.

May 29, 1974

Syria and Israel agree to a disengagement on the Golan Heights, ending 81 days of artillery duels.

November 13, 1974

Yasir Arafat addresses the UN General Assemby with a pistol on his hip.

March 25, 1975

Saudi King Faisal is assassinated by his nephew.

Kuneitra was not an agricultural center. Its strategic position near the Israeli front proved suitable to the location of rear facilities for the Syrian army, including command and control centers for the entire front-line area. The Syrians concentrated at least half their army in the front-line area, of which Kuneitra was the capital. Military installations, barracks, support centers, fuel and ammunition dumps were constructed. (The Officers' Club was the largest building in town.) As a result, the sources of livelihood of the inhabitants changed from primitive peasant agriculture to service to the army.

On May 5, 1974—much before Israel's alleged destruction of the town—*London Times* correspondent Eric Marsden reported that Kuneitra, which once "had about 17,000 residents plus a Syrian army garrison . . . is in ruins and deserted after seven years of war and dereliction. It looks

---

April 1975

Civil war erupts in Lebanon.

June 5, 1975

Suez Canal is reopened.

September 1, 1975

Egypt and Israel sign second disengagement agreement which returns Sinai passes and Abu Rudeis oil fields to Egypt.

November 10, 1975

UN General Assembly declares Zionism a form of "racism."

July 4, 1976

Israeli rescue of 103 passengers of hijacked Air France aircraft in Entebbe, Uganda.

October 1, 1977

U.S. and Soviets issue joint declaration on Geneva conference.

November 15, 1977

Israeli Prime Minister invites Anwar Sadat to address the Israeli Knesset.

November 19, 1977

Egyptian President Sadat arrives in Israel.

September 17, 1978

Egypt, Israel and the United States sign Camp David peace accords.

March 26, 1979

Egypt, Israel and the United States sign Egyptian-Israeli peace treaty.

Syrian Minister of Defense Mustafa Tlas told the Syrian National Assembly in December 1973 of the following example of "supreme valor" by Syrian troops:

> "There is the outstanding case of a recruit from Aleppo who murdered 28 Jewish soldiers all by himself, slaughtering them like sheep. All of his comrades in arms witnessed this. He butchered three of them with an ax and decapitated them. In other words, instead of using a gun to kill them, he took a hatchet to chop their heads off. He struggled face to face with one of them and throwing down his ax managed to break his neck and devour his flesh in front of his comrades. This is a special case. Need I single it out to award him the Medal of the Republic? I will grant this medal to any soldier who succeeds in killing 28 Jews, and I will cover him with appreciation and honor his bravery."

like a wild west town struck by an earthquake. . . . Nearly every building is heavily damaged and scores have collapsed. . . . "

MYTH

"Arab aims in 1973 were primarily political, meant to bring Israel to the negotiating table."

FACT

As recapitulated by Herzog in *The Arab-Israeli Wars,* "The political purpose of Egypt and Syria was to strike two heavy blows against Israel in order to break the log-jam which had occurred in the Arab-Israeli conflict since the cease-fire in August 1970. These strategic blows were designed to force the hands of the superpowers and oblige them to pressurize Israel to return to the 1967 borders, without requiring any Arab country actually to sign a peace treaty with Israel—a development that, in the eyes of the Arabs, would have to be avoided in order to prevent granting any form of legitimacy to Israel in the Middle East. In short, their aim was to move the clock back to the eve of the Six Day War in 1967 as far as Israel-Arab relations were concerned."

9

The Peace Process
1973-1982

MYTH

"Anwar Sadat began the initiative that led to the Israeli-Egyptian peace treaty and he should receive most of the credit for it."

FACT

The peace drive did not begin with President Sadat's visit to Jerusalem in Nov. 1977. Though the visit itself was a dramatic act of courage and statesmanship, it came only after several months of behind-the-scenes contacts between Israeli and Arab leaders, which included secret missions by Israeli Foreign Minister Moshe Dayan to Morocco.

Nevertheless, Israel's warm reception of Sadat was *not* as dramatic as Sadat's gesture of going to Jerusalem. "For Israel to equal the drama," said Simcha Dinitz, former Israeli ambassador to the United States, "we would have had to declare war on Egypt, maintain belligerent relations for 30 years, refuse to talk to them, call for their annihilation, suggest to throw them into the sea or the Nile, conduct military operations, infiltration and terrorism against them, declare economic boycotts, close the Strait of Tiran to their ships, close the Suez Canal to their traffic, and say they are outcasts of humanity. Then Mr. Begin would go to Cairo and his trip would be equally dramatic. Obviously we could not do this because it has been our policy to negotiate all along."

MYTH

"Egypt took greater risks by signing the peace treaty than Israel."

FACT

Egypt's President Sadat took greater personal political risks by negotiating peace with Israel, but Israel's Prime Minister Begin took far greater national security risks. The risk the Egyptian leader took was a personal one, that he and perhaps his regime would fall. Tragically, on the eighth anniversary of the Yom Kippur War, he was assassinated. Egypt, of course, lived on.

The risk Begin took, however, was a national one—that Israel would be faced with new threats and perhaps even destruction. Israel gave up tangibles (land, oil, air bases, strategic depth) in exchange for intangibles (pledges).

This is not to say that Egypt's concessions were unimportant. In the context of traditional Arab attitudes, its decision to recognize Israel was momentous. It also signed a peace treaty in advance of an expressed willingness by other Arab countries to do the same, and it gave up its insistence that Israel agree to total withdrawal from the West Bank prior to an Israeli-Egyptian accord.

But Israel offered to give up the entire Sinai peninsula, three times the size of Israel proper, and to relocate its defense line. It also agreed to dismantle the military government in the West Bank and Gaza, withdraw its troops to specified areas, and work toward Palestinian autonomy. The Begin government made these concessions despite the fact that no Palestinian Arab willing to recognize Israel stepped forward to speak for the territories, and despite Israel's claim to sovereignty over the areas.

MYTH

"The autonomy framework agreed to at Camp David provided nothing for the Palestinian Arabs on the West Bank and Gaza. The Camp David drafters should have recognized the necessity of a Palestinian state."

FACT

The Camp David frameworks signed on Sept. 17, 1978, provided for an autonomous administrative council for the West Bank and Gaza inhabitants for a transition period of five years. Under this plan the Palestinian Arabs would be able to conduct their own domestic affairs. The framers of the Camp David accords saw the necessity to omit military and foreign policy portfolios, which are functions of a sovereign state, from the administrative council.

The United States officially opposes the establishment of an independent Palestinian state. In all likelihood, such a state would be a Soviet client under PLO domination and a threat to Israel and moderate Arab countries.

In 1979, President Jimmy Carter told a press conference that he had "never met an Arab leader that in private professed a desire for an independent Palestinian state. Publicly, they all espouse an independent Palestinian state—almost all of them—because that is what they committed themselves to do at Rabat [the 1974 Arab League summit conference]. But the private diplomatic tone of conversations is much more proper. . . ."

In a 1979 column in *The Washington Post*, Ronald Reagan warned that if "policies should serve to weaken Israel either through building the basis for a radical Palestinian state on her borders or through providing her with insufficient military assistance, the tasks of Kremlin planners dealing with the Middle East would be enormously eased and a determined barrier to Soviet expansionism in the region would have been withdrawn."

Israel has no obligation to anyone to participate in the formation of a new Palestinian Arab state. It took the West Bank from Jordan and the Gaza Strip from Egypt in a defensive war. If Israel has an obligation under international law to negotiate with anyone over the West Bank it is with the party from whom it took the territory—Jordan, but Jordan's annexation of the region was itself illegitimate. Before 1967, the West Bank and Gaza had been under Arab rule for 19 years with no thought given to forming a Palestinian state. The Arabs rejected a Palestinian state when the UN proposed it in 1947. Thus, it is ironic that Arabs demand that Israel do for the West Bank and Gaza what they were unwilling to do at a time when Israel had no say in the matter.

The final status of the West Bank-Gaza could be one of five possibilities: an indefinite period of autonomy; a territorial division between Israel and Jordan, some kind of shared-sovereignty arrangement between the two countries; confederation with either Jordan or Israel; or integration into Israel.

MYTH

"Autonomy for Palestinian Arabs in the West Bank and Gaza is not enough to satisfy their aspirations."

FACT

If the Camp David agreements had dictated that autonomy was the ultimate solution to the status of the West Bank and Gaza then the idea indeed would not meet the needs of the Palestinian Arabs. But autonomy was designed as an interim arrangement. The accords provided for Egypt, Israel, and any Palestinian Arabs and Jordanians willing to participate, to negotiate the formation of a self-governing authority for the areas that would sit for five years. By the end of the first three years of that interim period, the negotiators were to work out a permanent solution to the status of the West Bank and Gaza. The Camp David accords provided an invitation to Palestinians to participate in the determination of their future.

Just before starting his spring 1988 Middle East peace shuttle, Secretary of State George Shultz said that if people realized how much progress on autonomy Israel and Egypt had agreed to before talks broke down in early 1982, they would be surprised. By early 1982, official Israeli talking points—then confidential—on the power and scope of the self-governing authority, noted that after free elections "the Palestinian Arabs will for the first time have an elected and representative body, in accordance with their own wishes and free choice, that will be able to carry out the functions assigned to it as an administrative council."

Those powers covered: administration, justice, agriculture, finance, civil service, education and culture, health, housing and public works, transportation and communications, labor and social welfare, municipal affairs, local police, religious affairs, industry, commerce and tourism. In rejecting autonomy and a transition period, the Arabs rejected an opportunity to advance their own definition in the final status negotiations agreed to by Israel. In labeling such openings "capitulationist," as the PLO and other extremists did, in refusing to come forward during the Israeli-Egyptian autonomy talks or any time thereafter through the "uprising" of early 1988, Palestinian Arab leadership confirmed the observation of U.S. and Israeli diplomats that they "never missed a chance to miss an opportunity."

MYTH

"The Israeli-Egyptian treaty had to be linked to progress toward implementation of West Bank-Gaza autonomy because Israel would not otherwise live up to its commitments on the occupied areas."

FACT

Autonomy was Israel's idea, not that of Egypt or the United States. It was Israel's idea to dismantle the military government in the West Bank and Gaza.

The Sinai and West Bank-Gaza frameworks were designed to be independent of each other because while the parties at Camp David could be reasonably certain about their own intentions, they had little control over the actions of third parties—such as the Palestinian Arabs and Jordanians—whose cooperation is necessary for the West Bank-Gaza framework to succeed. A strong link between implementation of the Israeli-Egyptian treaty and implementation of the West Bank-Gaza autonomy plan would have given those who oppose peace with Israel a veto not only over the West Bank-Gaza plan but over an Israeli-Egyptian accord as well.

MYTH

"Israel is content with its bilateral treaty with Egypt and does not want a comprehensive Middle East peace settlement."

FACT

Every government in Israel's 40-year history has favored a comprehensive settlement and has stated a desire to talk peace with the leaders of any or all of the neighboring Arab states. One of the peace frameworks Israel signed at Camp David stated explicitly that its principles were designed to serve as the basis for peace treaties "between Israel and each of its neighbors—Egypt, Jordan, Syria and Lebanon." The push for a quick-fix, comprehensive settlement, however, has tended to to undermine what has already been achieved between Israel and Egypt.

As the Egyptian-Israeli peace treaty demonstrated, the

way to achieve an overall Middle East peace settlement is through direct, bilateral negotiations.

MYTH

"At Camp David, Israel agreed to halt the construction of settlements for five years. Within months, Israel had violated the accords by establishing new settlements on the West Bank."

FACT

The five-year period agreed to at Camp David was the time allotted to negotiations on sovereignty over the West Bank. The Israeli moratorium on West Bank settlements was only for the duration of negotiations on the Egyptian-Israeli peace treaty.

Israel's position on this interpretation received unexpected support from Anwar Sadat, who told the *Middle East News Agency* on Sept. 20, 1978, "We agreed to put a freeze on the establishment of settlements for the coming three months, the time necessary in our estimation for signing the peace treaty."

MYTH

"Israel's defense needs decreased as a result of the peace treaty with Egypt and it therefore requires less military assistance from the United States."

FACT

No nation on earth—particularly one that has relatively recently conceded large amounts of territory to a former enemy—would throw away its arms after signing a peace treaty. No one can be sure that Sadat's successors always will honor the treaty. President Hosni Mubarak repeatedly has been criticized by Egyptian Islamic fundamentalists and by some secular left-wing figures as well, for adhering to the treaty. His Defense Minister, Abdel Halim Abu Ghazallah, has made contradictory statements regarding Egypt's pan-Arab defense commitments and military planning which still see Israel as Egypt's top potential threat. At any rate, other Arab countries have denounced the Camp David accords and still do not recognize Israel's right to exist.

For these and other reasons, Israel's defense needs have

increased as a result of its treaty with Egypt. The largest cost, perhaps as much as $17 billion, involved Israel's military withdrawal from Sinai and the relocation and reconstruction of the Sinai defense facilities in the Negev desert.

MYTH

"The Arabs recognized Israel's right to exist in the Fez peace plan of 1982. The plan is a far-reaching compromise by the Arab states."

FACT

The Fez Plan, issued on Sept. 9, 1982, was part of the final declaration issued by an Arab summit conference meeting in Morocco. In many ways it was a reissuance of a plan presented by Saudi Crown Prince, later King, Fahd in Nov. 1981. The plan was proposed at a time when the Arab world was in considerable disarray: The PLO had just been expelled from Beirut; Syrian forces had been defeated in Lebanon; Lebanese President Bashir Gemayel had begun negotiating peace terms with Israel; and President Reagan issued his own peace initiative just days before.

The Fez Plan called for total Israeli withdrawal from the territories captured in 1967, including east Jerusalem; dismantling of settlements; recognition of the PLO as sole representative of the Palestinians; and the establishment of another Palestinian Arab state.

The summit rejected the Camp David Accords and President Reagan's plan. The plan did not recognize Israel. It only proposed that "the Security Council guarantees peace among all states of the region . . . " That formulation is actually a step backwards from the Fahd Plan which at least had the Arabs affirming the "right of all countries to live in peace." The Arab emphasis on a major role for the Security Council also demonstrates a desire to keep the Soviet Union involved in the region in a way that might insulate Arab countries from having to hold direct, bilateral talks with Israel, which would imply recognizing Israel as an equal.

MYTH

"The Reagan plan, based on the Camp David Accords, is the best route today to reach peace in the Middle East."

FACT

The Reagan plan was presented to Israel's government on Aug. 31, 1982, and delivered as a speech by President Reagan on Sept. 1. In both presentations the United States in effect departed from the Camp David Accords.

There were positive elements in the plan. The President reaffirmed the U.S. commitment to Israel's security needs and rejected the establishment of a second independent Palestinian Arab state after Jordan. But, in abandoning the principles of the Camp David Accords, the United States rejected the only agreed-upon framework for Middle East peace.

The Reagan plan was particularly troublesome as it related to Jerusalem. It stipulated that the city should remain undivided but that its final status should be resolved in negotiations. In short, the Reagan initiative put all of Jerusalem—east and west—on the negotiating table. No Israeli government is prepared to negotiate over Jerusalem's sovereignty. The city is Israel's capital. It will remain undivided under Israel's control.

Camp David left open the ultimate status of the West Bank and Gaza. The Reagan plan clearly tilted toward Jordanian control. In addition, while Camp David stipulated a three-month settlement freeze, the Reagan proposals called for a "real" and indefinite freeze—again predetermining the outcome of an issue that was to be negotiated.

MYTH

"The 1988 Shultz initiative reflected only the positive elements of the Reagan plan, and Israel was to blame for blocking it."

FACT

The Shultz proposals, outlined in letters to Israeli Prime Minister Yitzhak Shamir and Jordan's King Hussein, were only a few weeks old when, in March 1988, Jordan and Syria criticized them in nearly identical terms, suggesting that Hussein had given a virtual veto to Syria's extremist leader, Hafez Assad. Jordan retreated from the idea of a joint delegation with non-PLO Palestinian Arabs which would talk with Israel. Instead, it insisted on a separate seat for the PLO, regardless of whether it met U.S. conditions, including explicitly endorsing UN Security Council Resolutions 242 and 338, ceasing terrorism and recognizing Israel.

Further, Jordan demanded an authoritative international conference, to be convened by the five permanent members of the Security Council, including the Soviet Union and China, which did not have diplomatic relations with Israel.

Israeli Foreign Minister Shimon Peres, who endorsed Shultz's initiative, had believed that Hussein in 1987 had agreed to a conference without power to impose a settlement or to veto any agreement arrived at in direct, bilateral talks held under the auspices of an "international opening."

Shamir, who strenuously objected to Shultz's early emphasis on "land-for-peace" as a central element to his proposal, nevertheless did accept the idea of an international opening to direct talks, even with Syria, and repeated his support for autonomy and eventual final status negotiations. He accepted a suggestion by the United States for Israeli-Jordanian-Egyptian talks on the sidelines of the Dec. 1987 Washington summit between President Reagan and Soviet leader Mikhail Gorbachev; Hussein refused. Shamir later said he would participate in such negotiations in the shadow of the 1988 Moscow superpower meeting. But again there were no Arab takers.

Meanwhile, Palestinian Arab residents of the West Bank and Gaza acceded to calls—and threats—by the PLO and local leaders of the uprising not to meet with Shultz despite the secretary's invitation and conciliatory statements to them.

10

Boundaries

MYTH

"The creation of the State of Israel in 1948 changed border arrangements that had existed for centuries."

FACT

The boundaries of Middle East countries were fixed largely by the Great Powers after the defeat of the Ottoman Empire in World War I. Lines were drawn arbitrarily and with little regard for economic or strategic necessity.

The French took over the area now known as Lebanon and Syria. The British received the remainder of the Fertile Crescent: Palestine and Iraq.

In 1923, the League of Nations recognized the French mandates. Soon the borders were redrawn. In 1926, Lebanon was separated from Syria and made an independent state.

Britain installed Faisal, who had been deposed by the French in Syria, as the ruler of the new kingdom of Iraq. Later, in 1922, to appease the Arabs, the British made Faisal's brother Abdullah the emir of the newly created province of Transjordan, which incorporated all Palestine east of the Jordan River.

MYTH

"Israel has been an expansionist state since its creation."

FACT

On numerous occasions, Israel has withdrawn from territories captured in *defensive* wars.

In Sept. 1983, Israel withdrew from large areas in Lebanon, to positions south of the Awali River.

In 1985 it completed withdrawal from Lebanon except for a three-to-nine mile-wide security zone just north of the Israeli border. The zone—patrolled by about 2,000 members of the Israeli-backed South Lebanon Army, and up to an estimated 1,000 Israel Defense Forces troops—was necessary since no central Lebanese government authority existed to prevent repeated attempts by Palestinian Arab and Shi'ite Moslem terrorists to infiltrate Israel.

As part of the 1974 disengagement agreement, Israel returned to Syria territories captured in the 1967 and 1973 wars.

Under the terms of the 1979 Israeli-Egyptian peace treaty, Israel withdrew from the Sinai Peninsula in April 1982 for the third time; it withdrew from large parts of Sinai in 1949 and from the entire peninsula in 1957.

Israel's willingness to make withdrawals in exchange for either an armistice or a peace treaty shows that security, not extra land, has been its priority.

MYTH

"The West Bank is part of Jordan."

FACT

The Jordan River was the frontier between Palestine and Transjordan after Britain divided Palestine in 1922.

Mandatory Palestine as recognized by the League of Nations consisted of the entire territory that presently comprises the State of Israel, the West Bank of the Jordan River, and the Hashemite Kingdom of Jordan. In 1922, the British arbitrarily suspended the applicability in the province of Transjordan of the provisions of the Mandate which called for the Jewish National Home. This step entirely removed Transjordan from the possibilities of Jewish immigration and development, restricting them to that portion of Palestine west of the Jordan River.

Legally, however, Transjordan remained part of Mandatory Palestine, and British rule continued until 1946, when the formal partition of Palestine occurred.

In 1948 Abdullah's Arab Legion invaded western Palestine seizing the West Bank and the Old City of Jerusalem. Transjordan formally annexed the West Bank in 1950 and changed its name to Jordan.

Under the partition resolution, the West Bank had been allocated to the proposed Arab state; thus most West Bank Arabs opposed Jordan's takeover.

Only two governments, Britain and Pakistan, recognized the annexation *de jure*.

The United States never recognized Jordan's annexation *de jure*. Similarly Washington never recognized Jordan's sovereignty over the Old City of Jerusalem. On July 29, 1977, Secretary of State Cyrus Vance stated, "It is an open question as to who has legal rights to the West Bank."

MYTH

"Israeli settlements are illegal and are obstacles to peace. They are in violation of the Geneva Convention."

FACT

Numerous legal authorities dispute the charge that the settlements are "illegal." International law scholar Stephen Schwebel, in the *American Journal of International Law*, explained Israel's legal position: (a) A state acting in lawful exercise of its right of self-defense may seize and occupy foreign territory as long as such seizure and occupation are necessary to its self-defense. (b) As a condition of its withdrawal from such territory, that state may require the institution of security measures reasonably designed to ensure that that territory shall not again be used to mount a threat or use of force against it of such a nature as to justify exercise of self-defense. (c) Where the prior holder of territory had seized that territory unlawfully, the state which subsequently takes that territory in the lawful exercise of self-defense has, against that prior holder, better title.

According to former State Department official Eugene Rostow, UN Resolutions 242 and 338 give Israel legal rights in the West Bank. "The Israelis are now in the West Bank as the occupying power under the Security Council Resolutions of 1967 and 1973," Rostow wrote. "They have a right to remain until full peace is made." Israel's claim to the territory is superior to Jordan's, Rostow explained, "since Jordan's presence in the West Bank was the result of its aggression in 1948, while Israel's arose from the exercise of its legitimate right of self-defense in 1967 . . ."

As for Israel's adherence to the Fourth Geneva Convention, lawyer Rita Hauser, in testimony before the House International Relations Committee on Sept. 21, 1977, explained the convention's non-applicability in this case. Hauser, a former U.S. representative to the UN Human Rights Commission, stated: "The restrictions contained in the convention as to a military occupier presuppose that a registrate sovereign was a signatory to the convention.

"The West Bank and Gaza were unlawfully occupied by Jordan and Egypt, respectively," Hauser explained, "as a result of Arab failure to accept the 1947 resolution of the General Assembly which partitioned the former British Palestine Mandate into two parts, and the consequent war which was ended by the armistice prior to the June 1967 war . . . Israel nevertheless has stated that it acts in accordance with the humanitarian provisions of the convention and has attempted to administer the territories on that basis."

Based on the legal evidence, Ronald Reagan concluded that the Jewish villages on the West Bank are not illegal.

"The charge by the [Carter] Administration at the time those settlements first started that they were illegal is false. . . . All people—Moslems, Jews and Christians—are entitled to live on the West Bank," Reagan told a press conference in Oct. 1980. He reiterated his opinion four months later, after taking office.

After many people had said for years that Israel's Sinai settlements were obstacles to peace, those settlements were evacuated as part of a peace agreement with Egypt. Settlements and security often go hand in hand but, as the Sinai case indicates, Israel is willing to make territorial concessions in exchange for the only other guarantee of its security: genuine peace.

MYTH

"The Israeli settlements have displaced thousands of Arabs and have taken hundreds of acres of Arab land."

FACT

As a matter of policy, most settlements established prior to formation of the national unity government in 1984 were located in uninhabited or sparsely populated regions; that government placed a virtual freeze on new settlements, although some existing ones continued to expand. Israeli governments generally have avoided placing the settlements in densely populated areas. In 1979, an attempt to establish a settlement on private Arab land was rejected by Israel's Supreme Court on the grounds that it was not required for security purposes. As a result of this policy, *few Arab residents have been displaced.*

The bulk of the land used for the new communities has been in the categories of state domain, ownerless, or private property owned by absentee landlords. When the owners could be located, they were given the choice of cash compensation or alternative land. About 45% of the land on the West Bank is either state owned, of uncertain ownership, or owned by absentee landlords.

An examination of the location of the West Bank (Judea and Samaria) settlements indicates that the clear majority have been placed along the sparsely inhabited Jordan Valley or along the "green line," the pre-1967 armistice lines—a further indication of the security function even suburban "bedroom" settlements near Tel Aviv and Jerusalem—were meant to serve. Indeed, many of the Jewish villages are on the sites of former Jordanian army and police bases, and have been integrated into the Israeli defense network.

Even under a formula for Israeli withdrawal from the West Bank with minor border modifications, many of these settlements would remain within the new borders of Israel.

Large tracts of land on the West Bank have been legally purchased by Israelis or by the Jewish National Fund. According to one report, the JNF purchased more than $7 million worth of West Bank property from absentee landlords in 1975 alone.

After 1982, a major development occurred on the West Bank: Arab landowners began selling large tracts to private Israeli contractors. New towns have been built and thousands of Israelis have moved into new homes. By 1987 an estimated 65,000 Jews were living in the villages and towns established in the West Bank, the Gaza Strip and Golan Heights—excluding new neighborhoods of Jerusalem. Nevertheless, the Arab population of these territories had grown to approximately 1.4 million, up from about 950,000 in 1968. The economic boom stimulated by Israeli control in 1967 "led to a real increase in the gross national product; in Judea and Samaria it rose by 400% and in the Gaza district by 430%." (*Judea, Samaria, and the Gaza District, 1967-1987: Twenty Years of Civil Administration*, Office of the Co-ordinator of Government operations in Judea, Samaria and Gaza District, Ministry of Defense).

Yet Arab reaction to land sales has been extreme: Jordan has sentenced to death *in absentia* several Arabs who sold land to Jews.

While many residents of the government-sponsored settlements cite national and historic justification for their return to Judea and Samaria, in numerous cases they can claim modern title to the land as well. Several of the communities existed prior to the 1948 war but were overrun by Arab armies in their attack against Israel. Kfar Etzion, Massuot Yitzhak, Ein Zurim and Revadim, for instance, fell to Arab forces in May 1948 and their defenders were captured or massacred. Sons and daughters of these communities' defenders were among the first to return after the 1967 war. A Jewish community existed in Hebron for centuries until Arab riots and resultant massacre in 1929 forced Jews to flee.

MYTH

"Israel has no right to hold on to the Golan Heights."

FACT

The international frontier between Syria and Palestine, arbitrarily determined by the United Kingdom and France after World War I, placed the Golan Heights in Syria. It gave that country a great military advantage over Israel.

The mountain plateau, ranging in height from 400 to over 3,000 feet, rises steeply east of the Sea of Galilee, the Huleh Valley and Israel's towns in the north. From this vantage point, the Syrians constantly attacked Israel's farmers and fishermen and hindered economic development.

The Syrians mounted campaigns against the Israeli project to drain the Lake Huleh swamps, interfered with Israel's comprehensive water plan, and repeatedly threatened to undertake an extravagant project to divert the headwaters of the Jordan (the waters of the Hasbani and Banyas rivers) up over the Golan Heights and southwest to Jordan. The project would have transformed Israel into a desert.

During the Six-Day War, Israelis scaled the escarpment and occupied the 400 square-mile area in the Golan. The territory represents only 0.5% of Syria's 71,498 square miles, but is crucial to the safety of Israel's towns and the preservation of her water resources.

Incidentally, the Golan shows much archeological evidence of Jewish settlement in ancient and Talmudic periods.

MYTH

"Israel illegally annexed the Golan Heights in 1981, a move clearly contrary to international law and UN Resolution 242."

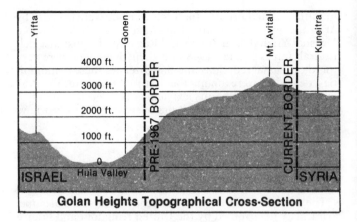

Golan Heights Topographical Cross-Section

FACT

The Israeli Golan Heights law passed on Dec. 14, 1981 extends Israeli civilian law and administration to the residents of the Heights, replacing the military authority which ruled the area for 14 years. The new law does not annex or extend Israeli sovereignty over the region. It does not impose Israeli citizenship on the Golan's non-Jewish inhabitants, as would be required by formal annexation.

More importantly, as Israeli leaders have made clear, the law does not foreclose the option of negotiations on a final settlement of the territory. It, therefore, is consistent with UN Security Council Resolutions 242 and 338.

For 21 years Israel has been prepared to negotiate with Syria. For 21 years, Syria has been implacably opposed not only to negotiations but to Israel's very right to exist.

"The Syrian refusal for 14 years to negotiate a treaty of peace has made any agreed territorial adjustment impossible," Professor Julius Stone of the California Hastings College of the Law wrote following the Israeli Knesset decision. The renowned jurist argued, "There is no rule of international law which requires a lawful military occupant, in this situation, to wait forever before putting the control and government of the territory on a permanent basis. Many international lawyers have wondered, indeed, at the long-suffering patience which led Israel to wait as long as she did before establishing that permanent basis."

80

In 1977, Ronald Reagan addressed this issue:

"The real issue in the Middle East had to do with the Arab refusal to recognize that Israel has a right to exist as a nation. To give up the buffer zones Israel took in the Six-Day War, could be to put a cannon on her front walk aimed at her front door by those who have said she must be destroyed."

In 1988, President Reagan's Secretary of State, George Shultz, was asked by Associated Press if he agreed with Israel's Foreign Minister, Shimon Peres, that Israel should not return to its pre-1967 lines:

"Absolutely. 'No' to a Palestinian State. 'No' to a return to the borders."

MYTH

"Israel's demand for defensible borders is unrealistic in this era of missiles and long-range bombers capable of crossing vast territories."

FACT

Aerial attacks have never defeated a nation, as history illustrates with the blitz bombing of England in World War II or with the bombing of North Vietnam in the 1970's. Instead, nations are conquered by troop invasion and occupation.

By definition, defensible boundaries would prevent or at least impede such a ground assault. On the other hand, the pre-1967 borders, indefensible in character, encouraged Arab attempts to cut Israel into sections to hasten its destruction.

In 1983, Israel received an unexpected endorsement for its call for defensible borders when the Pentagon declassified a June 29, 1967 memorandum from the U.S. Joint Chiefs of Staff.

In the memo, the Joint Chiefs concluded, "From a strictly military point of view, Israel would require the retention of some captured territory in order to provide militarily defensible borders."

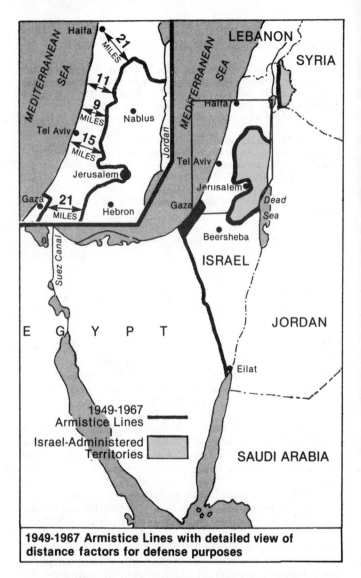

1949-1967 Armistice Lines with detailed view of distance factors for defense purposes

Specifically, the Joint Chiefs recommended a defense line down the middle of the West Bank "as a minimum." The hills of the West Bank, if possessed by Jordan, would offer it a "route for a thrust to the sea" which could "split the country [Israel] in half," the Joint Chiefs warned. The new defense line "would widen the narrow portion of Israel and provide additional buffer for the airbase at Beersheva."

From a military point of view, the memorandum also recommended Israeli retention of the Golan and Gaza strip. "The organization of an adequate defensive position" in the Jerusalem area required that "the boundary of Israel be positioned to the east of the city," which, in effect, endorses Israel's refusal to redivide Jerusalem.

In an era of weapons like the Stinger anti-aircraft missile—smuggled by mule into Afghanistan to lethal effect against Soviet aircraft in the mid- and late-1980's—Israel must ensure that no hostile force controls the mountain tops of Judea and Samaria. Otherwise, the ability of its air force to spread a protective umbrella over even the pre-1967 territory of "Israel proper" would be jeopardized.

MYTH

"The Yom Kippur War and Arab success in penetrating Israeli positions prove the uselessness of defensible borders."

FACT

The strategic depth the occupied territories afforded Israel actually underscores the importance of defensible borders. This depth allowed Israeli troops to absorb the Arabs' surprise attack, regroup and counter-attack while reserves mobilized in safety. Unlike earlier wars, populated areas were not under fire. (Previously, Israeli civilians were prey to even small arms and mortar fire.) KELT and FROG missiles fired by Egyptian and Syrian forces fell on defense positions and not on densely-populated centers. Flight times to Israeli cities from Egyptian bases were three times longer than in 1967. An attack of the 1973 magnitude on pre-1967 Israel would have meant the overrunning of major Israeli population areas.

The arguments used against Israel's demand for "defensible borders" are based on an erroneous definition of the term. Defensible borders are not borders that are impregnable, but borders that, if breached, still allow for the defense of the country and its population centers. Far from proving the obsolescence of the defensible borders concept, the Yom Kippur War clearly proved its continuing validity.

The drastically increased accuracy and destructiveness of tactical, or battlefield weapons, as well as strategic missiles, since 1973 only heightens the need for the buffer zones around the "heartland" of a threatened and tiny country like Israel. Losses to the standing army in the initial hours of any future surprise attack could be several times more serious than those suffered by the Israelis in the 1973 war.

11

Israel and Lebanon

MYTH

"Israel cannot claim that its 1982 invasion of Lebanon—against an ill-equipped PLO—was a defensive war."

FACT

A defensive act is one devoted to resisting or preventing aggression. For over a decade the PLO threatened civilian life in northern Israel. Israel attempted to curb this aggression through retaliatory strikes against PLO bases in Lebanon. Israeli air strikes and commando raids, however, were unable to stem the growth of the PLO army—to more than 15,000 gunmen on the eve of the invasion—along Israel's border.

The opposition that Israel faced was neither ill-armed nor ill-equipped. The PLO had stockpiled large caches of Soviet arms and long-range artillery. Furthermore, Syrian air-defenses assisted the PLO. Israel was under no obligation to wait for a Syrian-PLO onslaught against its northern towns before striking at the PLO bases and eliminating its arsenals.

MYTH

"The PLO posed no real threat to Israel. At the time of Israel's attack, the PLO had been observing a year-long ceasefire."

FACT

For seven years, Israel's northern settlements endured attacks from PLO artillery positioned in southern Lebanon. Lebanon also served as a base for terrorist raids into Israel's interior.

In 1978, Israel mounted the Litani operation to push back the PLO. Israel withdrew voluntarily after two months and United Nations forces entered the region. However, terrorists reinfiltrated the area and attacks and raids on Israel's civilian population continued. U.N. forces proved unable or unwilling to stop the terrorists. As Jill Becker wrote, referring to developments in 1981, "The UNIFIL [United Nations Interim Forces in Lebanon] command entered into treaties of cooperation with the PLO, by which they agreed to admit PLO officers and men into the area under their control for access to observation posts. Despite this atmosphere of friendly cooperation, there were still some armed clashes between them, in which more UNIFIL soldiers were killed" (*The PLO: The Rise and Fall of the Palestine Liberation Organization*, 1984, St. Martin's Press). In 1987, the *Jerusalem Post* was still reporting episodes such as the one in which "Israel Defense Forces soldiers were fired upon from behind a South Lebanese Army position, and the gunmen then retreated inside a U.N. Army post belonging to the Nepalese contingent. They then continued to fire from that UNIFIL position . . ." This group of 50 Shi'ite radicals apparently had learned from PLO examples.

Philip Habib, President Reagan's special envoy to the Middle East, negotiated a ceasefire along Israel's northern border on July 24, 1981. The PLO violated the ceasefire 148 times. Furthermore, the PLO used the ceasefire to transform itself into a conventional army, stockpiling enough Soviet weapons to fully arm five infantry brigades.

The shooting of Israel's ambassador to Great Britain, Shlomo Argov, on June 3, 1982 was not the *cause* for Israel's operation into Lebanon, rather it was the final straw. In response, the Israeli Air Force attacked two known PLO bases in Beirut. The PLO then launched a 24-hour attack on

---

Documents captured during the 1982 war attest to the PLO's intentions to hit Israeli civilian targets. One such document, dated July 1981, read:

"Blessings of the Revolution!

The supreme Military Command decided to concentrate on the destruction of Kiryat Shmona, Metulla, Dan, Shaar Yeshuv, Nahariya and its surroundings.

Kiryat Shmona: will be divided between the units and shelled with improved Grad rockets.

Metulla: will be shelled with 160mm morters.

Nahariya and its surroundings: will be shelled with 130 mm guns."

---

civilian centers in northern Israel, in which over 1,000 shells were fired at 23 settlements.

Only then was Operation Peace for Galilee mounted to ensure the safety of Israel's northern settlements in the face of constant, concerted and escalating PLO threats.

Former Secretary of State Henry Kissinger defended the Israeli operation on June 16, 1982: "No sovereign state can tolerate indefinitely the build up along its borders of a military force dedicated to its destruction and implementing its objectives by periodic shellings and raids."

MYTH

"Israeli action in Lebanon violated Lebanese sovereignty and international law."

FACT

The Israeli operation was not directed against Lebanon, but rather a terrorist group within Lebanon's borders yet beyond the Lebanese government's control.

Lebanese sovereignty had been violated since 1969 when the PLO first infiltrated Lebanon and began to establish a state-within-a-state. Syria entered Lebanon in 1976 and established itself as the local authority. For the six years prior to Israel's operation, Lebanon, as a sovereign government, had ceased to exist. More than 60% of its land was controlled by foreign hands.

Israel did not violate international law. Article 51 of the United Nations Charter ensures the basic right of self-defense. This right was exercised by the United States when Soviet missiles were found in Cuba in 1962, and by Great Britain in the 1982 Falkland dispute.

Furthermore, international law guarantees a country the right to enter foreign soil to remove an armed threat which the host country cannot control.

MYTH

"The PLO was in Lebanon legally. Agreements between Lebanon and the PLO permitted PLO camps on Lebanese soil."

FACT

Once thousands of PLO gunmen infiltrated into Lebanon in the late 1960's and early 1970's, attempts were made to control them through signed agreements. None of these agreements were implemented or adhered to by the PLO.

87

In 1969, Arafat signed the "Cairo Agreement" whereby he pledged that the PLO would not shell Israel from Lebanon; that the PLO would not operate bases in southern Lebanon; and that there would be no PLO military training in refugee camps.

After years of violations, the Lebanese army moved against the PLO in 1973. The fighting ended with the signing of the Malkert Agreement wherein the PLO promised to remove heavy weapons from refugee camps; end terrorist activity in Lebanon; and cease using refugee camps as training bases.

Again, the PLO flagrantly violated the agreement. After the Lebanese civil war and Syrian intervention, the PLO signed the Shtaura Agreement in 1977. The PLO agreed to restoration of Lebanese sovereignty in all of Lebanon; to relinquish control of the refugee camps; to surrender all heavy weapons; to cease importing arms and ammunition; and to stop military training programs.

The PLO flouted the agreements, and by 1982, was virtually a sovereign power within Lebanon. With the PLO weakened after its ouster from Beirut in 1982—and by Syrian-backed dissidents from Tripoli in 1983—momentum shifted. By 1987 the Lebanese parliament was able to recommend revocation of the Cairo Agreement.

MYTH

"Life in southern Lebanon under the PLO was orderly. The Israeli occupation actually disrupted normal life."

FACT

Despite PLO claims of protecting the Palestinians and Lebanese of southern Lebanon and providing them with various social services, life under the PLO was anything but normal.

The PLO entered Lebanon in large numbers after 1970, when it was expelled from Jordan. In Jordan the terrorists had disrupted civilian life and threatened government stability. After being driven out of Jordan, the PLO was denied permanent settlement and independent action in Syria.

In weaker Lebanon, the PLO seized whole areas of the country, evicted residents, terrorized the population and usurped Lebanese governmental authority. Houses were appropriated for ammunition dumps. Cars were stopped arbitrarily on the streets and taken at gunpoint. And, Lebanese teenagers were kidnapped by the PLO, to be released later with their fingers cut off so that they could not fire weapons for the opposition.

The majority of the Lebanese population opposed the PLO occupation and welcomed Israel as marking the end of what one southern Lebanon resident described as the "complete anarchy . . . imposed by the Arafat gang" (Halil Shamariyeh, *Ma'ariv*, July 16, 1982).

On Oct. 14, 1976, Lebanese Ambassador Edouard Ghorra told the UN General Assembly that the PLO was bringing ruin upon his country. "Palestinian elements belonging to various . . . organizations resorted to kidnapping Lebanese—and sometimes foreigners—holding them prisoners, questioning them, torturing them and even sometimes killing them . . . ." The Islamic fundamentalist hijackers and kidnappers who plagued Lebanon in the middle- and late-1980's followed the example set earlier by the PLO—and at times appeared to cooperate with them.

MYTH

"Syrian forces entered Lebanon to serve as a peacekeeping force at the request of the Arab League. Today, Syria has legitimate security interests in Lebanon."

FACT

The Syrians did not enter Lebanon at the request of either the Lebanese government or the Arab League.

In May 1976, Syrian troops crossed into Lebanon to aid Christian Lebanese in preventing a take-over by a PLO-Moslem alliance. Not until five months later, in Oct., did the Arab League legitimize the Syrian occupation by declaring the Syrian troops to be the majority of an "all-Arab peacekeeping force" in Lebanon.

At the Fez Conference in Sept. 1982, the Arab League refused to renew the mandate that legitimized the Syrian presence in Lebanon. The Lebanese government of President Amin Gemayel later said that Lebanon did not want Syrian troops to remain on its soil.

Syria is not in Lebanon as a legitimate peacekeeping force, but rather as a foreign power attempting to impose its will on a sovereign nation.

Indeed, Syria considers all of Lebanon to be an integral

part of "Greater Syria." As early as July 1976, Syrian President Assad was openly declaring, "Syria and Lebanon have always been one country, one people."

As a result of Syria's designs on Lebanon, it refuses to maintain official, diplomatic relations with Beirut. Syria, it is widely believed, was responsible for the assassinations of President-elect Bashir Gemayel in 1982. Syria's redeployment of troops in and around Beirut in 1987 and 1988 highlighted Damascus' divide-and-conquer approach to Lebanon. Ostensibly, the Syrian army entered to quell bloody fighting between warring militias. Several of the militias, however, were Syrian-backed.

MYTH

"Israeli raids into Lebanon killed innocent civilians and were illegal."

FACT

Following an April 1979 terrorist attack that killed four Israeli civilians—including two small children—Israel announced that it would aggressively seek out terrorist bases rather than wait for terrorist attacks.

This policy was defended later by then-National Security Adviser in the Reagan White House, Richard V. Allen. In an interview in Feb. 1981, Allen stated, "To the extent that one reaches to the source of terrorism then, of course there is ample justification for taking action. . . . Reaching to the source is generally recognized as hot pursuit of a sort, and therefore justified."

When civilian lives were lost during Israeli raids, the fault must be assigned to the PLO terrorists, who deliberately located their bases within population centers and refugee camps in order to use the civilians as shields.

Israeli attacks against terrorist concentrations were not indiscriminate. According to American news accounts, dozens of terrorist raids were thwarted and scores of terrorists killed. In one Israeli raid in June 1979, the coordinating committee for terrorist operations was wiped out.

Israel's response is legitimate self-defense. On Oct. 1, 1974, on the Senate floor, the late Sen. Hubert Humphrey discussed Israel's attacks against terrorist bases. The Senator declared, "It has been made abundantly clear by eminent international legal scholars that Israel's retaliatory raids into Lebanon . . . are countenanced by international law, and constitute 'legitimate self-defense' as cited in the Foreign Assistance Act of 1961 ... Israel's actions on Lebanese territory are also based on the inherent right of Israel to self-defense in accordance with Article 51 of the UN Charter."

MYTH

"Proof of Israel's brutality against Arabs can be seen in Israel's bombing of downtown Beirut in July 1981. More than 500 civilians were killed."

FACT

On July 17, 1981, Israeli planes struck the PLO command center in Beirut. The targets—Fatah's operational headquarters, the offices of the Iraqi-controlled Arab Liberation Army, and the headquarters of the Democratic Front for the Liberation of Palestine—were located in the middle floors of three buildings. PLO families and other civilians lived in apartments beneath and above the offices.

The Israeli attack on the PLO did not take place in a vacuum. It occurred in the midst of a conflict in which the PLO had declared war on the civilian population in Israel's Galilee.

During early 1981, the PLO had reorganized into a terrorist army. Heavy weapons had arrived from Libya and the Soviet Union.

The *Sunday Times* of London reported on July 19, "Earlier this month, rocket-launchers, guns, tanks and anti-aircraft missiles were observed moving southwards across the Zahrani and Litani rivers. . . . The Israelis are particularly concerned about the new 40- and 20-barrel mobile Katyusha rocket launchers, which have a range of 18 miles and are the main weapon used by the PLO [against] civilian targets in Galilee."

The PLO also received T-55, T-54 and T-34 tanks; 130mm, 150mm, and 57mm cannons, armored personnel carriers; SAM-7 and SAM-9 anti-aircraft missiles; and heavy mortars.

The Israeli attack on the PLO headquarters was designed to disrupt and destroy the PLO's ability to attack Israel's civilians. According to news accounts, there were less than 300 casualties, and many of them were officers or members of the terrorist organizations.

The PLO is known for its exaggerated reports of casualties—both those inflicted on Israelis and those incurred by Palestinian Arabs. One month prior to the Beirut incident, a PLO advertisement in the *Christian Science Monitor* charged that "more than 500 people . . . had been killed in the previous month by Israeli military air raids and attacks." The *Monitor* ran a retraction two weeks later, which said:

> "The Lebanese government in Beirut estimates that about 100 persons were killed from May 25 to June 25. Of these about 90 resulted from Syrian shelling, about 10 from Israeli attacks. The total number killed since April 1 is about 70. The great majority of losses resulted from shelling by Syrian forces. . . . "

By the end of July 1981, an uneasy ceasefire was arranged by U.S. envoy Philip Habib. The PLO, however, continued its military buildup of tanks, heavy artillery, and rockets. PLO raids against the Christians and Moslems in southern Lebanon continued, as well as terrorist bombings in Israel's towns and attempted forays across Israel's borders.

MYTH

"Israel's action in southern Lebanon caused 10,000 civilian deaths and left 600,000 homeless."

FACT

These figures, which were widely circulated in the first few weeks of Israel's 1982 incursion into Lebanon, were supplied by the Palestinian Red Crescent, headed by Yasir Arafat's brother, Fathi Arafat. These figures were repeated by sources who had no access to the combat areas in southern Lebanon.

The inaccuracy of these figures is readily apparent—only 510,000 individuals resided in all of southern Lebanon. International Red Cross officials later denounced the figures presented by the Palestinian Red Crescent.

Israel took special measures to avoid civilian casualties, but the stationing of PLO armaments and men in civilian centers raised the civilian death count.

Critics of Israel forget or ignore the death and destruction caused in large part by the PLO and Syrian occupation of Lebanon dring the era of the Lebanese civil war, which resulted in an estimated 100,000 killed, 250,000 wounded,

800,000 Christians and 500,000 Moslems homeless, and 32,000 orphaned children from 1970 until Israel's operation. (Source: American Lebanese League, *New York Times*, July 14, 1982.) According to wire service reports, by mid-1987 another 20,000 had been slain in that country's continuing chaos, and several times that number added to the list of wounded—the result of *intra-Arab* enmity.

MYTH

"The PLO was willing to leave Beirut in the summer of 1982 and save the civilian population from further attack, but Israel made this impossible."

FACT

Within the first week of Israel surrounding terrorist positions in west Beirut, Lebanese leaders asked the PLO to leave. Walid Jumblatt, the leader of a coalition of leftist Lebanese allied with the PLO, told Arafat to "face reality" and leave Beirut in order to save the capital from destruction.

However, for over a month the PLO proved itself intransigent, trying to exact a political victory from its military defeat. Arafat declared his willingness "in principle" to leave Beirut, then subsequently refused to go to any other country; the PLO demanded American guarantees of safe transit, then rejected President Reagan's offer of a Sixth Fleet escort; Arafat sought American recognition of the PLO, yet refused to fulfill the American precondition of recognition of Israel's right to exist.

Only when Israel stepped up its military pressure, through heavy aerial and artillery bombardments of PLO positions on Aug. 4th and 11th, did the PLO drop its demands and agree to leave without concessions. Following Israeli penetration of PLO positions in the south and east, Arafat dropped his demand for deployment of a multinational force before PLO withdrawal and reduced the timetable for withdrawal to two weeks. Israel compromised by accepting deployment of the multinational force after only a partial terrorist withdrawal.

The siege of Beirut was prolonged not by Israel's action, but by PLO intransigence. Arafat and the rest of the PLO leadership virtually held the city hostage; by negotiating the PLO's retreat—while Western news media portrayed the siege as Israeli aggression—Israel chose the tactic that

93

would spare the most lives, both Israeli and Lebanese.

MYTH

"Israel was directly responsible for the massacre of thousands of Palestinian refugees at Sabra and Shatilla."

FACT

Sabra and Shatilla, two refugee quarters in southern Beirut, were the sites of terrorist bases. Captured PLO members reported, for instance, that the "European base" for the training of German, British, Irish and Italian terrorists was located in Shatilla.

On Sept. 16, 1982, members of the Maronite Christian Phalange militia entered the camps. When Israeli soldiers ordered them out they found 460 dead, including 15 women and 20 children. Among the dead were Palestinians, Lebanese, Pakistanis, Iranians, Syrians, and Algerians, according to Lebanese police.

The Phalange committed the massacre in the refugee camps, an act which should be viewed as part of the internecine warfare that has plagued Lebanon. The massacre was in retaliation for the assassination of President Bashir Gemayel, the leader of the Maronite Christians, and 25 of his followers, two days earlier. Massacres have been—and continue to be—part of the political warfare among Lebanon's numerous sects for more than a century.

Israel had allowed the Phalange to enter Moslem west Beirut in an effort to transfer authority to the Lebanese, and Israel took responsibility for that decision. The Kahan Commission of Inquiry, formed by the Israeli government in response to public outrage and grief, found that Israel was indirectly responsible for not forseeing the possibility of Phalange violence.

While the massacre was a tragic event, it is important to note that Israel did not absolve itself from blame, but rather accepted its responsibility and instituted the recommendations of the Commission, including the dismissal of Defense Minister Ariel Sharon and General Raphael Eitan, the Chief of Staff of the Israeli Army.

It is ironic that there was little or no reaction in the Arab world. While more than 300,000 people demonstrated in Israel, there was no public reaction to the massacre in any Arab country. An inquiry conducted by the Lebanese government, undertaken months after the Kahan Commission, found the Lebanese free of responsibility and placed all the blame squarely on the shoulders of the Israelis.

Former Secretary of State Henry Kissinger summed up the Kahan Commission of Inquiry as a "great tribute to Israeli democracy that they could accept such a heavy responsibility by such high-level people. It is true that there are very few governments in the world that one can imagine making such a public investigation of such a difficult and shameful episode."

To illustrate the double standard frequently applied to Israel: no worldwide outcry was heard in May 1985 when Shi'ite Moslem militiamen attacked the Shatilla and Burj el-Barajneh camps of the Palestinian Arabs. According to U.N. officials, 635 were killed and 2,500 wounded. During the two-year intermittent "camps war" between the Syrian-backed Shi'ite Amal group and Palestinian gunmen largely loyal to Arafat, more than 2,000—including many civilians—reportedly were killed. A footnote to the combat was that Amal, made up of Lebanese, fought to prevent the PLO from reestablishing itself in the camps and from re-instituting its pre-1982 reign of terror over Lebanon.

MYTH

"Israel seeks to extend its northern border to the Litani River; Israeli policies in southern Lebanon prove this."

FACT

During the first round of Lebanon's bloody civil war (1975-1976), inhabitants of southern Lebanon—Christian, Druze and Moslem—turned to Israel for assistance after the savage fighting cut off the region's services and markets. Villagers came to Israel's border seeking medical assistance, fuel and water. In a humanitarian gesture, Israel opened the border, initiating its "Good Fence."

In the first year of the Good Fence, over 25,000 Lebanese received medical attention at Israeli first-aid stations and clinics, with over 1,000 hospitalized in Israel. Food staples and jobs were made available to Lebanese unable to work in their old jobs, and who were not hostile to Israel. Israeli agricultural experts have helped Lebanese farmers increase their yields and market their products.

In March 1978, PLO terrorists from southern Lebanon

attacked Israeli civilians along the Tel Aviv coast, killing 34. In response, Israeli forces attacked terrorist concentrations in southern Lebanon, pushing the terrorists northward. Israel withdrew voluntarily after two months and United Nations forces entered.

Terrorists reinfiltrated the region. By 1979, an estimated 2,000 Palestinian gunmen had reestablished operations in southern Lebanon, attacking Israelis and Lebanese Christians and introducing new and heavier arms. The PLO was establishing a terrorist army, even within the UN-controlled areas. It was the PLO that sought to dominate the southern Lebanese regions.

MYTH

"Israel's deployment of its troops in southern Lebanon is the first step toward the annexation of that territory."

FACT

Israeli officials have repeatedly stated that Israel does not covet one inch of Lebanese territory. The withdrawal from Lebanon in 1985 confirmed that. The relatively small force deployed in southern Lebanon protects towns and villages

in northern Israel and Moslem and Christian towns in southern Lebanon from terrorist attacks.

Meanwhile, in 1988, between 25,000 and 30,000 Syrian soldiers still occupied much of eastern and northern Lebanon. Thousands of other armed men, some loyal to Iran, others to Syria, many members of various Palestinian terrorist groups, and more who belong to the numerous Lebanese sectarian militias, also contributed to the anarchy which overwhelmed Lebanon and at times threatened to spread south.

Syrian troops must withdraw and terrorist groups be disarmed and dispersed for Lebanon to be reconstituted finally as a sovereign and independent nation.

12

The United Nations

MYTH

"The United Nations plays a constructive and objective role in Middle East affairs. Accusations of pro-Arab or pro-PLO bias are false."

FACT

Starting in the mid-1970's, the Arab-Soviet-third world bloc supported a growing PLO lobby at the United Nations. Particularly in the General Assembly—where 9.5% of the world's population commands two-thirds of the vote—the Arab, Soviet and third world countries voted as a unit to pass resolutions which served the PLO cause. In 1974, for example, the General Assembly invited a pistol-packing Yasir Arafat to speak before it. In 1975, the Assembly awarded permanent representation status to the PLO's Zehdi Labib Terzi, who together with "Information Director" Hassan Abdel Rahman opened a sizable office in midtown Manhattan. Also that year, the Assembly adopted the Soviet-backed, Arab-promoted resolution which obscenely equated Zionism—the Jewish response to anti-Jewish racism—with racism.

As Chaim Herzog, then Israel's UN Ambassador, noted, the world organization developed an Alice-in-Wonderland perspective on Israel. "In the U.N. building . . . she would only have had to wear a Star of David in order to hear the imperious 'Off with her head' at every turn . . . .

"The PLO takes credit for a dastardly bomb explosion in Jerusalem and then cites General Assembly Resolution 3236 as the legitimization of its activities, to which the UN responds by inviting the representative of that criminal organization to sit at the Security Council table." Resolution 3236, adopted in 1974, in effect reiterated the PLO's plan for destroying Israel, Herzog wrote *(Who Stands Accused? Israel Answers Its Critics*, Random House, 1978).

Bloc voting also made possible the establishment of the pro-PLO "Committee on the Inalienable Rights of the Palestinian People" in 1975. The committee recommended to the General Assembly a program to achieve Palestinian Arab rights: it has organized meetings, issued pro-Palestinian UN stamps, and prepared films and draft resolutions on the "Question of Palestine."

The committee's first report was presented in 1976 and recommended the establishment of an "independent Palestinian entity" and "full implementation of the inalienable rights of the Palestinian people," incldding their return to the Israeli part of Palestine. The committee also recommended that the General Assembly observe Nov. 29 (the day the UN voted to partition Palestine in 1947) as the "International Day of Solidarity with the Palestinian People." The day has since been observed at the UN with anti-Israel rallies, films and exhibits.

In Dec. 1977, the PLO was given additional exposure at the UN when a Special Unit on the Palestinian People was established as part of the UN Secretariat. The Special Unit's mandate was to provide additional staff support to the "Rights Committee" and to publicize its work.

A result of the pro-PLO committees has been the undermining of the UN's goals and daily workings, according to former U.S. representative to the UN, Seymour Maxwell Finger. The committees have "hurt the Secretariat staff's morale and public perception of the impartiality it should have," Finger noted. "Such one-sided Assembly decisions do not help the standing and integrity of the UN."

Aside from the committees, the excessive number of Arab professionals on the UN Secretariat also contributes to pro-PLO bias. The United Nations' "professional job rules" provide that jobs must be distributed fairly among members, with job quotas for citizens from each country. Yet Arab countries have been routinely overrepresented, with Palestinian Arabs occupying many posts. And the role of Kurt Waldheim as Secretary General of the UN during the period that organization welcomed the PLO has yet to be fully examined. Waldheim, whose Nazi past was revealed before his 1986 election as president of Austria, did not act to mediate the 1973 Yom Kippur War until Israel took the offensive, and routinely made decisions agreeing with Soviet positions.

The United States actively opposed the establishment of both the Palestinian Rights Committee and the Special Unit on the Palestinian People. Senator Daniel Moynihan

(D-N.Y.), who served as U.S. Ambassador to the UN in 1975, declared that the establishment of the two committees made the UN Secretariat "a party to a conflict between members of the UN, a clear violation of the charter." In a letter to Congress in January 1978, the Department of State said that it opposed these committees' "needless" expenses as well as their creation and recommendations. The United States has described their actions as "misguided" and "totally devoid of balance."

According to the Israeli UN Mission, the regular budget for the 1986-1987 UN session included more than $10 million for activities—the vast majority bureaucratic or public relations expenses—related to the Palestinian Arabs and debates on "the question of Palestine." These "debates," as the 1987 session again demonstrated, are merely a succession of anti-Israel harangues by PLO, Arab and third world representatives for whom "the question of Palestine" remains the question of Israel's right to exist.

MYTH

"Israel must implement all UN resolutions adopted on the Middle East."

FACT

Only the Security Council can pass resolutions which, if unanimously passed, are binding upon the members of the UN. As the UN charter explicitly states, the resolutions of the General Assembly are mere recommendations having no binding effect.

If the powers of the General Assembly seem weak on paper, they are even weaker in practice due to the phenomenon of Soviet, Arab and third world bloc voting. Bloc voting was invoked religiously on resolutions castigating Israel, and for a decade—from the middle 1970's to middle 1980's—crippled the Assembly's role as a legitimate international decision-making forum, especially on Middle East issues. But as the world oil glut weakened Arab nations' ability to play pressure politics, cracks appeared in the automatic majority. For example, the UN's 1985 "Women's Decade Conference" in Nairobi accepted a U.S. veto of a resolution declaring a Palestinian Arab right to self-determination. U.S. delegate Alan Keyes called the resolution "a tendentious political formulation" that could harm Middle East peace efforts. Egypt had previously pressed for a compromise which omitted critical references to Israel. Despite a walkout by delegates from some Arab, Soviet bloc and African countries during the speech of Israeli delegation chief Sarah Doron, the conference ended by deleting language equating Zionism with racism.

In 1985 and 1986, in the General Assembly itself, the annual Arab effort to challenge Israel's credentials appeared to weaken. In 1985, 83 countries backed Iceland's move to take no action on the Arab proposal, with 41 countries opposed, 18 abstaining and 16 absent. In 1986, on the same issue, the votes were 86 for no action, 41 opposed to Iceland's anti-challenge move, 14 abstaining and 17 absent.

As an alternative to expelling Israel, the Arab states, backed by Soviet-bloc and many nonaligned and third world nations, embarked on an effort to vilify Zionism, the philosophy behind Jewish nationalism. This campaign resulted in a General Assembly resolution adopted in Nov. 1975 which labeled Zionism a form of "racism and racial discrimination."

U.S. Ambassador Moynihan called the resolution "an obscene act." Herzog declared: "This day will live in infamy. Hitler would have felt at home in this hall." The vote was 72 to 35 with 32 abstentions and three delegations absent. The mechanical majorities commanded by the Arabs and their backers—there are 20 Arab delegations at the UN—assured the passage of this and virtually any anti-Israel resolution, no matter how extreme or absurd.

Even in the so-called humanitarian and specialized affiliates of the UN, the pro-Arab voting bloc has managed to politicize activities—resulting in a sharp backlash of support among American public opinion and in the U.S. Congress. Thus, in 1975, the United States withheld its funds from UNESCO because of its anti-Israel actions, and the United States withdrew from the International Labor Organization for two years because of its blatantly anti-Israel position.

The U.S. government withdrew from UNESCO at the end of 1984 because its policies "have, for several years, departed sharply from the established goals of the organization. We have regularly advised UNESCO of the limits of U.S. (and Western) toleration of misguided policies and programs, and of repeated management failures .... Extraneous politicization continues as does, regrettably, an endemic hostility toward the institutions of a free society—

particularly those that protect a free press, free markets, and, above all, individual human rights. UNESCO's [fiscal] mismanagement also continues . . . ."

What ailed UNESCO afflicted the UN as a whole, especially regarding Israel. As Ambassador Jeane Kirkpatrick told the *Washington Post* on Dec. 2, 1984, "It's fairly clear that among the Arabs the principal elements of unity are certain kinds of hostility to Israel and Israeli policies. As for Israel, I was not really aware until I came to the United Nations of the extent or the intensity of hostility to that nation . . . . The analogies drawn between Nazis and Israelis are practically a daily affair at the United Nations. It happens all the time—accusations of genocide, contempt for the notion that there is a rule of law in Israel, or that there is honor in Israel or that there is any kind of legitimacy about Israel. There is a readiness to believe anything about Israel, no matter how outrageous."

Her successor, Vernon Walters, told a Congressional committee a year later that in the General Assembly "there has grown up the nasty habit of singling out the United States for special condemnation in resolutions. It is a transparent ploy promoted by the Soviet Union and its henchmen, and they usually throw Israel in with the United States to attract Arab votes."

The U.S. Congress has voted to delete that portion of the U.S. UN contribution which would be earmarked for the two commitees set up by the General Assembly to publicize the cause of Palestinian Arabs.

As for Israel's—or America's—obligation to implement General Assembly resolutions, many, like 38/180D, adopted Dec. 19, 1983 by a 103 to 18 vote, undermine the national interests of both countries. That particular resolution determined that "strategic cooperation between the United States and Israel . . . would threaten the security of the region. [The General Assembly] calls on all states to put an end to the flow to Israel of any military, financial, and economic aid . . . ." Among U.S. aid recipients and friends voting *for:* Greece, Turkey, Thailand, the Philippines, Mexico, Brazil, Argentina, Venezuela, Peru, Morocco, Egypt, Oman, Somalia, Saudi Arabia and Jordan.

MYTH

"At the United Nations, Israel is a burden to the United States.

The U.S. delegation loses prestige with other nations by casting votes to protect Israel."

FACT

Bloc-voting by Soviet-dominated, Islamic, and third world nations can carry virtually any issue at the United Nations, but these votes are not cast only against Israel. "The influence of these voting blocs is so all-pervasive," Kirkpatrick told the Senate Subcommittee on Foreign Operations in March 1983, "aside from the United States, only Canada, New Zealand and Australia, and a very few others, exist out of voting blocs . . ."

Israel, Kirkpatrick explained, is one of those "very few others." Indeed, Israel is the United States' leading supporter at the UN. Of 20 issues of importance to the United States in 1982, she explained, Israel cast 86.2% of its votes with the United States. The Jordanian delegation, on the other hand, tied with Bulgaria at 20.8%.

Five years later the situation looked much the same. The 1987 State Department report on U.N. General Assembly voting showed Israel standing with the United States 80% of the time, more than any other country. Great Britain was second at 79.2%. NATO nations averaged 62.4% agreement with America, the Arab group 11% and the Warsaw Pact countries 10.3%. Specifically, Egypt—largest recipient of direct U.S. foreign aid after Israel—voted with the United States 14.4% of the time, Saudi Arabia 12.4%, Syria 5.8%.

13

The Refugees

MYTH

"Palestinian Arab refugees were the major victims of the 1948 war."

FACT

The Arab war in defiance of the 1947 UN partition resolution actually created *two* refugee problems—Arab and Jewish.

Although much has been said about the plight of the Arab refugees, little is heard about the 800,000 Jewish refugees—who, facing increased discrimination and an uncertain future, fled from the Arab states.

They had reason for apprehension. Their situation long had been precarious. During the 1947 UN debates, Arab leaders threatened them. Egypt told the General Assembly:

> "The lives of a million Jews in Moslem countries will be jeopardized by the establishment of the Jewish state."

Little is heard about these Jewish refugees because they did not remain refugees for long. Most were absorbed by their fellow Jews and became citizens of Israel. (Other Jewish refugees from Moslem countries found homes in Europe, the United States and Canada.)

But the less than 600,000 Arabs who left what is now Israel to escape the conflict did not fare so well with their brothers.

Instead of offering opportunities to the Arab refugees, most Arab governments rejected suggestions for resettling the refugees—claiming resettlement would remove the evidence of the world's crime against them. The Arab governments preferred to leave the burden of caring for the Arab refugees to the world community in general, and the United Nations Relief and Works Agency (UNRWA) in particular. Most of the financial burden has been carried by the United States.

The contrast in the reception of Jewish refugees in Israel

with the reception of Arab refugees in Arab countries is even more stark when one considers the difference in cultural and geographic dislocation experienced by the two groups. Most Jewish refugees travelled hundreds—and some travelled thousands—of miles to a tiny country whose inhabitants spoke a different language. Most Arab refugees never left Palestine at all; they travelled a few miles to the other side of a truce line, remaining inside the vast Arab nation that they were part of linguistically, culturally and ethnically.

MYTH

"Jewish atrocities in 1948 caused a mass Arab exodus."

FACT

Had the Arabs accepted the 1947 UN resolution, their refugee problem would not be an issue today. Palestinian Arabs would not have become "permanent refugees" but today would be living at peace in an independent Arab state if the Arabs had not gone to war. It is the Arab refusal to make peace with Israel which has needlessly and cruelly prolonged Arab displacement for 40 years.

Arab leaders have always tried to disown responsibility for the Arab flight and to blame it on the Israelis. But the truth is that Arab leaders stimulated the Arab departure. From Arab capitals came frightening radio broadcasts because they wanted to arouse the Arab world into a holy war against the Jews. Expecting a quick victory, they fabricated atrocity stories and promised departing Arabs that they would soon return to reclaim their property—and that of the Jews as well.

The exodus began with the departure of wealthy Arabs who preferred to wait out the war in Cairo and Beirut.

It was estimated that 20,000 of them left the country in the first two months of internal hostilities. By the end of Jan. 1948, the exodus was already so alarming that the Palestine Arab Higher Committee asked neighboring Arab countries to refuse visas to these refugees and to seal the borders against them. While the Arab armies were moving in, the Arab civilian population was moving out.

Ash Sha'ab, an Arab newspaper in Jaffa, wrote on Jan. 30, 1948:

"The first group of our fifth column consists of those

who abandon their houses and businesses and go to live elsewhere. . . . At the first signs of trouble they take to their heels to escape sharing the burden of struggle."

As Sarih of Jaffa excoriated Arab villagers near Tel Aviv on March 30, 1948, for "bringing down disgrace on us all" by "abandoning their villages."

Large voluntary evacuations occurred well before the April 10, 1948, attack on Deir Yassin. Thousands of Arabs evacuated the Sharon coastal plain between Tel Aviv and Haifa to move inland to the hills. Many took the time to sell their livestock to Jewish friends.

In Tiberias, when the Jewish community of 2,000 broke the siege by 6,000 Arabs on April 18, 1948, the Arabs suddenly departed, obviously in obedience to a directive. The British provided transport. The startled members of the Jewish Community Council issued a statement, declaring:

"We did not dispossess them; they themselves chose this course. . . . Let no citizen touch their property."

In Safed, 14,000 Arabs picked up and left one night, although they commanded every strategic part of the town and were facing only a small Haganah brigade and 1,500 Jewish civilians.

In one case, in the Ramle-Lod area, Israeli troops, seeking to protect their flanks, forced a portion of the Arab population to go to an area a few miles away that was occupied by the Arab Legion. But these people constituted less than 10% of the Arab refugees, and the report itself has been contradicted by other witnesses to the Arab flight. A study by *Jerusalem Post* reporter Benny Morris has dealt with several cases from the War of Independence in which Jewish troops reportedly drove out Arab civilians. However, these cases were the exceptions. Far more common were the refugees who fled in panic or at the explicit behest of Arab leaders. As Abba Eban noted in 1988, some of the flight could be ascribed to normal human behavior: the desire of civilians to get out of the way of war.

And some no doubt was based on the evacuees' fear that the Jews would behave to them as Arab armies often behaved to civilians in disputed territory.

MYTH

"Israel forced the Arabs to flee from Haifa."

> "There is no evidence of a long-standing and agreed Jewish policy to evict the settled population; on the contrary in the first half of 1948 there is considerable evidence that the Jews tried to prevent the flight . . . When the war was over, Arab journalists and broadcasters asserted on several occasions that the exodus was a planned Arab maneuver the main object being to clear the land and thus give freedom of action to the invading armies."
>
> Christopher Sykes, *Cross Roads to Israel,* 1973.

FACT

There was a mass Arab exodus from Haifa, where Jews and Arabs had lived in harmony, sharing responsibility for the municipal government.

The London *Economist,* on Oct. 2, 1948, carried a British eyewitness account:

> "During subsequent days the Jewish authorities, who were now in complete control of Haifa (save for limited districts still held by the British troops), urged all Arabs to remain in Haifa and guaranteed them protection and security. As far as I know, most of the British civilian residents whose advice was asked by Arab friends told the latter that they would be wise to stay. However, of the 62,000 Arabs who formerly lived in Haifa, not more than 5,000 or 6,500 remained.
>
> "Various factors influenced their decision to seek safety in flight. There is but little doubt that the most potent of the factors were the announcements made over the air by the Arab Higher Executive, urging all Arabs in Haifa to quit. The reason given was that upon the final withdrawal of the British, the combined armies of the Arab states would invade Palestine and 'drive the Jews into the sea,' and it was clearly intimated that those Arabs who remained in Haifa and accepted Jewish protection would be regarded as renegades."

Jamal Husseini, spokesman for the Arab Higher Committee, told the UN Security Council, on April 23, 1948:

> "The Arabs would not submit to a truce but they rather preferred to leave their homes in the town . . . and leave the town . . . they did."

The British police superintendent in Haifa reported in a secret cable to police headquarters in Jerusalem, April 26, 1948:

> "Every effort is being made by the Jews to persuade the Arab populace to stay and carry on with their normal lives, to get their shops and businesses open and to be assured that their lives and interests will be safe."

The late Golda Meir revealed in her autobiography that she had personally responded to Ben Gurion's instructions:

> "Ben Gurion had said: 'I want you to go persuade the Arabs on the beach to go back ... they have nothing to fear.'
>
> "I went immediately. I begged them to return to their homes, but they had only one answer. 'We know there is nothing to fear, but we have to go. We'll be back.' I was quite sure that they went not because they were frightened of us but because they were terrified of being considered traitors to the Arab cause."

The State Department in 1975 released the 1948 dispatches of the U.S. Consul General in Haifa, Aubrey Lippincott. He wrote on April 26, 1948, that "local mufti-dominated leaders" were urging "all Arabs to leave the city," and large numbers were going.

MYTH

"The massacre of hundreds of innocent Arab civilians by Jewish troops at Deir Yassin demonstrates that the Jews were no less terroristic in 1948—or at Kafr Kassem in 1956—than the PLO is today."

FACT

Unlike the PLO's almost exclusive focus on civilian targets, the 100 troops from the Irgun and Stern group that struck at Deir Yassin on April 10, 1948, targeted the village for its military importance. Deir Yassin was on the road to Jerusalem, which the Arabs had blockaded, and it housed Iraqi troops and Palestinian irregulars. Snipers based in Deir Yassin were a constant threat to the Jewish citizens in Jerusalem.

Arab civilians were killed at Deir Yassin, but that attack does not conform to the propaganda picture that the Arabs have tried to paint. The number of Arabs killed was generally reported to be about 250. In April 1983, however, Eric Silver of *The Guardian* (Britain) interviewed a survivor, Mohammed Sammour, who testified that 116 out of a population of 800-1000 were killed. "About three days after the massacre," Sammour explained, "representatives of each of the five clans in Deir Yassin met at the Moslem offices in Jerusalem and made a list of the people who had not been found. We went through the names. Nothing has happened since 1948 to make me think this figure was wrong."

Unlike the PLO's deliberate attacks on civilians, the killing of civilians at Deir Yassin was not premeditated. The attackers left open an escape corridor from the village and more than 200 residents left unharmed. After the remaining Arabs feigned surrender and then fired on the Jewish troops, some of the attackers killed Arab soldiers and civilians indiscriminately. Independent observers told *The Guardian* that among the bodies they found Arab men disguised as women.

On Oct. 29, 1956, the eve of the Sinai campaign, orders were issued by the Israeli Ministry of Defense to keep the Jordanian border area peaceful. The orders expressly prohibited interference with the normal work of the area's population. An Israeli regiment commander ordered an early evening curfew, and most of his unit commanders took the initiative of personally escorting Arab workers to their homes to avoid possible incidents. Unfortunately, however, through a breakdown in communications, one unit commander ordered his men to fire on curfew violators, and 47 inhabitants of Kafr Kassem, an Arab village, were killed.

The regiment commander was courtmartialed, dismissed from the army and sentenced to 17 years of imprisonment. The soldiers who had obeyed their orders were also tried and condemned to penalties ranging from seven to 15 years in prison.

What differentiates these incidents from Arab terrorist attacks is that they are exceptions rather than the rule. The only reason Arab sympathizers constantly raise Deir Yassin and Kafr Kassem is that they have little else to raise. This is in contrast to the nearly endless list of premeditated Arab bombings and attacks on tourists, hikers, schoolchildren and other civilians in Tel Aviv, Jerusalem, Ma'alot, Kiryat Shemona, Nahariya, Yiftach, and on the Coastal and Dimona roads. It is overshadowed by hijackings and other terrorist actions throughout Europe. There were many at-rocities committed by Arabs against Jews in 1948—such as the slaughter of 78 Jewish doctors and nurses on the road to Jerusalem's Hadassah Hospital—but these massacres have receded from memory, overwhelmed by the glut of more recent atrocities against Israel. Deir Yassin and Kafr Kassem, on the other hand, stand almost alone.

Also unlike PLO attacks, for which the perpetrators receive praise in the Arab world, the attack at Deir Yassin was immediately denounced by the Jewish leadership; most of the Jews in Palestine reacted to the news with horror. Had the attack taken place five weeks later—after the proclamation of statehood—those responsible probably would have been prosecuted.

Some Arabs have claimed that what happened at Deir Yassin caused the Arab exodus from Palestine—that the Arabs fled because they were afraid of bloodthirsty Jews. But the exodus began shortly after the UN voted to partition Palestine in Nov. 1947, more than four months before the attack at Deir Yassin. The Arab argument is further weakened by the fact that Palestine's Jews remained in their homes in the face of Arab atrocities that far outnumbered the Jewish attack on Deir Yassin.

MYTH

"Facts about the Arab flight are open to different interpretations."

FACT

There is ample testimony to confirm the facts about the Arab exodus.

The Research Group for European Migration Problems reported in its *Bulletin* for Jan.-March 1957:

"As early as the first months of 1948 the Arab League issued orders exhorting the people to seek temporary refuge in neighboring countries, later to return to their abodes in the wake of the victorious Arab armies and obtain their share of abandoned Jewish property."

On April 3, 1948, (before Deir Yassin), the Near East Broadcasting Station (Cyprus) said:

"It must not be forgotten that the Arab Higher Commitee encouraged the refugees' flight from their homes in

Jaffa, Haifa and Jerusalem and that certain leaders have tried to make political capital of their miserable situation."

On Aug. 16, 1948, Monsignor George Hakim, the Greek Catholic Archbishop of Galilee, said in an interview with the Lebanese newspaper *Sada al-Janub:*

"The refugees had been confident that their absence from Palestine would not last long, that they would return within a few days, within a week or two. Their leaders had promised them that the Arab armies would crush the 'Zionist gangs' very quickly and that there was no need for panic or fear of a long exile."

Emile Ghoury, secretary of the Palestine Arab Higher Committee, said on Sept. 6, 1948, in an interview with the Beirut *Telegraph:*

"The fact that there are these refugees is the direct consequence of the act of the Arab states in opposing partition and the Jewish state. The Arab states agreed upon this policy unanimously, and they must share in the solution of the problem."

John Bagot Glubb (Glubb Pasha), the former commander of the Arab Legion, confirmed in the London *Daily Mail* on Aug. 12, 1948, that "villages were frequently abandoned even before they were threatened by the progress of war."

The Jordanian *Ad-Difaa* (Sept. 6, 1954) put it bluntly:

"We were masters in our land, happy with our lot . . . but overnight everything changed. The Arab government told us: 'Get out so that we can get in.' So we got out but they (the Arab government) did not get in."

MYTH

"Israel encouraged the Arab exodus with verbal threats as well as deeds, thus frightening the populace into leaving."

FACT

Jewish leaders urged the Arabs to remain in Palestine and to become citizens of Israel. The Assembly of Palestine Jewry issued this appeal on Oct. 2, 1947:

"The Jewish people extends the hand of sincere friendship and brotherhood to the Arab peoples and calls them to cooperate as free and equal allies for the sake of peace and progress, for the benefit of their respective countries."

On Nov. 30, the day after the UN vote, the Jewish Agency announced:

"The main theme behind the spontaneous celebrations we are witnessing today is our community's desire to seek peace and its determination to achieve fruitful cooperation with the Arabs . . . . "

Israel's Proclamation of Independence, issued May 14, 1948, declared:

"In the midst of wanton aggression, we yet call upon the Arab inhabitants of the State of Israel to return to the ways of peace and to play their part in the development of the state, with full and equal citizenship and due representation in all its bodies and institutions, provisional or permanent."

Meanwhile, the Arab flight was in full progress.

In Feb. 1962, Salim Joubran, an Arab citizen of Israel, told American audiences the story of his own experience:

"The Arab High Command asked us to leave the country for two weeks to make the battle easier for them. They told us: 'A cannon cannot differentiate between a Jew and an Arab. Leave the country for two weeks and you will come back victorious. . . . ' I heard the Haganah microphone asking the Arabs to remain and live peacefully with their Jewish brethren. The late Jewish Mayor of Haifa also asked us to go back to our homes. The Histadrut, our trade union, was distributing leaflets asking the Arabs to come back. I still have that leaflet."

MYTH

"UN resolutions uphold the Arab refugees' right of repatriation."

FACT

Arabs base their demand for repatriation on the UN resolution of Dec. 11, 1948, which established the Palestine Conciliation Commission (PCC) for the purpose of negotiating an Arab-Israeli peace settlement. Paragraph 5 of that resolution called for:

"Agreement by negotiations conducted either with the Conciliation Commission or directly, with a view to the final settlement of all questions outstanding between them."

It was hoped that a quick solution of the refugee problem would be found in the context of a peace settlement.

The resolution does not recognize an unconditional *right* of return. This is the crucial point in dispute. Arabs have insisted that the refugees have a *right* to go back to Israel by virtue of this clause. The clause does not speak of any *rights*. It speaks of resettlement, as well as repatriation. But this is rarely cited.

All Arab states voted against that 1948 resolution. Nevertheless, paragraph 11 has become the central theme of their propaganda, while paragraph 5, calling for an Arab-Israeli peace settlement, is always ignored as are the qualifications in paragraph 11.

MYTH

"Israel blocked negotiations by the Palestine Conciliation Commission."

FACT

Early in 1949, the PCC opened negotiations at Lausanne. The Arabs insisted that Israel yield the territory won in the 1948 fighting and agree to repatriation.

The Israelis told the commission that the solution of the problem depended on the conclusion of peace. But Israel did make a substantial repatriation offer during these negotiations.

Israel said it would accept 100,000 refugees in a general settlement of the refugee problem. It was hoped that each Arab state would make a similar commitment. This offer was rejected.

On April 1, 1950, the Arab League adopted a resolution forbidding its members to negotiate with Israel.

The PCC made another effort to bring the parties together in 1951, but finally gave up. It reported:

"Since any solution of the refugee question would involve important commitments by Israel, she could not be expected to make them unless at the same time she received reasonable assurances from her neighbors as to her national and economic security."

The Commission itself was part of the problem. Writing of the late 1948, early 1949 period, historian Howard M. Sachar says the PCC "by its ineptitude ... hastened the destruction of whatever chances for peace still existed." *(A History of Israel*, Alfred A. Knopf, 1985.) Instead of acting quickly, the Commission dragged its feet; then, in Lausanne, it let the Arab states avoid direct bilateral negotiations with Israel, letting them participate as a bloc. "Under this format, no individual Arab dared take the initiative in expressing moderation .... The Arabs repudiated the pattern of the early armistice negotiations and declined to sit in the same room with the Jews."

MYTH

"There are 1,500,000 . . . 3,000,000 . . . 4,000,000 refugees."

FACT

The number of Palestinian refugees has always been vastly inflated by Arab propagandists.

Arabs who had lived in the area of Israel defined by the 1949 armistice agreements numbered about 750,000.

About 160,000 Arabs remained in Israel after the exodus. This means that the total number of bona fide Arab refugees who left Israel was about 590,000. Of these, 20% soon found permanent homes and resettlement in the Arab world, according to early UNRWA reports.

Yet later UNRWA reports began to speak of 1,300,000 refugees, and by the mid-1980's, of more than 2 million.

What accounts for the discrepancy?

When the fighting ended, many Arabs living in the territory seized by Jordan claimed that they were entitled to relief because they had been rendered indigent by the war. Many who had never lived in Israel were given the status of refugees. UNRWA then had no means of verifying the eligibility of those in the queues.

Padding of the rolls was prevalent. Deaths were not reported, and Arab governments resisted rectification of the lists. Ration cards were valued as currency.

The UN Economic Survey Commission reported on Dec. 28, 1949, that the number of non-refugees on the lists was as high as 160,000. In 1952, UNRWA stated:

"Whereas all births are eagerly announced, the deaths wherever possible are passed over in silence, so that the family may continue to collect rations for the deceased."

Henri Labouisse, UNRWA director, told a Palestinian refugee conference in Jerusalem, on July 20, 1955:

"There are refugees who hold as many as 500 UNRWA ration cards and there are dealers in UNRWA-approved clothing ration cards."

As late as 1984, official UNRWA population tables still carried the following qualification: "These statistics are based on the Agency's registration records, which do not necessarily reflect the actual refugee population owing to factors such as unreported deaths and births, false and duplicate registrations and unreported absences from the area of UNRWA operations. The agency presumes that the refugee population present in the area of UNRWA operations is less than the registered population."

The 1987 report included the following, less incriminating, qualification: "These statistics are based on UNRWA's registration records, which are updated continually. The number of registered refugees present in the Agency's area of operations, however, is almost certainly less than the population recorded . . ."

Of the two million-plus refugees claimed by UNRWA in 1985, 750,000 were Jordanian citizens of Palestinian Arab background. And only one-third of the claimed total actually lived in the camps. Some preferred the rent-free shelters, UNRWA schools and clinics, according to a 1985 study prepared for the Heritage Foundation. Danny Rubinstein, veteran *Davar* correspondent for the territories, noted in 1988 that after two or three generations the people are no longer refugees and the camps not camps but more like the poor neighborhoods of adjacent Arab towns and villages, with some people moving in and out for economic reasons.

MYTH

"History shows the repatriation of refugees—not resettlement elsewhere—is the best way to solve such problems."

FACT

Of the hundreds of recent articles and commentaries that have dealt with Vietnamese, Haitian or Cuban refugees, it is difficult to find one that calls for, or even talks about, repatriation. They speak only of resettlement of the refugees. Even for the recent refugees—the ethnic Chinese who have been expelled as opposed to the early refugees who simply fled—no voice has been raised to try to persuade Vietnam to take them back.

After World War II, there were some 40 million refugees throughout the world: Koreans, Jews, Hindus, Sikhs, Moslems, Chinese, Poles and Germans. In every case, resettlement—not repatriation—proved to be the answer.

According to Holborn's *World Refugees* (1960), West Germany, after World War II, absorbed and rehabilitated 9,688,000 displaced persons (5,978,000 from Poland, 1,891,000 from Czechoslovakia, and the rest from several other European countries). Austria received 178,000 Hungarian refugees in the aftermath of the Hungarian revolution of 1956 (Elfin Rees, *Century of the Homeless Man, International Conciliation, 1957*). Italy provided a home for 585,000 Italians displaced from territory ceded to Yugoslavia, and from various parts of Africa (UN *World Refugee Year Secretariat*). France gave permanent asylum to 1,372,000 refugees (including Algerian Moslems) displaced by the emergence of new sovereign states in North Africa and Indochina (*The New York Times*, December 1961, November 1962). The Netherlands, tiny and crowded, welcomed and settled 230,000 refugees from Indonesia (Kraak, *Repatriation of the Dutch from Indonesia*). Turkey resettled 150,000 Turks expelled by the communist regime in Bulgaria (Kostarisk, *Turkish Resettlement of Bulgarians, 1957*). There was an exchange of some 15 million between India and Pakistan. Finland absorbed 400,000 Karelians. After Bangladesh's war for independence from Pakistan in 1971—when the countries were still respectively East and West Pakistan—Pakistan agreed to resettle 360,000 Urdu-speaking Moslems "stranded" in Bangladesh. Many had spent years after the war in refugee camps.

Contributions to UNRWA—1985
(in thousands of U.S. dollars)

Donor	Amount U.S. $	Percentage of Total Contributions
A. Governments:		
—First 15 Governments:		
1. United States of America	75,000	43.1
2. Japan	13,680	7.9
3. Sweden	7,898	4.5
4. Norway	7,249	4.2
5. United Kingdom	6,556	3.8
6. Canada	6,306	3.6
7. Switzerland	3,397	2.0
8. Germany, Federal Republic of	3,110	1.8
9. Denmark	2,726	1.6
10. Saudi Arabia	2,200	1.3
11. Australia	1,408	0.8
12. Netherlands	1,379	0.8
13. Italy	1,276	0.7
14 Kuwait	1,100	0.6
15 France	1,024	0.6
—Other Governments	3,844	2.1
Subtotal, Governmental Contributions	138,153	79.4
B. Inter-Governmental Organizations: European Economic Community	24,091	13.8
Other Organizations	1,492	0.8
Subtotal	25,583	14.6
C. United Nations System	8,528	4.9
D. Non-Governmental/ Private Donors	1,918	1.1
Total	174,182	100.00

Source: *World Refugee Report,* September, 1986 United States Department of State, Bureau of Refugee Programs

Yet many Arabs still insist that Palestinian Arab refugees be repatriated in Israel. The PLO demands this "right-of-return" in its "covenant"; leaders of the 1988 "uprising" or *intifadah* in the West Bank and Gaza Strip called for the right-of-return in their underground leaflets even before demanding self-determination and statehood. Israeli Defense Minister Yitzhak Rabin said he could understand the Arab aspiration to return to Haifa or Jaffa, but could never accept it. Exercised by the one million-plus Palestinian Arabs who claim lands within Israel from before 1948, it would mean "national suicide" for the Jews, Rabin said. "Return" is not a humanitarian concern in this context, but an important political weapon in the Arab war against Israel in any boundaries.

MYTH

"Israel has refused to compensate Arab refugees for their losses."

FACT

After its failure to make any headway to secure an Arab-Israeli settlement, the PCC made a study of Arab property claims inside Israel. There was a preliminary valuation of $300 million.

Arab figures on this subject are wildly exaggerated. Arabs have demanded the appointment of a UN custodian to act as trustee over abandoned property. This proposal, based on the assumption that Arabs still own the property and its income, has been repeatedly rejected by Israel.

Its real purpose was political—to establish a form of UN trusteeship in Israel that would abridge Israel's sovereignty. The UN has been unwilling to set such a precedent.

Even so, Israel has offered to pay compensation for Arab property and has even declared that such payments need not wait for a peace settlement. In fact, through August 1975, the Israeli government paid to over 11,000 claimants more than 23 million Israeli pounds in cash and granted over 10,000 acres as alternative holdings. The claimants were paid on the basis of land value between 1948 and 1953 plus 6% for every year following the claim submission. On the other hand, hundreds of thousands of Jews who are now

Israeli citizens were forced to abandon property in Arab countries worth several billions of dollars—estimated at worth up to four times the holdings lost by fleeing Palestinian Arabs—and this will have to be taken into account in any settlement of "the refugee problem." Prof. Ya'akov Meron, a Hebrew University expert on international law, noted in a paper for the 1987 international conference of the World Organization of Jews from Arab Countries that by calling for a "just settlement of the refugee problem," UN Security Council Resolution 242 demanded international assistance for "all the refugees of the Arab-Israeli conflict, including hundreds of thousands of Jews from Arab lands." By rejecting Soviet and Arab pressure to mention Palestinian Arabs specifically in 242, the Security Council made it clear that all refugees—"Jewish refugees from Arab lands, and Arabs who had left Israel"—should be treated justly, Meron said.

Many years ago Israel released the blocked bank accounts—totalling more than $10 million—of Arab refugees.

MYTH

"The Arab states have taken the major responsibility and provided most of the funds for helping the Palestinian refugees."

FACT

Ever since 1948, the refugees have been under the care of the international community which has fed, housed, trained and educated them—at a cost of more than two billion dollars, expended by the United Nations Relief and Works Agency (UNRWA).

No collective group of refugees was ever treated with so much solicitude and concern by any international agency. But the Arab governments contributed little money or cooperation. In fact, Israel contributed more funds to UNRWA—over $11 million from 1950 to 1983—than most Arab states. The Saudis did not match Israel until 1973; Kuwait and Libya, not until 1980.

For years UNRWA encountered obstacles and resistance from the Arab host countries. It was refused diplomatic recognition. Its operations were impeded by duties, taxes and restrictive regulations.

UNRWA provided health and educational services, including university scholarships to the refugees, but it had to overcome their many psychological difficulties. At first the refugees rejected concrete houses, self-help grants, vocational training and visas for emigration.

But gradually, many changed their attitude. The refugees, as a class, live far better and longer and receive a better education than many Arabs who live in the squalor of the villages in the hinterlands of Egypt, Syria and Iraq.

Gradually, many Arab refugees have become integrated in Arab economies, as the late UN Secretary General Dag Hammarskjold had predicted—despite official Arab attitudes. UNRWA's 1986 report stated, among other things, that "direct relief assistance which dominated the agency's activities at the outset, gradually diminished in relative importance over the years as more refugees became self-supporting, largely through programs of general and vocational training."

On July 14, 1966, former Secretary of State Dean Rusk told a Senate committee:

> "There are almost half-a-million refugees who have registered refugee status but who, in fact, have jobs and some of them at some distance from the camps, living reasonably normal lives."

In later years, UNRWA's work was increasingly subverted, with some UNRWA officers supporting Arab terrorist activities. During the 1982 Israeli military operation in Lebanon, it was discovered that UNRWA's facilities had been used for training terrorists. The agency's own investigation (after Israel made its discovery public) found "that PLO military personnel had made unauthorized use of the Siblin Training Center . . . for about two years before 1982."

Incredibly, UNRWA claimed that the PLO activity was "unknown to the Agency's senior officials."

Twenty-two UNRWA staff members were arrested on the West Bank and Gaza between June 1980 and 1981, according to the report of the UNRWA Commission General. More than 200 staff members were arrested and detained by Israeli military forces during the 1982 operation because of their PLO-related activities.

In 1975, a reporter told of meeting a PLO information officer in Lebanon:

> "Jada said he was an employee of the United Nations Relief and Welfare Agency and took much pride in claiming that almost the entire agency had been proliferated

AN AMERICAN PRECEDENT

There is an instructive precedent in America's own history. During the American Revolution, many colonists who remained loyal to the Crown fled to Canada. In the peace negotiations, the British pressed the United States to permit the loyalists to return and to reclaim their property.

But the U.S. Congress was adamant. On Oct. 18, 1782, Congress issued the following instructions to John Adams, the U.S. minister plenipotentiary in the peace negotiations:

> "That with respect to those persons who have either abandoned or been banished from any of the United States since the commencement of the war, he is to make no stipulations whatsoever for their readmittance; and as to an equivalent for their property, he may attend to propositions on that subject only on reciprocal stipulation that Great Britain will make full compensation for all the wanton destruction which the subjects of that nation have committed on the property of the citizens of the United States."

On Nov. 26, 1782, four days before the preliminary treaty, Benjamin Franklin wrote Richard Oswald, the British negotiator:

> "Your ministers require that we should receive again into our bosom those who have been our bitterest enemies and restore their properties who have destroyed ours; and while the wounds they have given us are still bleeding!"

The peace treaty contained a provision that Congress "recommended" that the states permit the restitution of property. But there was no thought of repatriation. Everyone knew that the recommendation, which historians describe as "an empty formula to save the face of the British government," would not be accepted. It was not.

---

by 'soldiers of the revolution.' He escorted me to the agency's printing and graphics shop in Beirut where it appeared to me that dozens of people drawing UN salaries were pumping out PLO propaganda, posters and pamphlets, books and pictures, portraits of Yasir Arafat. I surmised that all this was being produced and paid for by the United Nations and perhaps, in the ultimate analysis, being largely financed by the United States." (*Faces Magazine*, Dec. 30, 1975.)

Only Jordan accepted the refugees as citizens and allowed them to work. This was a matter of self-interest. Jordan wanted to integrate them as Jordanians in order to obviate any attempt to form a Palestinian government which would threaten Jordan's rule of the West Bank. On the other hand, Lebanon did not accept the refugees as citizens because that would have hastened the end of Christian majority status. In Syria and Iraq, Palestinian Arabs were discriminated against but were able to obtain work.

Most Arab states refuse to grant citizenship to resident Palestinian Arabs. An advertisement placed in U.S. newspapers on June 8, 1976, by the government of Libya illustrates this point. The ad, which attempted to recruit Arab workers to Libya by offering citizenship and other incentives, explicitly barred Palestinian Arabs. The ad said: "The provisions concerning immigration for the purpose of naturalization under this Law, shall not be applicable to Palestinians."

Claiming that "the Arab land is but a home for all the Arab people," the government of Iraq undertook a policy of offering homesteads in underpopulated regions to Egyptian peasants—but not to Palestinian Arab refugees.

Similarly, Saudi Arabia failed to use unemployed Palestinian refugees to alleviate its manpower shortage in the late 1970's and early 1980's. Instead, thousands of South Koreans and other central and far east Asians were recruited to fill the Saudi employment ranks.

Thus, while jobs and land went begging in some Arab countries, many Palestinian Arabs were cooped up in densely-populated Gaza, where Nasser's rule was devoid of concern or compassion. In that congested purgatory, the refugees were virtual prisoners. Very few were allowed to emigrate; they were barred from Egypt, denied Egyptian citizenship, confined by strict curfews, and generally subjected to discrimination and repression. Nothing was done for Gaza's economic development.

Even Saudi Arabian radio, on March 10, 1962, likened Nasser's regime in Gaza to Hitler's regime in occupied territories in World War II.

"The Gaza is not a hell-hole, not a visible disaster. It is worse. It is a jail," wrote Martha Gellhorn after a visit. (*Atlantic Monthly*, Oct. 1961.)

14

The Palestinian Question

MYTH

"The Palestinian question is the core of the Arab-Israeli conflict. More than that, the Palestinian issue is the key to peace in the Middle East."

FACT

Arabs claim that the plight of the Palestinian Arabs is the heart of the Arab-Israeli conflict, which will not end unless the Palestinian question is solved. The truth is that the Palestinian Arab question is the *result* of the conflict—not the source. The real cause is the refusal of the Arab states to acknowledge Israel's right to exist as an independent Jewish state.

There would never have been a Palestinian question if the Arab governments had been ready to live in peace with Israel, if they had not gone to war to block the UN partition resolution in 1948, and if they had not repeatedly waged war to destroy the Jewish state.

The West Bank and Gaza were under Arab rule from 1948 to 1967 but the Arabs did not set up a Palestinian state, nor were they asked to by Palestinian Arabs or by non-Arab sympathizers who now claim that such a state is the panacea that will end the Middle East conflict.

The Palestinian Arab question could be swiftly solved if the Arab states and the Palestinian Arabs recognized Israel's right to exist in peace. The Palestinian Arab refugees could then be resettled among their own people, as they should have been long ago, in the vast Arab lands which extend over five million square miles and which have the oil, soil, and—most important—the money to rehabilitate them.

The claim that a solution to the Palestinian Arab question would bring Middle East peace is ludicrous. The tensions in the Middle East—the Iran-Iraq war; Shi'ite insurgency in the Persian Gulf and Lebanon; Libyan troublemaking in Sudan, Egypt, Tunisia and Chad; conflict between Morocco and Algeria over the southwestern Sahara; civil war in Sudan and Lebanon; tension between Syria and Iraq; and internal instability in Saudi Arabia, Morocco, Bahrain and, as a 1987 coup attempt demonstrated, in the United Arab Emirates—have little or no relationship to the Arab-Israeli conflict.

MYTH

"If the Israelis would accept the establishment of a separate West Bank and Gaza Strip state for Palestinian Arabs, the PLO would recognize Israel's right to exist."

FACT

The PLO was founded in 1964, when the West Bank and Gaza were under Arab rule. The "Palestine" it sought to "liberate" then, as now, was Israel within its pre-1967 borders.

PLO officials have made it abundantly clear that they would accept a separate West Bank state only as a first step toward their eventual objective of creating a Palestinian state in *all* of Israel. The Palestine National Covenant, adopted by the PLO in 1964, revised in 1968, amended in 1974, and reaffirmed in 1977, clearly states that the establishment of a Palestine "national authority" on any of the occupied territories evacuated by Israel would only be "a step on the path" to the total "liberation of Palestinian soil," (*See appendix for text of the Covenant.*) In 1977 and 1979, the PLO repeatedly spurned the many appeals of the Carter Administration to accept Resolutions 242 and 338 as a basis for negotiations with Israel. It did the same in 1985, 1986 and 1987—sometimes with intentionally vague language to encourage and deceive opinion in the West as to the possibility of evolving PLO "moderation." It has ignored pleas to rescind those parts of the Palestine National Covenant that call for the destruction of Israel. Reagan Administration officials repeatedly made it clear that the United States would be willing to talk with the PLO the minute that organization accepted 242 and 338, recognized Israel and stopped its terrorism. Yet the PLO never gave an unequivocal answer, let alone demonstrated a change in behavior. The reason is that, regardless of *tactics*, PLO strategy calls for the "liberation" of what is Israel. Most veteran leaders of the organization came from places inside the 1948 "green line"; so did most Palestinian Arab refugees living in Lebanon, Syria, Jordan and other countries. As Israeli Defense Minister Yitzhak Rabin told the *Jerusalem*

Post in 1988, a West Bank and Gaza Strip state provides no answer for them.

On June 1, 1980 The Fatah Revolutionary Congress Central Committee Conference issued a declaration in Damascus, Syria. Fatah vowed to "liquidate the Zionist entity politically, economically, militarily, culturally, and ideologically."

In Feb. 1983, the PLO's governing body, the Palestine National Council, met in Algiers. The commmunique released at the conference stated, "The PNC affirms the need to develop and escalate the armed struggle against the Zionist enemy."

Meeting in Algiers in 1987, the PNC restated allegiance to its "covenant" and previous resolutions.

MYTH

"A democratic secular state encompassing Israel, the West Bank and Gaza Strip will bring peace."

FACT

A popular myth propagated by the PLO has been that its goal of establishing a "democratic, secular Palestinian state" would bring peace to the Middle East; Jews and Arabs would live side by side in harmony.

The real intentions underlying the PLO proposal for a secular state in which Jews would live as Palestinians were illuminated in this major qualification: only Jews who were living in Palestine before the "Zionist invasion" would be considered Palestinians.

What would happen to those Jews who could not qualify?

During the 1930s, some Jewish leaders advocated the establishment of a binational state in Palestine, but no leading Palestinian Arabs joined them.

A Fatah spokesman declared, on Oct. 19, 1968, that a "solution" could be achieved by a "declaration of amnesty" to every Jew from an Arab state now living in Israel. He said that a Jew of Arab origin would be able to return to his "native land, a true Arab citizen enjoying every right enjoyed by the Arab native, as he was before. . . . If these Jews returned to their countries of origin, which we do not doubt that many of them would like to do, the problem would be solved to a great extent."

125

It should be emphasized that some 600,000 Jews came out of Arab countries to live in Israel after 1948 and that these Jews and their offspring, as well as Jews born in Israel, now comprise a substantial majority of Israel's population. They are as indigenous to the region as their Arab foes. Another 200,000 Jews from Arab countries moved to France, the United States and elsewhere. These Jews have never shown any inclination to return to Arab countries.

The shattering political conflict in Lebanon continues to

"Just Out Of Curiosity, How Is It We Never Got A Homeland During All The Years Our Arab Brothers Had The West Bank?"

exemplify Arab intolerance toward non-Islamic religious groups in the Middle East. The brutal "brother-against-brother" fighting between pro-Iranian and pro-Syrian Shi'ite Moslem militias in May 1988 in which more than 300 were killed and 1,000 wounded in just three weeks for control of the south Beirut slums testifies to the violent nature of even intra-Islamic disputes. About the same time, more than 120 pro- and anti-Arafat PLO gunmen died in renewed internecine PLO warfare in Lebanese refugee districts and more than 500 were wounded. Such "score-settling"—a feature of Palestinian Arab politics from British mandatory times onward—highlights the impossibility of a PLO "democratic, secular state." The lack of a secular, democratic state anywhere in the Arab-Islamic world says much about the forces opposing Israel.

MYTH

"The Palestinians do not have a homeland."

FACT

There already exists a Palestinian Arab state. It is called Jordan.

Jordan spans the whole of eastern Palestine, up to the Jordan River. A majority of its citizens east of the Jordan River are Palestinian Arabs, not to mention the West Bankers, who hold Jordanian citizenship. All Jordanians are, by geographic definition, "Palestinians," as are all Israelis. Movement of the Arab population, including the Palestinian refugees, took place *inside the historic area of Palestine.*

Many of Jordan's cabinet ministers and members of parliament have come from western Palestine. In the spring of 1988, Palestinian Arabs made up half the Jordanian cabinet. As Clinton Bailey, a Tel Aviv University specialist on Palestinian nationalism, put it, "How is Taher al-Masri, the Jordanian foreign minister, from Nablus, less Palestinian than Farouk Kaddoumi, the PLO's 'foreign minister?' " The major part of the country's economy and government administration is in the hands of former residents of western Palestine. More than half of the 2.7 million Jordanians on the East Bank have their origins in western Palestine. And approximately three-quarters of the inhabitants of Amman the capital, came from western Palestine.

These facts and figures mean that the Hashemite Kingdom of Jordan is actually a Palestinian Arab state. Both

King Hussein of Jordan and the PLO agreed in the past that Jordan was Palestine and Palestine was Jordan. In 1970, Yasir Arafat told correspondent Oriana Fallaci, "What you call Jordan is actually Palestine." In 1981, King Hussein declared, "The truth is that Jordan is Palestine and Palestine is Jordan."

By the mid-1980's, neither side sounded this theme so openly, Hussein preferring to emphasize the "Jordanian" nature of his inheritance, the PLO—for the sake of greater harmony with Arab states—emphasizing its "west of the river" focus. At the same time, Arab propaganda in the West became more strident in trying to deny and obscure Jordan's origins in mandatory Palestine.

MYTH

"The PLO itself condemns terrorism."

FACT

The PLO's long history of brutal violence—and its rush to claim credit for that violence—belies any condemnations of terrorism the group may have uttered for public consumption. A striking example was the PLO jubilation after the murder of Anwar Sadat in 1981.

From 1965 until the 1982 Israeli operation in Lebanon, 689 Israelis lost their lives and 3799 were wounded in PLO terrorist attacks. Outside of Israel, in Europe, Asia and Africa, Palestinian Arab terrorists killed 326 people and wounded 768 more in the same time period.

Beginning with the hijacking of an El Al airliner to Algiers in 1968, Arab terrorists have commandeered or attacked at least 45 other international civilian planes and machine gunned airline passengers at Lod (May 30, 1972—26 killed), Munich (Feb. 10, 1973—one killed), Athens (Aug. 5, 1973—five killed), Rome (Dec. 17, 1973—31 killed), Istanbul (Aug. 11, 1976—four killed), Beirut (June 19, 1985—1 killed), Malta (Nov. 23, 1985—67 killed), Rome (Dec. 3, 1985—13 killed), Vienna (Dec. 27, 1985—3 killed), Karachi (Sept. 5, 1986—21 killed), and Cyprus (April, 1988—2 killed), among others.

The PFLP-General Command proudly claimed responsibility for the Feb. 1970 mid-air explosion of a Swissair jetliner that killed 47 passengers and crew members, including Swiss, Germans and Israelis.

The world was outraged by the PLO slaughter of 11 Israeli athletes at the 1972 Munich Olympics. It was later proven that the Black September terrorists who carried out the atrocity were under the command of Fatah intelligence. Black September was directed by PLO leaders Mohammed Yusef Najjar, Salah Khalaf, Abu Daoud and Yasir Arafat.

In March 1973, eight Fatah terrorists stormed a diplomatic reception at the Saudi embassy in Khartoum, kidnapped and then murdered U.S. Ambassador Cleo Noel. Chargé d'Affaires George Moore and Belgian Chargé d'Affaires Guy Eid. Arafat was reported to have personally directed this action by radio from Lebanon.

The year 1974 was a particularly active one for Palestinian terrorists in Israel. Their atrocities that year at Kiryat Shemona, Ma'alot, Nahariya and Shamir left 52 dead and more than 100 wounded—most of them women and children.

One of the PLO's bloodiest atrocities took place on March 11, 1978 when Arab terrorists landed on Israel's coast and killed an American photographer, Gail Rubin. The terrorists then commandeered a bus along the coastal road, shooting and throwing grenades from the bus windows. When their deadly ride was finally stopped by the Israeli military, they had left 34 civilians dead and 82 wounded in their wake.

In Oct. 1985, PLO terrorists hijacked the ocean liner Achille Lauro. They murdered a wheelchair-bound American Jew, Leon Klinghoffer. Intercepted radio messages between the hijackers and shore indicated that the attack was directed by Mohammed Abbas, a member of the PLO Executive. Said U.S. Attorney General Edwin Meese, "We do have hard evidence as to the complicity of Mohammed Abbas."

Incredibly, the PLO denied not only its role, but also the murder of Klinghoffer. The PLO's Political Department head, Farouk Kaddoumi, told the UN Security Council that the report of the murder was "a big lie fabricated by the intelligence service of the United States." After the hijacking, Arafat issued his "Cairo declaration." In it he pledged to halt attacks against Israeli targets outside of Israel, the West Bank (Judea and Samaria) and the Gaza Strip. He reiterated the PLO's dedication to "armed struggle"—terrorist action—inside the "occupied territory." The "Cairo declaration" did not come close to meeting U.S. conditions for dealing with the PLO; in any case, it left Israeli civilians—men, women and children—as approved targets, as well as anyone else who happened to be in Israel while the organization continued its "military operations."

MYTH

"The PLO represents the national aspirations of the Palestinians."

FACT

The PLO was not founded by the residents of Arab Palestine, even though the East Bank (Jordan), West Bank (Judea and Samaria) and Gaza Strip were all under Arab rule when the organization was formed in 1964. Instead, it was set up in Egypt, under the chairmanship of a puppet of the Egyptian government, Ahmed Shukairy, and backed by Egyptian money and arms. It drew its manpower mainly from the refugee camps in the Gaza Strip, then under Egyptian control. The first meeting of the PLO's National Council was held in Arab east Jerusalem in May 1964.

Palestinian Arabs in Syria, Lebanon, Jordan and Iraq created their own competing organizations—all with similar names, all with a heavy emphasis on paramilitary or terrorist action, all enjoying the support of their host countries in varying degrees. Thus, when Fatah moved out of Syria's orbit, the Syrian government established As-Saiqa.

Terrorist groups mushroomed after the military defeat of Egypt and Syria in 1967. Each new organization had its own ideology—mostly a rehash of Marxist or Maoist doctrine covered by a patina of "national liberation" rhetoric in their names: the "Popular Front" or the "Popular Democratic Front" for the "Liberation of Palestine." Bitter differences centered on personal rivalries, conflicts among the host states, and tactics. Thus, almost since its inception, the PLO, as an umbrella for these groups, served more as an arena for political competition among the Arab states and for ideological feuding among its factions than as a voice for the aspirations of Palestinian Arabs.

This fractionalized view of the PLO was reiterated in Oct. 1983 by *Arabia—The Islamic World Review*, which wrote, " . . . the internecine squabbling, although limited, in the PLO is a microcosm of the wider Arab political setting both regionally and nationally . . . The Palestinian card was played in the past by Nasser, and nowadays by Qaddafi, Saddam Hussein and Hafez Assad. . . . The PLO is a conglomeration of organizations that are a reflection of inter-Arab divisions . . ."

All the groups are united on one point, however—the final goal of eliminating Israel and replacing it with an Arab state embracing all the territory of Mandatory Palestine. In 1968, when Fatah became the dominant group within the organization, Yasir Arafat assumed control.

In July of that year, the Palestine National Council (PNC) convened in Cairo and approved a revised Palestine National Covenant. All Palestinian terrorist organizations were represented. The PLO has never retracted any part of the covenant—which calls in numerous places for the elimination of Israel. (See Appendix.)

Leaders of the PLO and Fatah have sanctioned compromises for the sake of expediency. They brandished the slogan of a "secular, democratic state of Palestine in which Jew, Christian and Moslem will live side by side" in order to project an image in the West and camouflage the genocidal intent implicit in the covenant and displayed by PLO practice against fellow Arabs in Lebanon before 1982 (see Jillian Becker's *The PLO: The Rise and Fall of the Palestine Liberation Organization*, St. Martin's Press, 1984). By 1985 the organization was again engaged in deadly *internal* warfare in Palestinian camps in Lebanon.

The PLO occasionally flirted with Western peace proposals, and in 1983, 1985, and again in early 1987, Arafat went through the motions of negotiating with Jordan's King Hussein. In Feb. 1987, Hussein severed talks with Arafat, declaring that Jordan is "unable to coordinate politically with the PLO leadership until such a time as their word becomes their bond, characterized by commitment, credibility, and constancy." While much hopeful commentary was written at the time about Arafat's diplomacy, the real purpose and eventual result in both occasions, were to freeze any potential Jordanian moves.

Such deviations are condemned by the smaller terrorist organizations which rigidly oppose even the image of compromise at the expense of ideology and doctrine. In 1983, a Syrian-supported faction within the PLO broke away under the leadership of Abu Musa. Pitched battles were fought with the Arafat faction. Soviet-orchestrated reconciliation

131

at the 1987 Algiers PNC resulted in Arafat's reacceptance of "more radical" PLO factions like George Habash's Popular Front for the Liberation of Palestine and Naif Hawatmeh's Democratic Front for the Liberation of Palestine.

MYTH

"The PLO enjoys broad support among the inhabitants of the West Bank and Gaza."

FACT

The support the PLO has in the West Bank and Gaza was gained and held largely through bribery, intimidation, and murder. During the winter of 1977-78, the PLO murdered three West Bank Palestinian Arabs who were considered collaborators with Israel. In 1979, it assassinated an Islamic religious leader from Gaza who supported the Israeli-Egyptian peace treaty. The following year, PLO operatives killed three citizens of Silwan in the West Bank. And in 1980-81, a PLO terrorist ring killed a dozen prominent Gaza residents before it was finally broken up by Israeli authorities.

In Nov. 1981, Yusef al Khatib, a leader of the West Bank village councils was gunned down by the PLO, which viewed the councils as a threat to its control of the region. Khatib's son also died in the attack. Issam Sartawi, Arafat's designated "dove," was murdered by Abu Nidal in 1983. Although Arafat and Abu Nidal had long opposed each other, their respective factions took part in the reconciliation at the 1987 Algiers PNC. Zafer al-Masri, moderate mayor of Nablus, was gunned down, apparently by members of the PLO's Popular Front for the Liberation of Palestine, in 1986.

Rashid A-Shawa, viewed as a moderate Palestinian leader in Gaza, missed injury when a hand grenade was thrown at his home in Dec. 1983. After he indirectly criticized PLO obstruction of peace efforts after the breakdown in the Arafat-Hussein accord in 1986, arsonists struck a factory he owned.

By the mid-1980's, however, the organization, and Arafat as chairman, had gained popularity, especially as *symbols* of the Palestinian Arab movement, if not as an institution and leader who could provide any lasting political settlement. In 1986, a poll sponsored by *Newsday* and the Australian Broadcasting Company showed overwhelming support for Arafat and the PLO. However, the poll was conducted for *Al-Fajr*, the pro-Fatah east Jerusalem newspaper, and by students from Nablus' An-Najah University, a hotbed of anti-Israel activity. The survey, questions of methodology aside, showed large majorities in favor of terrorism and a 50% to 43% split between those favoring a West Bank and Gaza state *as the first step* and those who wanted continued struggle for a state including the territories and Israel from the outset.

The spontaneous outbreak of the *intifadah*, or uprising, in Dec. 1987, revealed, among other things, that the younger generation in the West Bank and Gaza had grown tired of waiting for Arafat—nom de guerre Abu Amar—and the other aging "Abu's" of the PLO leadership, to produce some tangible political gains. Criticisms from the Arabs of the territories in the early weeks of the violence about the overseas "Cadillac revolutionaries" stimulated PLO headquarters in Tunis to try to gain control over the Arabs in the West Bank and Gaza and the rioting.

Several news stories published in 1987 estimated the PLO's total assets at as much as $5 billion—most of it amassed after the organization was driven out of Lebanon by Israeli troops in 1982. "In 1983," according to journalist James Adams, "about $600 million in current-account income was generated for the PNF (Palestine National Fund). And of this, less than $100 million came in the form of donations from wealthy Palestinian or Arab nations; the balance was made up by investments all over the world. The total annual income of the various PLO factions runs to well in excess of $1.25 billion.

"This sum, which is greater than the total budget of some third world countries," Adams concludes, "makes the PLO the richest and most powerful terrorist group in the world."

MYTH

"The PLO is not a terrorist organization. It seeks only the establishment of a peaceful Palestinian Arab state."

FACT

Besides being committed to terrorist attacks against innocent Israeli civilians ("struggle in the occupied lands in all its forms," according to the PLO's 15-Point Program), the PLO was the most important member in the international terrorist network. It provided training, money, intel-

133

iigence and weaponry for terrorist movements in Ireland, Spain, France, Germany, Japan, Italy, Africa, Asia, and Latin America. Even American and Arab-American radicals trained in PLO camps.

The PLO has often stated its commitment to the "world forces of liberation and progress to foil all Zionist, reactionary and imperialist schemes" (10-Point Program). The PLO's threat, therefore, is not only to Israel but to liberal democracies throughout the world.

The PLO played a major role in the overthrow of the Shah of Iran, which led to the disruption of oil supplies to the West. In Feb. 1979, the PLO's Farouk Kaddoumi boasted: "Hundreds of Iranian *mujahaddin* (fighters) have fought with the Palestinian revolution since 1969." Ayatollah Khomeini's first official guest was Yasir Arafat—in recognition of the aid the PLO gave to the Iranian despot. In the late 1980's, as the Arab world tended to be more openly critical of Persian Iran and supportive of Arab Iraq in the war between the two countries, Arafat and the PLO began re-emphasizing ties to Iraq, where they maintained a major radio broadcasting facility and other important offices.

In April 1979, *The Washington Post* reported that the PLO had trained the soldiers of Ugandan dictator Idi Amin and that PLO troops had served as Amin's bodyguards and in his torture chambers.

In Jan. 1982, Yasir Arafat boasted that PLO pilots were serving in Nicaragua, and that other PLO terrorists were in El Salvador and the African nation of Angola, whose Cuban-supported government faced a strong guerrilla challenge. Addressing the General Federation of Palestinian Writers and Journalists in Beirut, Arafat explained, "The Palestinian identity is one of revolutionary struggle and universal in its character, not a racist movement."

In June 1979, the Sandinista press officer, George Mandi, told the Kuwaiti *Al-Watan* of the "longstanding blood brotherhood" between the PLO and the Sandinistas. "Many of us trained in PLO bases in Jordan . . . . In the early seventies, Nicaraguans and Palestinians fought side-by-side in Amman and other places, in the course of Black September's battles." According to intelligence sources, more than 80 Sandinistas were trained by the PFLP. Some took part in the four-plane hijacking by the PFLP which helped lead to Jordan's crackdown on the armed Palestinian Arab presence in the kingdom. A 1985 State Department report

134

confirmed that Sandinista gunmen did fight alongside the PLO in Black September. Patrick Arguello Ryan, a Sandinista killed in the unsuccessful Sept. 6, 1970 El Al hijack attempt, became a movement "martyr"; a major dam in Nicaragua was named in his honor. Arguello had trained in a PLO camp.

Palestinian sources told *The Wall Street Journal* on Jan. 14, 1982, that PLO relations with Salvadoran rebels were "relatively deep-rooted" because the leader of their Communist Party was of Palestinian Arab origin and visited the Beirut headquarters of the Palestinian terrorists.

The Israeli "Peace for Galilee" operation in June 1982 overran the PLO training camps in Lebanon and captured dozens of foreign "terrorists-in-training." Documents seized proved the PLO's role as the core of the international terrorist network. In 1980 and 1982, 2,300 terrorists from 28 countries were trained in PLO bases in Lebanon, the Israeli military reported after analyzing documents captured in Lebanon.

MYTH

"Given its own state, the PLO would moderate its views and move away from the Soviet Union. Such a state would not become a threat to anyone in the Middle East."

FACT

The PLO is supported, trained and armed by the Soviet Union. Until the late 1960's, Soviet support for the PLO was indirect, coming through Arab states. Following the 1967 defeat of the Arab states, however, Soviet support for the PLO grew. After a PLO attack on an El Al plane in Switzerland in 1969, *Pravda* declared, "The act was carried out by patriots defending their legitimate right to return to their homeland."

PLO terrorists received political training at the Patrice Lumumba Univerity in Moscow. Military training was given in Crimea, near Simferpol, as well as in Hungary, Bulgaria, Yugoslavia, Czechoslovakia and East Germany. Documents captured in the 1982 war in Lebanon showed extensive PLO training in Cuba, North Korea, Pakistan, India, Vietnam, and China.

During the summer of 1979, the PLO's representative to the UN, Zehdi Terzi, admitted, "The Soviet Union and all the socialist countries . . . give us full support—diplomatic, moral, educational and also they open their military academies to some of our freedom fighters."

When asked whether Yasir Arafat received orders from the Soviet ambassador in Lebanon—as charged by a defector from the PLO—Terzi admitted that Arafat met with him weekly. "I think sometimes he should meet with him twice a day," Terzi stated.

The claim that a PLO-led state would be too busy to foment violence in the Middle East is unfounded. States like Cuba and Libya have not been too busy domestically to inhibit their incitement of violence around the world. The dangers from a PLO state—not just to Israel but to the entire Middle East and to the movement of oil throughout the world—cannot be underestimated.

As to the assertion that a PLO in charge of the West Bank and Gaza Strip would be too preoccupied to threaten Israel, Arafat's lieutenant, Salah Khalaf (Abu Iyad), told the Lebanese newspaper *Al-Safir*, in a Jan. 25, 1988 interview: "The establishment of an independent Palestinian state on the West Bank and the Gaza Strip does not contradict our ultimate strategic aim, which is the establishment of a democratic state in the entire territory of Palestine, but rather is a step in that direction."

After the failures in 1967 and 1973 by Arab armies to defeat Israel militarily, the theory of the destruction of Israel in stages returned to favor among many Arabs in gen-

'HIJACKED AN ITALIAN SHIP, MURDERED AN ELDERLY JEW IN A WHEELCHAIR, REINFORCED U.S.-ISRAELI RELATIONS, INCREASED THE CLIMATE OF VIOLENCE FURTHER... MY, MY, WHAT ELSE DID YOU DO TO US?'

eral and Palestinians in particular. As Intisar al-Wazir (Um Jihad), wife of Abu Jihad, explained to the Kuwaiti newspaper *Al-Anba*, on March 17, 1988, ". . . The PLO must establish a Palestinian state on every inch of Palestinian territory which is liberated. This is the interim goal: one state beside the other . . . . The establishment of a Palestinian state [in the territories] will be the launch-point for the liberation of the territory of Palestine from the [Mediterranean] sea to the [Jordan] river."

Arafat himself takes care not to foreclose this objective, as in a June 11, 1987 interview with *The New York Review*: ". . . I have to respect exactly all the resolutions which have been adopted by the PNC [Palestine National Council, the PLO's 'parliament']. So I will repeat exactly one of the important resolutions. We said we are ready to establish our independent state in any part from which the Israelis withdraw or which is liberated. Any part. The moment they withdraw from Gaza, I will establish my state there in Gaza. If they withdraw from Jericho, I will raise my flag in Jericho." Elsewhere in the interview Arafat makes it clear—as do the other PNC measures he mentioned—that there is no place for "a strange body" like a Zionist state in the region.

MYTH

"The United States should negotiate with the PLO."

FACT

The official U.S. position is that it will not recognize or negotiate with the PLO until the PLO recognizes Israel's right to exist and accepts UN Resolution 242. The policy is both morally and strategically sound. The United States made this policy commitment as part of the 1975 Sinai II Accord; it was reaffirmed on numerous occasions by Presidents Carter and Reagan. In 1985, this policy was passed by Congress, signed by the President and codified into law.

The Anti-Terrorism Act of 1987 reinforced U.S. policy toward the PLO by ordering the closure of PLO offices in Washington, D.C. and New York. The law declared, "The PLO and its affiliates are a terrorist organization and a threat to the interests of the United States and its allies." The U.S. position makes clear that there can be no reward for terrorism and intransigence. Only if the PLO becomes a serious and peaceful political organization can it be considered a legitimate party to negotiations. This policy also underscores U.S. support for the Egyptian-Israeli peace treaty to which the PLO has pledged its violent opposition.

As former Secretary of State Henry Kissinger wrote in the May 15, 1988 *Washington Post:* "Much of expert opinion deplores the 1975 American undertaking not to negotiate with the PLO unless that organization accepts the state of Israel and Security Council Resolutions 242 and 338. These experts choose to ignore the phrasing of that pledge, which did not create a new policy, but rather 'reaffirmed existing U.S. policy' carried out by three previous administrations of both parties for 11 years.

"The PLO was formed in 1964 while Israel was within its 1967 borders. The PLO carried out terrorist raids for three years before Israel occupied Gaza and the West Bank. Its program calls for a secular Palestinian state within the borders of historic Palestine—a euphemism for the destruction of Israel. To be sure, there are Palestinians claiming to speak for the PLO who hint at coexistence with Israel. But no PLO leader has ever been prepared to put that proposition before the PLO governing body. Even the ambiguous language of Resolution 242, which was carefully crafted after the 1967 war to permit each side wide latitude in interpretation, has proved too precise for the PLO, which cannot bring itself to accept that resolution's call for a 'just and lasting peace within secure and recognized borders.' "

15

Arab Treatment of Jews

MYTH

"Arabs cannot possibly be anti-Semitic as they are themselves Semites."

FACTS

The terms anti-Semite, anti-Semitism, and anti-Semitic were coined in Germany by Wilhelm Marrih 1879 to refer to the anti-Jewish manifestations of the period and to give Jew-hatred a more scientific-sounding name. The terms refer specifically to hostility towards Jews and have no relevance to other Semitic groups. Arabs, like any other people, can indeed be anti-Semitic.

Further, the often-heard claim that Jews and Arabs, as "Semites," are cousins seems to have little basis in ethnic ties. David Shipler, in *Arab and Jew: Wounded Spirits in a Promised Land*, (Times Books, 1986), explained that "the term 'Semitic' was coined in 1781 by the German scholar, A. L. von Schlozer, to identify a family of related languages, including Hebrew, Arabic, Aramaic and others. He derived the word from Shem, one of Noah's three sons, giving the unintended impression that all those who spoke Semitic languages shared a common ancestry, and thereby setting in motion a process of labeling that may have distorted biblical history and anthropology.

"In the nineteenth century, the narrow linguistic definition of 'Semitic' gradually broadened into the concept of race, and the notion grew up in European writings that a Semitic group of people existed with quite specific characteristics of appearance and culture. Modern archaeological excavations and other research have led some contemporary scholars, most notably S. O. Goitein, to break that link between language and race, to conclude that there is no basis for the idea that the varied peoples who spoke Semitic languages also share physical and social traits."

MYTH

"Arabs are only anti-Israel and have never been anti-Jewish."

FACT

Jews were sometimes treated better in some Arab countries than in some Christian lands in Europe. But Jews were no strangers to persecution among the Arabs. The few Jews remaining in the Arab world today are severely discriminated against and, for the most part, forbidden to leave.

Albert Memmi, the Tunisian-born writer and political theorist, writes, "It is not Zionism that has caused Arab anti-Semitism, but the other way around, just as in Europe. Israel is a rejoinder to the oppression suffered by Jews the world over, including our own oppression as Arab Jews. From the time my friends and I were 12 years old, long before [the Holocaust in Europe], we conspired, amid an Arab world that had always been hostile, for the construction of a Jewish state."

The founder of Islam, Mohammed, was intolerant of nonbelievers and expelled or exterminated those who refused to convert. Many Jews died at the hands of Moslems, and many others were forced to pay exorbitant taxes or live in *mellahs*, Arab ghettos for Jews. It was Baghdad's Caliph Haroun al Rashid who invented the yellow badge of shame which Jews were ordered to wear in 807 A.D.—setting a precedent that would be followed centuries later in Europe.

More than 6,000 Jews were massacred in Fez, Morocco in 1033. In 1066, more than 5,000 were murdered by Arab mobs in Granada. In Libya, Ali Burzi Pasha murdered hundreds of Jews in 1785. Eighteen Jews were killed in Tunis in 1869. In Morocco, more than 500 Jews were murdered between 1864 and 1880.

Jewish populations were continuously harassed by Islamic restrictions and under ever-present physical threat. Riots in which dozens were slain occurred in Iraq in 1941, in Libya in 1945, in Egypt in 1946 and 1948, Syria in 1948, and Yemen in 1947 and 1948.

"Never," writes Memmi, "except perhaps for two or three eras with very clear boundaries in time, such as the Andalusian period . . . have the Jews lived in the Arab countries otherwise than as diminished people in an exposed position, periodically overcome and massacred so that they would be acutely conscious of their position."

He concludes, "If we leave out the crematoria and the murders committed in Russia from Kishinev to Stalin, the

140

sum total of the Jewish victims of the Christian world is probably no greater than the total number of victims of successive pogroms, both big and small, perpetrated in the Moslem countries."

In a May 15, 1975 article in the Lebanese daily *An-Nahar*, Sabri Jiryis, a PLO official and former director of the Institute for Palestinian Studies in Beirut, wrote: "This is not the place to describe how the Jews were removed from Arab countries where they had lived for centuries; how they were ignominiously expelled after their property had been confiscated or acquired at a nominal sum. It is impossible to justify the matter by saying that it was the past regimes in the Arab world, aided by the imperialist power, which worked in coordination with Zionism that did it . . . The historical results ensuing from such an operation cannot be wiped out by such simple pretexts . . . . There is no need to say that the problem of those Arab Jews and their transfer to Israel is not merely theoretical, at least as far as the Palestinians are concerned. It has a very practical repercussion on the future of the Palestinian problem."

Jews were never permitted to live in Jordan or Saudi Arabia. Indeed, Jordanian Civil Law No. 6 (paragraph 3) stipulated, "any man will be a Jordanian subject unless he is Jewish."

MYTH

"Jews—and Christians—as 'People of the Book', are protected under Islamic law."

FACT

This argument is rooted in the traditional Islamic concept of the *"dhimmi,"* which means "protégé" or "protected person," as the French authority Jacques Ellul has noted. But, "one must ask: 'protected against whom?' When this 'stranger' lives in Islamic countries, the answer can only be: against the Moslems themselves. The point that must be clearly understood is that the very term 'protégé' implies a latent hostility" (from the foreword to *The Dhimmi: Jews and Christians Under Islam*, by Bat Ye'or, Fairleigh Dickinson University Press, 1985).

Dhimmi status—from the treaty or *dhimma* between the non-Islamic group and its Moslem rulers—was concessionary; it was granted and could be unilaterally revoked. It "meant that in reality the protected person had *no genuine rights*," according to Ellul. This view persists, and "for the conquering Islam of today, those who do not claim to be Moslems do not have any human rights recognized as such. In an Islamic society, the non-Moslems would return to their former dhimmi status, which is why the idea of solving the Middle East conflicts by the creation of a federation including Israel within a group of Moslem peoples or states, or in a 'Judeo-Islamic' state, is a fantasy and an illusion."

Echoing Memmi, Ellul added that historically, anti-Jewish outbursts, the equivalent of European pogroms, were quite numerous in Islamic lands.

Dhimmi status remains an issue today. As Bat Ye'or noted, Lebanon's president-elect, Bashir Gemayel stressed the theme in a speech on Sept. 14, 1982: "In the name of all the Christians of the Middle East, and as Lebanese Christians, let us proclaim that if Lebanon is not to be a Christian national homeland, it will nonetheless remain a homeland for Christians . . . .

"Yasir Arafat has transformed the church of Damur into a garage. We forgive him, and . . . we will rebuild it. Had we been in Egypt or Syria, perhaps we would not even have had the right to rebuild a destroyed church.

"Our desire is to remain in the Middle East so that our church bells may ring out our joys and sorrow whenever we wish!

"We do not want . . . to be transformed into citizens existing in the 'dhimmitude' of others! Henceforth, we refuse to live in any 'dhimmitude'!"

Several hours later he was assassinated. The Lebanon-based Syrian Social National Party—linked to Syrian military intelligence—reportedly was responsible.

MYTH

"Jews who return to Arab countries would live as free and equal citizens."

FACT

The PLO's suggestion that Jews born in Arab states would leave the democracy of Israel to live under oppressive Arab

142

dictatorship is preposterous.

In 1975, the Iraqi government issued an invitation for all former Iraqi Jews to return "home." Only one former Iraqi in Israel was known to have accepted the invitation. When Iraqi officials told Western reporters in Baghdad that "a trickle" of Iraqi Jews had returned, newsmen started referring to Yusef Navi as "Mr. Trickle." After a year in Iraq, Navi re-emigrated to Israel.

The exodus of Oriental Jews from Arab countries did not come as any surprise. For centuries, Jews of the Arab world lived as second-class citizens, oppressed by discriminatory taxes, restrictions on their freedom, and acts of violence.

On the anniversary of Mohammed's birth in April 1972, Egyptian President Sadat cited Mohammed's treatment of the Jews as justification for his refusal at that time to negotiate with Israel:

> "The most splendid thing our prophet Mohammed did was to evict them from the Arabian peninsula. We know their history with our prophet. They are mean and treacherous people."

The remnants of Jewish communities still in Arab countries at the time of the Six-Day War suffered brutal vengeance at the hands of the Arabs, and the few thousand who remain today in Syria live in extreme fear. As a result, most of the Arab world is *Judenrein*.

Nearly every Arab government has declared Islam its state religion. Yet the PLO claims that Oriental Jews who return to the Arab countries can expect to enjoy "every right."

The Situation Today

Syria

1948 Jewish population: 45,000
1987: 5,000
Damascus was the site of a blood libel and pogrom which killed many Jews in 1840.

Even before the 1967 war, Jews in Syria were terrorized by night arrest, interrogations, imprisonment and torture. Jews were not permitted to leave the Damascus ghetto. After the war their situation worsened.

An airport road was paved over the Jewish cemetery in Damascus; school examinations were scheduled on Saturdays to prevent Jewish participation.

Jews are singled out on identity cards. Palestinian Arab refugees are housed in the Jewish quarter to harass residents.

Until 1976, Jews were not permitted to leave the country, to go more than four kilometers from their place of business, to sell immovable property, to work for the government or banks, to have telephones and driver's licenses, to bequeath property to heirs. The state confiscated the property of those who escaped. Most Jews working for Arab merchants were dismissed. There were numerous reports of torture and murder of Jews trying to flee the country.

In Dec. 1975, *The Chicago Daily News* interviewed a 24-year-old Jewish woman who had escaped from Syria the year before. Fearing Syrian officials would retaliate against her relatives in Damascus, the refugee gave her name only as Jamile.

Four of her friends, Jamile related, were killed trying to flee Syria, their bodies "completely burned and disfigured by acid."

Describing life in Syria, she said: "After primary school, there was no high school for us, and no chance to work in an office or bank. We were forbidden this kind of work. We were surrounded by hatred. Sometimes there were attacks on us when we went to the synagogue."

Richard Schifter, Assistant Secretary of State for Human Rights and Humanitarian Affairs, May 3, 1988:

". . . The situation of the Jewish community in Syria is one of our major human rights issues with the government of Syria. We have voiced our concerns and opinions on this subject at the highest levels of the Syrian government and we will continue to do so."

After 1976, in an apparent effort to improve its image in the West, the Syrian government lifted some of its restrictions against the Jewish community. However, emigration is still forbidden, and identity papers are still stamped with the term "Musawi," identifying the bearer as a Jew. Jews are usually permitted to sell a house or car only if they can prove the money is being used to buy a replacement. Agents of the *Muhabarat* (the Syrian secret police) are reported to be present at all synagogue services. While Jews may now travel between cities, they must sign out before leaving one city and report to police on arriving at their destination. In 1988 it was difficult for Jews to obtain permission to travel abroad, and those who did posted a deposit, which in the past varied from $2,000 to $10,000. They also had to leave close relatives behind.

Government agents patrolled the Jewish quarter, and most Syrian Jews feared being seen in public with foreigners.

In July 1977, after months of negotiation at the highest governmental levels, Syrian President Assad permitted 12 Jewish women to marry men of the Syrian Jewish community in New York and to emigrate. However, there are an estimated 500 Jewish women still in Syria unable to find Jewish husbands there. A decade later some intermarriage was reported; more young men were able to escape Syria than women, leaving the latter with fewer prospective Jewish spouses.

In 1979, there were numerous reports of Jews, some as young as eight, being arrested on suspicion of trying to flee the country. There was also a report of a Jewish family that managed to escape to Lebanon, only to be recognized by a Syrian soldier in Beirut, arrested, and sent back to Syria.

Thirteen Syrian Jews, including four women and seven children, were able to escape to Turkey by motorboat in 1979. But an unsuccessful escape attempt in the same year left a young Jewish woman gravely wounded. She was eventually permitted to go to the United States for surgery, but she had to leave her four small children behind, and her husband was arrested.

In 1980, two Jewish women in Aleppo were raped by Syrian security men who were supposedly searching for members of the Moslem Brotherhood.

In Dec., 1983, Lilly Abadi, then pregnant, and her two children—aged four and seven—were stabbed and shot in the Syrian city of Aleppo by unknown assailants.

In 1987, the secret police seized several Jewish men. No formal charges were lodged but, according to the American Jewish Committee, the men were suspected of trying to escape from the country or of having returned from unauthorized trips abroad.

The men reportedly were mistreated while in custody. In

May 1988, the secret police still held at least eight Jewish men; a ninth, teenager Mousa Khalife, had been released. As a result of brutal beatings while incarcerated and subsequent formation of blood clots, Khalife faced possible amputation of his legs.

At the same time, several young Jewish women reportedly were kidnapped and forced to marry Syrian or Palestinian men.

Syria's attitude toward Jews was reflected in its continued sheltering of Alois Brunner, one of the most notorious Nazi war criminals still believed to be at large. Brunner, a chief aide to Adolf Eichmann, told the *Chicago Sun-Times* in a 1987 telephone interview from his Damascus home that he regretted nothing and would do it all again. All Jews "deserved to die because they were the devil's agents and human garbage," he said.

Brunner, 75, reportedly advised the Hafez Assad regime on "security matters." For years Syria denied that it hosted him; after West Germany requested Brunner's extradition, Damascus replied that he committed no punishable crimes.

Iraq

1948 Jewish population: 125,000
1987: Fewer than 300

The 2,700-year-old Jewish community of Iraq has suffered horrible persecution.

The 1941, Mufti-inspired, pro-Nazi coup of Rashid Ali sparked rioting and pogroms in which dozens died. There were vicious anti-Jewish riots in 1947 and most Jews fled to Israel in 1951.

In 1952, Iraq's Hashemite government ended the emigration right of Jews and publicly hanged two Jews after falsely charging them with hurling a bomb at the Baghdad office of the U.S. Information Agency.

With the rise of competing Ba'ath factions in 1963, the Jews were condemned to purgatory. Synagogues and schools were sequestered, the sale of property was forbidden, freedom of movement was curbed, and all Jews were forced to carry yellow identity cards.

After the Six-Day War there were more virulent measures: Jewish property was expropriated; Jewish bank accounts were frozen; Jews were dismissed from public posts; businesses were shut; trading permits were cancelled; telephones were disconnected. Jews were placed under house arrest for long periods or restricted to the cities or their living quarters. Emigration was prohibited.

All these restrictions were contained in statutes and regulations, specifically Iraqi Law Number 64 of 1967 and Iraqi Law Number 10 of 1968.

Persecution was at its worst at the end of 1968. Scores were jailed upon the "discovery" of a local "spy ring." Nineteen were sentenced to death in staged trials and hanged in the public squares of Baghdad; others died of torture.

Baghdad Radio, Jan. 27, 1969, called upon Iraqis to "come and enjoy the feast." Some 500,000 men, women and children paraded and danced past the scaffolds where the bodies of the hanged Jews swung; the mob rhythmically chanted "Death to Israel" and "Death to all traitors."

This barbaric display brought a world-wide public outcry which Iraqi President Bakr dismissed as "the barking of dogs."

Another 18 Jews were hanged in secret between 1970 and 1972. Jews were also forced to house Palestinian Arabs and raise money for Al Fatah and other terrorist groups.

The Ba'ath party apparatus grew in 1972 and Jews began to disappear, their possessions seized by rapacious officials who posted signs on their houses that the "Jewish occupants have fled the country."

Nazeim Kazzar, head of the secret police, ordered the murder of five members of the Reuven Kashkush family on April 12, 1973, in retaliation for the Israeli assassination of Palestinian Arab terrorist leaders in Beirut the day before.

The only bright spot in the recent past of Iraq's Jews is that international pressure after the public hangings in the late 1960's led the government to quietly allow most of the remaining 2,500 Jews to emigrate in the early 1970's, even while leaving other restrictions in force.

Most of Iraq's remaining Jews are too old to leave. They are pressured by the government to turn over title (without compensation) to over $200 million worth of Jewish community property, apartments, schools, hospitals and fields (*New York Times*, Feb. 18, 1973).

Libya

1948 Jewish population: 40,000
1987: Unknown, believed none.
A savage pogrom on Nov. 5, 1945 killed hundreds. Jews

were burned in their shops, hurled from rooftops and balconies or beaten to death. Almost every synagogue was sacked. In June 1948, Libyan rioters murdered another 14 Jews.

After the 1967 Six-Day War, the Jewish population of 4,500 was again subjected to brutal pogroms in which 100 were killed, sparking a near-total exodus.

In Feb. 1970, Muammar Qaddafi's regime confiscated all Jewish property and cancelled all debts owed to Jews since June 5, 1967 (Libyan Law Number 14, Feb. 7, 1970). Jewish claims for compensation totaling millions of dollars were cancelled (Libyan Law Number 57, May 9, 1970). Homeless Jews were herded into special camps. Today, Libya's ancient Jewish community has been all but obliterated.

According to a 1983 State Department report, "virulently anti-Jewish broadcasts on Libyan radio were the apparent cause of anti-Jewish violence in 1982 in portions of Tunisia within broadcasting range." The Department reported that in a June 1985 speech Qaddafi "cited the Prophet Muhammad as stating that Judaism and Islam cannot coexist in the land of the Arabs." In Sept. of that year he again made virulent broadcasts calling for anti-Jewish violence in Tunisia and Morocco.

Lebanon

1948 Jewish population: 20,000
1987: 90
Fighting in the 1975-76 Moslem-Christian civil war swirled around the Jewish quarter in Beirut, damaging many Jewish homes, businesses and synagogues. Most remaining Lebanese Jews emigrated *en masse* in 1976, fearful that the growing Syrian presence in Lebanon would curtail freedom of emigration. The remaining community has no rabbi.

Jews, like other innocent civilians, have been killed in the savage fighting of the civil war. In the mid-1980's the "Organization of the Oppressed of the Earth" claimed responsibility for the kidnappings of nine Lebanese Jews—most were leaders of what remained of the country's tiny Jewish community. Four of those kidnapped were later found murdered. News stories suggested that the "Organization of the Oppressed" was, like Islamic Jihad and Revolutionary Justice Organization, another label of Hezbollah, the pro-

Iranian Shi'ite Moslem "Party of God." Hezbollah—in its various guises—was believed responsible for the kidnappings of about two dozen Westerners, including at least 10 Americans, in Lebanon from 1985 through 1987.

North Yemen

1948 Jewish population: 54,000
1987: 1,200
Early in 1948, looting occurred after six Jews were accused of the ritual murder of two Arab girls. The imams of Yemen always treated Jews as infidels. Jews could not ride on horseback, carry arms, own property, or build houses taller than those of Moslem landlords.

Virtually the entire Jewish community was believed to have emigrated to Israel in 1949-50, but late in 1976, an American diplomat travelling in a remote region of northern Yemen came across a small Jewish community. The diplomat reported, on the basis of conversations with several Jews there, that the community appeared to be secure and free to emigrate.

The State Department Human Rights survey reported in 1983 that Moslem Yeminis "frequently are heard to regret the past emigration of Yemini Jews, many of whom were skilled craftsmen and played a special role in Yemini society. At least one American Jewish organization has been allowed to distribute Hebrew books and materials to the Yemeni Jewish community."

Prior to a visit by *Yediot Achronot* journalist Dr. Amnon Kapeliuk in 1984, the number of Jews in North Yemen was estimated at 500 to 600. But Kapeliuk put the number at 1,100 and since then most observers estimated 1,200 to 2,000 Jews in Yemen. Some reports—not corroborated—asserted that as many as 6,000 remained. Access to the community is difficult.

The spring 1988 issue of *Shofar*, the magazine published by the World Union of Jewish Students, noted that a former Yemenite Jew now living in Israel recently received "two letters, without return addresses, through the offices of an international organization. The letters were sent by relatives in North Yemen three years ago . . . . The letters relate, among other things, that many Jews in Yemen are abandoning their faith and converting to Islam, owing mainly to a lack of women in the Jewish community."

South Yemen

1948 Jewish population: 7,000
1987: None

The ancient Jewish tribes of the Hadramaut are now in Israel. Mob violence during the Six-Day War killed several Jews; the British government, then in Aden, evacuated all the remaining 350 Jews on June 18, 1967.

Tunisia

1948 Jewish population: 110,000
1987: 3,500

During the June 1967 war, Jews were attacked by rioting Arab mobs. Synagogues and shops were burned. The government denounced the outbreaks and President Habib Bourguiba apologized to the Chief Rabbi, promising compensation.

The government appealed to the 20,000 Tunisian Jews to remain but did not prevent anyone from leaving. Many emigrated to France.

The military court sentenced two youths to 15 years for burning the Great Synagogue. Others were convicted of attacking the American and British embassies and looting Jewish property.

In 1982, there were attacks on Jews in the towns of Zarzis and Ben Guardane. According to the U.S. State Department, the Tunisian government "acted decisively to provide protection to the Jewish community."

In 1985, a Tunisian guard opened fire on worshippers in a synagogue in Jerba, killing five people, four of them Jews. But following Israel's Oct. 1, 1985 bombing of PLO headquarters near Tunis, "the government took extraordinary measures to protect the Jewish community," the State Department noted.

Morocco

1948 Jewish population: 300,000
1987: 7,000

There were riots directed against Jews and one economic boycott initiated in 1967 by the Istiqlal Party. The infamous, anti-Semitic *Protocols of the Elders of Zion* was published in Morocco in 1967.

King Hassan has tried to protect the Jews, however, and in 1988 Morocco had one of the more tolerant environments for Jews in the Arab world. Many Moroccan Jews in Europe, the Westen Hemisphere and even Israel travel to Morocco to see friends or relatives. Nevertheless, the Jewish middle class has virtually disappeared. Younger Jews are eager to leave, and there have been recent cases of harassment in the passport processing of Jews of Moroccan extraction carrying French passports.

However, the State Department reported that Moroccan Jews held some leading positions in the business community as recently as 1986. One served as president of the administrative chamber of the Supreme Court; another was a parliamentary deputy. In July 1986, King Hassan publicly hosted Israeli Prime Minister Shimon Peres at Ifrane, in Morocco, as part of the effort to initiate an Arab-Israeli peace process. Two months later Hassan met with a delegation of Jews of Moroccan origin, including an Israeli Knesset member. Hassan's meetings with Israelis were condemned by Syria and other Arab radicals.

Algeria

1948 Jewish population: 150,000
1987: 500
The majority of Algeria's Jews left with the French in 1962. A French organization tracing 6,000 missing persons who disappeared between 1953 and 1963, reported that 600 Jews were living in mobile forced-labor camps in inhumane conditions.

Egypt

1948 Jewish population: 75,000
1984: 200
Egypt's Jews have lived in a relatively free climate since 1970, but prior to that they were as restricted as any other Jewish community in the Arab world.

When war broke out in 1967, homes and property were confiscated. The government forced all 2,500 Jews to register.

More than 600 heads of families were put in the Abouzabel prison near Cairo, while 200 were taken to the Al Barraga jail near Alexandria. The Grand Rabbi of Alexandria, Jacques Nefussi, and the Chief Rabbi of Cairo, Chaim Douek, were arrested. A few elderly prisoners were released, but the rest were harshly treated. Some were tortured, most were beaten or crammed into stifling, crowded cells.

In 1979 the Egyptian Jewish community became the first in the Arab world to establish official contact with the Jewish state. But by the time Cairo Jews welcomed Prime Minister Menachem Begin of Israel to their synagogue, a week after the Israeli-Egyptian peace treaty was signed, the community had become too small and grown too old for any kind of renaissance. Egyptian authorities have permitted major repairs and renovations to several Egyptian synagogues. But these measures may be too late. Services are held in only one synagogue, and there are no kosher butchers. *The Los Angeles Times* reported in 1983 that an attempt was made to import 11 bottles of wine and other supplies for the Passover holiday, but the items were blocked by customs officers who considered the items "political" and levied a $1,500 duty. The goods had to be abandoned.

Jews in Non-Arab Middle East Countries

Ethiopia

1862 Jewish population: 250,000
1987: 10,000 (estimated)

Struggling against the peril of extinction in the northwest Ethiopian province of Gondar, is the dwindling community of black Jews. They are called Falashas in Amharic, a term signifying landless outsiders. They refer to themselves as Beta Israel—House of Israel. According to their tradition, they are an ancient Jewish sect which has been living in Ethiopia since at least the fourth century. They claim to be descendants of King Solomon and the Queen of Sheba, whose son Menelik settled in Ethiopia.

The ritual of Ethiopian Jews is based primarily on the Bible; they have only recently been introduced to the Talmudic traditions. As is customary in traditional Judaism, they observe the Sabbath and holidays, pray in synagogues and eat kosher foods.

Prior to the 16th century, Ethiopian Jews were a self-governing and economically independent community with a population estimated at one million. By the 17th century, however, Christian and Moslem forces began to weaken the community through land confiscation, enslavement and forced conversion. In recent years, they have lived as second-class citizens, caught in the cross-fire of a civil war and suffering from famine and persecution.

Under the reign of Emperor Haile Selassie in the mid-1900's, Ethiopian Jews were permitted to practice their religious traditions, but were still unable to own land or emigrate freely. Following the 1974 revolution which deposed the Emperor, the new Marxist government, disapproving of the Ethiopian Jews' Zionist orientation, stepped up the anti-Semitic campaign.

Writing in the *New York Times* after "Operation Moses" was revealed, William Safire noted:

"... For the first time in history, thousands of black people are being brought to a country not in chains but in dignity, not as slaves but as citizens."

Today, the Jews remaining in Ethiopia after the "Operation Moses" exodus to Israel are facing extinction. For the Jews still in Ethiopia, life is a prisoner's struggle for survival.

Iran

1978 Jewish population: 80,000
1987: 30,000

The fate of the Jewish minority in Iran is in the hands of Islamic fundamentalists who, ruling by the Islamic code, have refused to extend full protection of rights to the Jews. Although they have lived in Iran for over 27 centuries, the Jews of Iran are today forbidden employment in government agencies, denied entrance into teachers colleges and expelled from teaching positions. Since the Iranian revolution, more than 40,000 Jews have left the country (stripped of their holdings), more than 400 have been detained in jail, and at least 10 have been executed by firing squads on trumped-up charges.

Some of those executed were charged with "importing honey from Israel," "receiving letters from relatives in Israel," "cooperation with Zionism and the state of Israel" and "corruption on earth." Such charges reflect Khomeini's febrile anti-Israel stance, under which Zionist or Jewish communal affiliations translate into acts of felony.

Khomeini views the Israeli-Arab conflict as an Islamic

struggle. As he told *Der Spiegel* in 1979, the Iranian Islamic Republic would break relations with Israel "because we do not believe there is any legal justification for its existence. Palestine belongs to the Islamic space and must be returned to the Moslems." He maintained close cooperation with the PLO; indeed, Yasir Arafat was the first foreign visitor he received after taking office. Khomeini expressed his gratitude for the training, weapons and money his forces received from the PLO by turning the Israel embassy building over to Arafat.

In July 1987, during the Mecca pilgrimage riots in which more than 400 people died, Iranian demonstrators chanted "Death to the United States, death to the Soviet Union, death to Israel!"

In his book, *Confronting Israel*, Khomeini exhorts all Moslems:

"Oh brothers! Let us not regard this holy and sacrificial war as a war between Arabs and Israel. Let us regard it as a war of all Moslems together against Jews and their leaders. It is the responsibility of all the Islamic governments with their peoples, with all their forces, and potential, to aid and support fedayeen [guerrillas] on the lines of fire."

Turkey

Before 1948: 80,000
1987: 22,000-25,000

Turkey—like Iran—is basically non-Arab in history and culture, but with a Moslem majority. Unlike Iran after the Shah, Turkey after a 1980 military coup maintained a secular, pro-Western outlook. It continues to maintain diplomatic relations with Israel. As George Gruen, director of Israel and Middle East Affairs of the American Jewish Committee, noted, "the military officers who seized power in Ankara . . . reaffirmed Turkey's basic commitment to secularism and alignment with the Western world."

By 1987, the country was again functioning as a parliamentary democracy, after adoption of a new constitution and regular elections. "The position of the Jewish community had been endangered not by overt anti-Semitism, which is restricted to small extremist fringe groups, but by the economic difficulties, political instability and left- and right-wing terrorism that beset Turkish society," according to Gruen.

Syria reportedly has sponsored anti-Turkish terrorism by separatist groups such as the Armenian Secret Army for the Liberation of Armenia (ASALA). Kurdish rebels also operated against the government and population near the Turkish border with Iraq and Iran.

In Sept. 1986, the Turkish Jewish community was horrified when at least two Arabic-speaking terrorists, posing as tourists, attacked worshippers in Istanbul's Neve Shalom Synagogue with automatic weapons and grenades, killing 24. People claiming to speak for the "Palestine Revenge Organization," "Islamic Resistance" and "Defense of Islam," among others, claimed responsibility. However, Turkish and Israeli authorities suspected Abu Nidal's "Fatah Revolutionary Council"; an Iranian connection also was suggested by some.

16

Arab Treatment of Other Minorities

MYTH

"Arabs were always tolerant of minorities in their midst."

FACT

The Jews are not unique.Every minority has suffered discrimination and worse under Arab rule.

CHRISTIANS

In Lebanon

Prior to the 1967 war, an ominous phrase about Jews and Christians was heard in the Arab world: "First the Saturday people, then the Sunday people." Historian Bernard Lewis has written: "The Saturday people have proved unexpectedly recalcitrant, and recent events in Lebanon indicate that the priorities may have been reversed" (*Commentary*, Jan. 1976).

On Oct. 2, 1977, Patrick Seale wrote in the London *Observer*, "Secular nationalism throughout the Arab world has lost ground to a militant revival of Islamic orthodoxy, making all minorities tremble."

Tens of thousands of Christian Arabs have died in the Lebanese civil war, which by the end of 1986 had resulted in approximately 130,000 fatalities out of a population estimated at three million.

In April 1975, Lebanese Maronite bishops issued a resolution protesting " vigorously against the abuse of the sacredness of churches and places of worship, desecration of Holy Places, firing at monasteries, hospitals and ambulances . . . attacks on ecclesiastics . . . as well as monks and nuns."

In 1975 and 1976 anti-Christian sentiment erupted in Lebanon where ideological and class warfare also split along Moslem-Christian lines. Cries for a *jihad* (Moslem holy war) were frequent. The description of the siege and destruction of Damour in Jan. 1976, in Becker's *The PLO*—based on the eyewitness account of Maronite Father Mansour Labaky—reveals the wanton brutality of the PLO and its allies at the time. These included Syrians, Lebanese Sunni Moslems, other Lebanese militia, and mercenaries from Iran, Afghanistan, Pakistan and Libya. Not only were the bodies of some of the town's residents—men, women and children—mutilated, but "in a frenzy to destroy their enemies utterly, as if even the absolute limits of nature could not stop them, the invaders broke open tombs and flung the bones of the dead into the streets" (Becker, pages 122-126).

"In all, 582 people were killed in the storming of Damour. Father Labaky went back with the Red Cross to bury them. Many of the bodies had been dismembered, so they had to count the heads to number the dead." The rest of the city's 25,000 residents had been driven from their homes; Damour was turned into a PLO center, the Church of St. Elias used as a garage and target range.

In Egypt

Coptic Christians may total between six and eight million of Egypt's 50 million people *(The History of Egypt*, P. J. Vatikiotis, 1985, Johns Hopkins University Press). U.S. government sources note that the Egyptian government "almost certainly" underestimates the figure.

An early twentieth century Coptic leader was assassinated by a Moslem motivated by religious fanaticism and nationalism, leaving the Copts "further terrified" as to their status, according to Vatikiotis. "Throughout the 1970's, there were recurrent Coptic-Moslem clashes in various parts of the country including the burning of churches and rival militant Coptic and Muslim demonstrations in Cairo and its surrounding districts, as well as in Upper Egypt, especially in Assiut."

Again, in 1987, "there were several outbreaks of sectarian violence in areas of Upper Egypt which have a large Coptic population, and two less serious incidents in the Delta," the State Department's *Country Reports on Human Rights Practices* noted.

The president of the American Coptic Association, Shawky F. Karas, reported on prospects for Egyptian Copts: "Job discrimination is at all levels. The Christians [between

10 and 15% of the population] are denied leadership positions. No Christian is a college dean, a police commissioner, a city manager, or a province governor. There are two Christian Egyptian ambassadors out of more than 120 ambassadors. Christian college students are exposed to harassment by Moslem students (*Christian Science Monitor*, Dec. 9, 1976).

In Sept. 1977, some members of Egypt's National Assembly tried unsuccessfully to legislate capital punishment for any Moslem converting to Christianity. In Oct. 1977, Coptic churches were desecrated.

A new outbreak of anti-Christian actions erupted in 1981. In June of that year, according to Egyptian government figures, anti-Copt riots in a Cairo slum neighborhood left nine Christians and seven Moslems dead. Independent sources estimated the number of dead as high as 70 or 80.

In Aug. 1981, a grenade was thrown at a Coptic church, killing three Christians and two Moslems.

One month later, Egyptian President Anwar Sadat banished the Coptic leader, Pope Shenouda, to a monastery in a secluded desert oasis. In April 1983, an Egyptian court rejected Shenouda's appeal, upheld the decree and recommended that a new pope be selected. The Coptic community defied the court, and Shenouda remained the Coptic leader. He was released from his seclusion in 1985.

In Libya

Soon after Muammar Qaddafi's Revolutionary Command Council took control of Libya in Sept. 1969, more than 4,000 Italians were ousted and forced to abandon property, money and belongings. Some 25,000 more were subsequently expelled.

The Libyan government proclaimed its "aim to avenge the past. . . . The feeling of holy revenge runs in our veins." The Cathedral of the Sacred Heart in Tripoli was converted into the Gamal Abdel Nasser Mosque on Nov. 26, 1979 (*Washington Post*, Nov. 27, 1979).

KURDS

The Kurds are a tribal people inhabiting the mountainous Zagros region now divided by the modern borders of Turkey, Iraq, Iran, Syria and the Soviet Union. The Kurds antedate Islam, tracing their ancestry back 4,000 years. While they accepted Islam, mostly as Sunni Mos-
158

lems, they have rejected the social and political influence of the Arabs. They have insisted on maintaining their own language, traditions and tribal leaders. The Kurdish population numbers well over 10 million, with at least three million in Turkey, more than 2.5 million each in Iran and Iraq, 500,000 in Syria and 200,000 in the USSR.

Although living contiguously across national borders, the Kurds have failed to develop a united nationalist strategy for an independent Kurdish state. Instead, they have fought for autonomy in each country in which they live. The Kurds have traditionally secured arms and assistance from adjacent states, and during times of harsh repression they have been able to take refuge with neighboring tribes. Their struggles for autonomy have been met with brutality bordering on genocide.

In Syria

When Syria split from Egypt in 1961, the new Syrian regime began a drive to destroy the Kurds as an ethnic group through discrimination and repression.

In Aug. 1962, Syria instituted the "Arab-Belt" plan, forcing the Kurds to evacuate the arable Jezrieh region and to emigrate or settle in desert areas. Half of Jezrieh's 300,000 Kurds were stripped of their citizenship.

The Arab-Belt plan, according to the Arab press, was formulated to "save Arabism in Jezrieh," although Arabs represented less than 20% of the Jezrieh population. It was later extended to all Kurdish areas in northern Syria.

The Kurds of the Belt area are not alone; all the Kurds in Syria suffer: They have no schools or newspapers; their political party is illegal; they are denied expression of Kurdish culture; they cannot publish books in their own language; and they are denied military and civil service positions unless they declare that they are "Arabs," rather than Kurds.

In Iraq

Iraq's genocidal war against the Kurds began in 1961 and has continued through the present. At times, according to the *New York Times*, the Iraqis have used bombs, rocket-type artillery, napalm and even poison gas against Iraqi Kurdish positions and towns, in the struggle to suppress Kurdish nationalism. Even so, the Iraqi government asked

159

Kurdish Gen. Mustafa Barzani to commit his forces in the war against Israel in 1967. Barzani repeated his reply in an interview with Eric Rouleau of *Le Monde* in Jan. 1969:

"Three days before the outbreak of the war between Israel and the Arabs, the Baghdad government sent emissaries to me requesting that I place Kurdish army units at their disposal for the war against Israel. I replied, 'For six years you have been fighting us, trying to wipe out the Kurdish people, so how can you come now and ask for my help?' "

Despite a peace treaty between Barzani and the Ba'ath government guaranteeing Kurdish autonomy, Iraqi troops, fearing for the safety of the Kirkuk oil fields, attacked Kurdish villages in the summer of 1973. *The Teheran Journal* (June 27, 1973) reported that 10 Kurds were killed and 22 wounded by Iraqi government aircraft and artillery.

In March 1974, the Iraqi Ba'ath Party tried to impose its own plan for Kurdish "autonomy" under which it would select Kurdish representatives as well as the head of government. The Kurds refused, and the Iraqi army began its fifth major offensive against Kurdish areas.

The attacks were merciless. Napalming and bombing by the Iraqi air force resulted in the partial or total destruction of 15 Kurdish towns and 205 villages. Massacres were common. More than 100,000 Kurds fled to camps in Turkey and Iran.

On April 24, 1974, Iraqi jets bombed and strafed the town of Qal'a Dizeh, hitting a primary school, market place and two university dormitories. More than 130 were killed and 300 wounded (*Washington Star*, Sept. 2, 1974).

The forces of General Barzani suffered a devastating defeat following the withdrawal of support from Iran and the United States. Thus ended the Kurdish struggle for autonomy. Barzani died in exile in the United States in 1979.

In recent years, Amnesty International has expressed concern over the fate of the Kurdish minority which comprises nearly one-quarter of Iraq's 15 million people. Hundreds of Kurdish elderly, women and children were arrested because family members had belonged to Kurdish forces. As a result of its war with Iran, Iraq has carried out mass execution of members of Iraqi Kurdish tribes that side with Iran. As many as 20,000 young Kurdish men have been detained in desolate areas.

Since 1975, the government of Iraq has conducted a wholesale relocation of the Kurdish population. At least 50,000 persons have been forcibly removed from strategic areas. Other sources place the number as high as 300,000. Tens of thousands of Arab Iraqis have been moved into former Kurdish areas. In a 1987 "campaign to pacify parts of Kurdistan by razing a large number of Kurdish villages, displacing their inhabitants" *(State Department Country Reports, 1987)*, tens of thousands of Iraqi Kurds were displaced and—according to diplomatic sources quoted in the American press—at least one hundred villages and towns were destroyed.

Kurdish political and cultural institutions have been savagely suppressed, and draconian army and police control has been extended throughout the Kurdish area. There have been periodic reports of mass imprisonment of suspected Kurdish rebels. Numerous community leaders have been exiled or executed.

Iraq established a facade of Kurdish autonomy which camouflages a continuing campaign to crush Kurdish nationalism and secure total Baghdad government control of the oil-rich Kurdish areas.

In Oct. 1976, Iraqi agents attempted to assassinate Dr. Ismet Cheriff Vanly, a prominent Kurdish nationalist spokesman, in Lausanne, Switzerland.

Iraq bombed Kurdish villages in Iran, and in the mid-1980's repeatedly allowed Turkish ground and air forces to cross into Iraq to strike anti-Turkish Kurdish rebels. And in March 1988, in an assault which put the oppression of the Kurds on the front page—briefly—Iraqi jets dropped poison gas bombs on the Iraqi Kurdish town of Halabja, and adjacent villages. The area had recently been seized by Iranian troops. Casualties—mostly civilian—were estimated at up to 5,000 dead, with many more wounded.

In Iran

The Iranian Kurds were long victims of repression by the Pahlavi regime. The Kurds fought with the revolutionaries against the Shah and, following his deposition and the disintegration of the Iranian armed forces, appealed to the new Khomeini government for autonomy. Their appeal rejected, the Kurds rallied behind their religious leader, Sheik Ezzedine Hosseini, and the Kurdish Democratic Party leader, Ali

Ghassemlou, and began attacking army and revolutionary guard outposts throughout the region. At Khomeini's command, the new Iranian army struck back with heavy artillery and mass executions.

The Arab and Iranian governments have continuously used the Kurdish populations in other states to stir up trouble for neighboring governments when it served their purpose. Weapons and other supplies are provided to the various Kurdish groups for a time, and then cut off at the whim of the supplier, leaving the rebel Kurds at the mercy of the various central governments.

BLACKS

It is estimated that 500,000-600,000 black Africans were slaughtered in Sudan in the war which the Arab north pursued against the south for 14 years after Sudan gained independence in 1959. As one black leader put it, "With the Arabs we are dead anyway" (*New York Times*, April 15, 1968). Sudan's population of more than 21 million is split between "two distinct cultures—Arab and black African," the State Department noted in 1987. And traditionally the Arab north dominated the black African south. "Southerners coming north looking for work or to escape the war face social discrimination by the Muslim Arab majority" *(Country Reports on Human Rights Practices, 1987)*.

Sudan closed the south to the outside world and tried to bar reporters. Grim reports trickled out. UN figures in the *Journal de Geneve* (Sept. 9, 1967) indicated that 33,000 Sudanese refugees fled to Zaire and 55,000 to Uganda. The South Sudan Liberation Front told the UN that from 1962 on, one million had died and 300,000 had fled to neighboring countries. The *Times* article, however, pointed out that Sudan had some success in persuading its neighbors to help it clamp down on and trap the refugees, barring their escape.

In 1972, the regime of President Gaafar Nimiery signed a peace agreement with the Anyanya rebel leadership. But Islamic law was imposed on Christians as well as Moslems and fighting resumed in southern Sudan in 1983. By the end of 1987, thousands more in the Christian and animist south had been killed. In 1986 the post-Nimiery government began arming some Arabic-speaking Moslem tribes to fight the rebels of the Sudanese People's Liberation Army. Instead, the tribes reportedly used their new automatic weapons to continue old conflicts, sometimes massacring non-Moslem Dinka tribesmen, stealing their cattle and taking their children as slaves. Massacres of hundreds, perhaps thousands of Dinka were reported in 1987 at Al Daein and Wau.

In some respects, the situation in Chad was similar to that of the Sudan. At independence from France in 1960, civil war broke out among many of the 200 tribal and ethnic groups. Also like Sudan, Chad is divided largely between an Arabic-speaking Moslem north and a black African Christian and traditional/animist south. Fighting between groups and regions cost more than 100,000 lives in the country's first two decades of independence.

Beginning in 1973, the conflict was exacerbated by Libyan intervention when Libya's Qaddafi sent troops to seize the Aozou Strip, a large section of northernmost Chad believed by some to contain minerals including uranium.

In 1980, Libya sent 7,000 troops into Chad at the invitation of then-President Goukouni Oueddei to put down a revolt led by Hissein Habre. But the Libyans remained as occupiers. In 1982, Habre's nationalist forces overthrew Goukouni's government. Libya, determined to keep Chad subservient, according to the State Department, reorganized Goukouni's troops and sent air and ground forces to save them after additional defeats.

With help from France, Zaire, and the United States, Habre's men defeated Goukouni's troops in 1986. In 1987, the Chadian army drove the Libyans themselves back to a small part of the Aozou Strip.

Regardless of its outcome, however, the incessant fighting not only contributed to Chad's impoverishment, it illustrated the bloody cleavage between Africa's Arab-Islamic north and its black Christian and traditional center and south.

SLAVERY

The Arabs, who ran the world's black slave markets for centuries, continued to engage in the slave trade among themselves into the 1980's.

Recent incidents of chattel slavery have been cited in Saudi Arabia—which "abolished" it years ago—and in Mauritania, Kuwait, Yemen, Oman, Qatar and Sudan, according to British correspondents and observers.

Britain's Anti-Slavery Society noted that slavery was legal in much of the Arab world until 1962 and that vestiges of the practice survive today.

In the case of Mauritania, however, the Anti-Slavery Society charged that slavery still flourished openly in this decade. In late 1981, the society accused the Arab League member of maintaining "at least 100,000 slaves and 300,000 semi-slaves." Although the Mauritanian government decreed the abolition of slavery in July 1980, the British anti-slavery group labelled the decree a maneuver to improve Mauritania's international standing.

As late as 1987 the State Department noted that "forced labor . . . [as] the vestiges of slavery" still existed in some parts of Mauritania. Despite the government's 1980 decree, "some persons whose ancestors for generations have worked without pay for a particular family still occupy positions of servitude . . . ." Freed slaves could choose to remain in servitude in exchange for bread and board.

The government of Mauritania did ask for UN assistance for a mass media campaign to help erase the remaining traces of slavery.

Former Black Panther leader Eldridge Cleaver, who returned to the United States in 1975 from self-imposed exile in Algeria, reported in *The Boston Herald American* in Jan. 1977, that "having lived intimately for several years amongst the Arabs, I know them to be amongst the most racist people on earth. This is particularly true of their attitude toward black people. . . . Many Arab families that can afford to, keep one or two black slaves to do their menial labor. Sometimes they own an entire family. I have seen such slaves with my own eyes."

In 1987, the *New York Times'* reporter Alan Conwell, in a column on Kuwait, wrote: " 'There is a tradition in the whole [Arabian] peninsula of slavery,' a West European diplomat said. 'To be a Kuwaiti is to be very privileged,' the diplomat went on. 'But if you are a foreign worker, you stand to be exploited and live, by Kuwaiti standards, in very bad conditions.' "

As open slavery has diminished in the Arab world, especially in the Arabian peninsula, the demand for what are essentially indentured servants has grown, with tens of thousands of East Asians being imported as long-term contract laborers. These laborers are virtually unprotected, their pay, working and living conditions being almost totally up to their Arab employers.

MYTH

"Women's rights are now protected in the Arab world."

FACT

In most Arab countries, the *Shari'a,* or Islamic law, defines the rules of traditional social behavior, and under that law women are accorded a role inferior to that of men.

As Daniel Pipes points out in *In the Path of God: Islam and Political Power,* (1983, Basic Books), "In the Islamic view, men and women are seen as partaking of the same sexuality . . . . [In fact] female sexuality is thought of as being so powerful that it constitutes a real danger to society." Therefore, unrestrained females constitute "the most dangerous challenge facing males trying to carry out God's commands (for it is the men who have the far heavier religious burden)." In combination, females' "desires and their irresistible attractiveness give women a power over men which rivals God's.

"Left to themselves," Pipes continues, "men might well fall victim to women and abandon God. *Fitna* would result, that is, civil disorder among believers." In traditional thought, Pipes notes, women pose an internal threat to Islamic society similar to the external one represented by the infidel.

Traditionally, the Arab woman marries at a young age to a man of her father's choice. A husband is entitled to divorce at any time, even against his wife's will, by merely declaring verbally that this is his intention. An Arabic saying, "A woman never knows whether she is going to eat the meal she is cooking," reflects this tenuous marital status.

Although the image of the egalitarian woman is slowly developing within Arab society, it remains largely confined to urban centers and upper-class circles. Ritual sexual mutilation of females remains common in North Africa and the Arabian peninsula.

The lot of Arab women is especially bleak in Saudi Arabia and the other Persian Gulf states. A study by UNICEF released at the 1975 International Women's Year Conference in Mexico City concluded that women in oil-rich Oman, Kuwait, Qatar and the United Arab Emirates now living in urban environments were, for the most part, even more secluded than when their husbands were laborers. Petro-dollars have bought these women leisure time, maids, tele-visions and time-saving appliances, but no political or civil rights. Despite a labor shortage and the example of immi-grant Egyptian, British and Palestinian Arab working women, these Persian Gulf countries have a tiny indigenous female work force.

In Saudi Arabia, as the State Department's 1987 *Country Reports* notes: "Women do not enjoy equality with men. By Koranic precept, a daughter's share of an inheritance is less than that of her brother. Women must demonstrate legally specified grounds for divorce, but men may divorce without grounds. In Shari'a court the testimony of one man equals that of two women.

"Women may travel abroad only with the written per-mission of their nearest male relative. Employment oppor-tunities for Saudi women either in the civil service or with public corporations are extremely limited. In practice their employment is largely restricted to the teaching and health care professions.

"In public, women are required to dress with extreme modesty. Free but segregated education through the uni-versity level is now available to Saudi women. The number of civil service jobs open to women (in segregated offices) has increased recently. Polygamy is becoming less common, particularly among younger Saudis."

In a much publicized case, a Saudi princess, Misha, was executed in public in 1977 after she attempted to escape from Saudi Arabia with her lover. Her husband, who had deserted her, had refused her a divorce, and the royal family had opposed her romance. Her lover was beheaded at the command of the brother of Saudi Arabia's late King Kha-lid.

Arab Women in Israel

Unlike her counterpart in the Arab world, the Arab woman in Israel enjoys a legal status equal to that of men. Legislation embodied in Israel's 1951 Equal Rights of Women Law states: *"The same laws shall apply equally to men and to women in all legal matters, and those laws which discriminate against women shall be unenforceable."*

Israeli law recognizes a woman as the natural guardian of

166

her children and grants her equal status with men in matters of inheritance. Every woman over the age of 18 has the right to vote and to be elected to public office.

The results of this profound change for Arab women are evident not only in the rise in Arab and Druze school attendance, but also in the impact of educated women in the social and economic spheres of Israeli society. In 1948, only 15% of Arab girls attended primary school; by 1973 the rate had increased to 93% in the rural areas and 99% in the cities. In 1952 there was only one Arab woman enrolled in the Hebrew University; today there are hundreds.

Despite the advantages enjoyed by Israeli women compared to their counterparts in Arab countries, the International Women's Year Conferences—in Mexico City in 1975 and in Copenhagen in 1980—decided to condemn Zionism. They made no reference to the countries—including Saudi Arabia, Kuwait, Oman, Qatar and the United Arab Emirates—that deny women the right to vote.

At the concluding UN Women's Decade Conference, in Nairobi in 1985, the "Zionism-equals-racism" big lie failed. Former Congresswoman Bella Abzug, asserted at Nairobi that the "Zionist movement means a place to go in order not to be discriminated against. Zionism is a liberation movement, part of the right of people everywhere to self-determination."

Maureen Reagan, chairwoman of the U.S. delegation, announced prior to the conference that the United States would walk out with Israel if Zionism was condemned. When Arab states and Iran lost their usual third world support, Israeli delegate Naomi Chazan said, "I think it came from the pent-up frustration of women who have come to the conference to work on women's issues and who had gotten tired of seeing all their work fall apart over the word 'Zionism.' "

And partly, perhaps, it came from delegates who saw the absurdity of condemning Zionism—a philosophy compatible with women's equality in the Middle East—being attacked by veil-wearing Iranian women and Arab bloc delegates who were legally second-class citizens in their own lands.

The 1987 *Country Report* noted that in Israel "women participate freely in the political process and account for more than 40% of the political party membership. Ten [of

120] members of the Knesset and two of the judges of the Supreme Court are women .... Women's rights in Israel are protected by law as well as by governmental and private organizations .... Over 40% of the university graduates are women, as are 39% of the work force ...." Israel's Arab women, like Israeli Arab men, have "equal rights under the law in most respects, and Israeli Arabs have made substantial education and material progress since the founding of the state."

In May 1988, an Arab woman, Nili Karkabi, was a candidate for the Labor Party's Knesset list.

MINORITIES IN OTHER MOSLEM NATIONS

Baha'is

The Shi'ite fundamentalist regime in Iran has declared a holy war against the peaceful Baha'i sect. Since the Islamic revolution in 1979, at least 200 Baha'is have been executed or tortured to death; thousands have been driven from their homes. Khomeini's followers, acting on orders issued by the government, have confiscated Baha'i properties, expropriated Baha'i-owned corporations, closed Baha'i schools, discharged Baha'is from their jobs and desecrated their temples. Baha'i marriages have been denied recognition; as a result, Baha'i wives have been arrested and charged with prostitution.

Preaching the unity of the human race, the Baha'i religion claims 300,000 adherents in Iran. The Baha'i believers, a 19th century offshoot of Islam, are now treated as heretics whose existence is intolerable to the Moslem militants.

"It is the beginning of the second Holocaust," said Baha'i exile Artin Mahmondi, whose mother and cousin were executed in Dec. 1981. Indeed, Khomeini's policy of systematic persecution of the Baha'is bears a frightening resemblance to Nazi barbarism. Denied the right to emigrate, or identification cards necessary to purchase food and fuel, the Iranian Baha'is fear that outright genocide will be the culmination of the Moslem reign of terror.

According to Amnesty International, "the imprisonment of Baha'is appears ... to indicate a deliberate government policy of religious persecution."

A sixteen-year-old Baha'i, Bijan Talebi, was stoned to death in a village near Tehran in early Oct., 1986 "by a group of fanatics who have previously harrassed Baha'is," according to the U.S. government. Washington reiterated President Reagan's 1985 Human Rights Day condemnation of "rampant religious persecution" of Baha'is in Iran.

After Talebi's death, "the body had been hanged to suggest suicide, but local police certified that death was caused by injuries sustained in the stoning." When Bijan's mother brought the murder to the attention of the authorities, she, a son, and a cousin were arrested and held in solitary confinement.

Although the Khomeini government joined a 1981 UN consensus in adopting a declaration on elimination of all forms of religious intolerance, persecution of Baha'is continued. In 1987, about 500 of 800 Baha'is jailed for charges such as "crimes against God," "corruption on earth," and "Zionism" were released. But many—their sentences nearly completed—remained subject to prosecution. At least five Baha'is were executed during 1987.

Even the UN Human Rights Commission has adopted a resolution deploring the oppression of Baha'is in Iran.

MYTH

"Despite previous problems, governmental attitudes toward human rights have improved recently in the Arab world."

FACT

In 1987 at the United Nations, "representatives of traditionally hostile Arab nations . . . joined to fight the recognition of an Arab human-rights group. The group, the Arab Organization for Human Rights, has applied for consultative status with the United Nations Economic and Social Council. The group was set up in 1983 in Cyprus because its founders were not sure they would be welcome in the Arab world" (*New York Times*, March 5, 1987).

The organization later was able to move to Cairo and worked with Amnesty International, the Arab Lawyers' Union and similar groups, the newspaper reported. It added that "the problem is that some Arab countries consider any charges of rights violations as interference."

In discussion of the group's request, "the Soviet Union aligned itself with the Algerian observer in expressing reservations . . ." Arab opponents persuaded Oman, the only Arab member on UNESCO at the time and neutral at first on the application, to oppose it. The *Times* noted that "most Arab countries have not ratified the international human rights conventions . . . Syria and Iraq, sworn enemies, banded together with Algeria to back Oman." In the end, the Arab Organization for Human Rights' request for consultative status was denied; the group said it would submit a new application in 1989.

Just as the United States has used the status of human rights in the Soviet Union as an indicator of the sincerity of latter's proclaimed peaceful intent, so does Israel measure the Arab world. As Dan Schueftan, an Arab affairs expert at Hebrew University's Truman Institute has noted, "Practically every Arab regime came to power through violence, maintains power through violence and probably will lose power by violence." He added that once Israel's neighbors begin to recognize the individual rights of their citizens and evolve toward more consensual politics, they will be more likely to recognize Israel's rights and to deal with it non-violently.

17

Israel's Treatment of
Minorities/The Uprising

MYTH

"Israel discriminates against its Arab citizens and treats them as second-class citizens."

FACT

Israel is one the most open societies in the world. Its 775,000 Arab citizens (604,000 Moslems, 101,000 Christians and 74,000 Druze, according to 1987 Central Bureau of Statistics estimates), have a far higher standard of living than most Arabs in Arab lands. They have equal voting rights. Arabs held seven of the 120 seats in Israel's Knesset in 1988. Arabic, like Hebrew, is an official language in Israel. There are approximately 400 Arab educational institutions, with more than 220,000 students, almost 20 times as many students as in 1948 although the Arab population has increased fivefold in those 40 years. Every child under 14, Arab and Jew, must go to school. This means that 90% of Arab children attend school compared with 45% before Israel was established. The 1981 State Department *Country Reports on Human Rights Practices* stated that Israel's "Arab population had a literacy rate of 64%—one of the highest in the Middle East."

There is, to be sure, a gap between Israel's Jews and its Arabs but it is more social and psychological than economic or legal. The gap is based mainly on the 40-year state of war maintained by the Arab states against Israel. The 1987 *Country Reports on Human Rights Practices* says that "despite some governmental and private efforts to bridge the gap, there is little social interaction between Israeli Arabs and Israeli Jews, and Israeli Arabs tend to feel estranged from the mainstream of Israel society and political life." Some of this estrangement must stem from the Israeli Arabs' own strong (83% in 1983) identification as Palestinians, not as Israelis, as noted by Haifa University sociologist

Sammy Smooha. Nevertheless, it is difficult to think of another country where an ethnic minority related to neighboring enemy countries can live as freely.

The thousands of Arab refugees who returned to Israel under the family reunion scheme after fleeing the 1948 war were granted full citizenship. Arabs have belonged to the Israel Federation of Labor (Histadrut) since 1960. They receive equal pay.

According to government statistics, there were more than 169,000 Arab citizens in the Israeli civilian work force in 1984, out of a total work force of more than 1.4 million.

Although Israeli military authorities once restricted freedom of movement in certain border areas for security reasons, these restrictions were ended in 1966.

An Arab communist, Tawfik Zayyad, was elected mayor of Nazareth in 1975 in a free election, despite his anti-government views, and has been reelected since then. He also was elected to the Knesset in 1977, and reelected in 1981 and 1984.

The sole distinction which Israel makes between Jewish and Arab citizens is that Arabs are not *required* to serve in the Israeli army. This is to avoid any conflict of conscience. (Yet there are Arab volunteers including Bedouin soldiers serving in crack paratroop units.) Compulsory military service is applied to the Druze and the Circassian communities at their own request. Some of the economic and social gaps between Israeli Jews and Israeli Arabs results from differences in military service. Veterans qualify for many benefits not available to non-veterans, including new household subsidies, university scholarships and certain government employment opportunities.

During the 1967 and 1973 wars, there was no Arab sabotage or disloyalty behind Israel's lines. Arabs voluntarily took over essential jobs, contributed money and donated blood. In the 1980's, there were scattered incidents of terrorism involving Israeli Arabs.

MYTH

The election to the 11th Knesset of Rabbi Meir Kahane—who favors expulsion of Israel's Arabs—is evidence that Israel is becoming a racist society."

FACT

Kahane received 26,000 votes in the July 1984 elections. He was the choice of one percent of the population. His views are overwhelmingly rejected by Israelis and are, in fact, antithetical to Israel's basic laws, which protect minority populations. Kahane's election was the result of Israel's democratic electoral process. Individuals who support the PLO and the Communist party also won a few seats.

Early in 1988, polls showed that Kahane's *Kach* party might win three or four seats in elections scheduled for late 1988.

But an anti-racism law passed by the Knesset in August 1986 may actually bar Kahane or other extremists on the right and on the left of the political spectrum from running in future elections. A 15% popular vote for ultra-rightist Le Pen in France's 1988 presidential election did not make France anything other than a democracy; a several seat gain for Kahane would still signify his rejection by the overwhelming majority of Israeli voters. The political phenomenon of Kahaneism should be seen as the mirror image—in miniature—of the anti-Jewish Arab racism with which Israel has been forced to contend for more than four decades.

MYTH

"Israel's Arabs may have all legal rights, but they are denied entry into schools of higher education."

FACT

There are no barriers to Israel's colleges and universities, only academic standards that must be met. As primary and secondary Arab schools within Israel improve, more and more Arab students are meeting those academic standards. In 1987, the government proposed a budget-cutting measure which would have required university students who had not served in the military to pay much higher fees. Jewish students joined Arabs in protesting the two-tiered system; eventually the scheme was dropped.

In 1975, there were 600 Arab students in Israeli universities. Today, there are six times as many. (In that same period Arab women students increased their numbers from 40 to 525.) Over 500 Arab students are enrolled in graduate programs.

MYTH

"Thousands of Arabs are held in Israeli jails—tortured, beaten and killed. Arabs speaking out are imprisoned without trial."

FACT

As of Oct. 1982, Israeli jails held about 1,600 Arab prisoners, nearly all of whom were captured while on terrorist missions against Israel or in possession of arms and sabotage plans. None was held under administrative detention.

In 1985, Israel exchanged more than 1,100 convicted terrorists and terrorist suspects—including murderers—for three Israeli prisoners of war who had been captured in Lebanon. Hundreds of those exchanged were permitted to remain in the West Bank (Judea and Samaria) and the Gaza Strip after they pledged to desist from terrorism. There followed a series of terrorist attacks, including killings, against Israeli civilians in the territories and inside the "green line." Defense Minister Yitzhak Rabin then reintroduced measures such as preventative detention.

Nevertheless, such detention was used sparingly until several months into the Palestinian Arab uprising or *intifadah* which began in Dec. 1987. As of May 1988, Israel held approximately 1,700 Palestinian Arabs in preventative detention for six-month terms, which could be renewed. The measure was one of those credited by Israeli authorities with greatly reducing the level of violence associated with the uprising without increasing the number of casualties.

Israel's prisons are open to inspection at any time by the Red Cross and any other legitimate international body which chooses to investigate them. Suspected terrorists are guaranteed trial and right of appeal.

The death penalty, which had been used by Jordan, has been applied just once, and not in relation to even the most heinous act of Arab terrorism. The only convicted criminal Israel has ever executed was Adolph Eichmann, who was in charge of the Nazis' "final solution." Convicted Nazi death camp guard John Demjanjuk—"Ivan the Terrible" of Treblinka—was sentenced to death in April 1988. He appealed his conviction to the Israeli Supreme Court in June; the appeal was to be heard late in the year.

The U.S. government has rejected claims of propagandists that Israeli authorities were torturing Arab prisoners as a matter of policy. According to the State Department's 1978 *Country Reports on Human Rights Practices*, "We know of no evidence to support allegations that Israel follows a consistent practice or policy of using torture during interrogations."

In March 1979, Leo Nevas, vice-chairman of the United Nations Association of America and the chairman of the American Bar Association's UN Committee, toured Israeli prisons and interviewed Arab prisoners. Nevas rejected the charges of systematic torture. "If you ask me," he told reporters, "the Israelis are more indulgent over many issues concerned with the rights of the individual than a number of democratic Western countries I could name. And that is without taking into account the situation of war and terrorism that Israel has to deal with and the rest do not."

In cases of brutality by individual interrogators, the Israeli government has punished those responsible. For example, in 1976 when a prisoner was beaten to death, both the officer in charge and the soldiers under his command were convicted of manslaughter and sentenced to prison terms. In 1982, two Israeli women soldiers accused of beating a woman with sticks during interrogation were found guilty and imprisoned.

However, in 1984 two terrorists officially reported to have died in the hijacking of a commuter bus were photographed alive in army custody immediately after the incident. Then, in 1987, Israel's Supreme Court upheld the appeal of a Circassian Army officer, Izat Nafsu, overturning his conviction of conspiring with terrorists. Nafsu already had served more than seven years of an 18-year sentence.

These cases in particular led to formation of the Landau Commission. Former Supreme Court Judge Moshe Landau, former Mossad and Northern Command chief Yitzhak Hofi, and State Comptroller Yaakov Maltz investigated the methods of Israel's General Security Services, better known as the Shin Bet.

They found that since 1971 the Shin Bet had routinely used "harsh interrogation methods" and then committed perjury about the practice to assure court acceptance of confessions by terrorist suspects. It was reported that before 1967 there were relatively few interrogations of terrorists, and these followed Supreme Court rulings against "physical pressure." But in 1971, with Israel in control of the West Bank and Gaza Strip, the number of cases rose, and defense lawyers began putting the interrogators themselves on the stand.

Shin Bet operatives believed that without physical pressure, terrorist suspects trained—unlike ordinary criminals—to obstruct and mislead questioners would not confess. And court testimony might compromise their sources and methods. So to maintain their high success rates in thwarting terrorism, some agents began breaking the law to obtain confessions, the commission found. That had to be stopped "for the moral resilience of Israeli society and of the (Shin Bet) as a part thereof...."

While finding that the "political, judicial and military authorities did not know of the . . . practice of perjury," the commissioners recommended that the Attorney General and military courts permit retrials in response to all "justified requests" submitted in the wake of their report. Interestingly, few requests were made, apparently confirming another commission conclusion, that the illegal methods were "not meant to convict innocent persons."

The Landau Commission did agree that "limited and clearly delineated psychological and physical pressures may legitimately be exerted in the interrogation of those suspected of terrorism" and it proposed precise guidelines for the Shin Bet to adopt. Such pressures were principally to consist of "vigorous and lengthy interrogation, with the use of strategems, including acts of deception." Physical pressure was not to involve either bodily or mental torture.

After the commission reported, Israeli leaders including Prime Minister Yitzhak Shamir, Foreign Minister Shimon Peres and President Chaim Herzog reiterated that no one in Israeli society could be permitted to view himself or herself as above the law.

Meanwhile, investigations of other specific torture charges have shown that many are fabrications. Other claims have been based on medical illness or injuries suffered years prior to arrest. And in some cases, investigators have discovered that injuries were caused by fellow prisoners who, acting as a "court of inquiry," tortured prisoners severely in an attempt to learn in what way and to what extent they had cooperated with the police.

MYTH

"Israel mistreats Arabs on the West Bank and Gaza and denies them political leadership."

FACT

After Israel captured the West Bank in 1967, the traditional pro-Jordanian leadership continued to hold office, and Jordan continued to pay the salaries of many of these civil servants. Municipal elections were held in 1972 and 1976, on the basis of expanded voter rolls that enfranchised women and non-landowners. The 1976 election brought to power Arab mayors of a radical, pro-PLO bent: Mohammed Milhem, in Halhoul; Fahd Kawasmeh, in Hebron; Bassam Shaka, in Nablus; Karim Khalaf, in Ramallah; Ibrahim Tawil, in El Bireh.

According to the Israeli weekly *Newsview* magazine (March 23, 1982), these mayors actually represented various PLO factions: Shaka, Kawasmeh and Milhem—Fatah; Khalaf—Popular Front for the Liberation of Palestine; Tawil—Democratic Front for the Liberation of Palestine.

In 1978, these mayors and other radicals formed the National Guidance Committee, which vigorously opposed any accommodation with Israel, attempted to stir up broad allegiance to the PLO on the West Bank, and incited rejection of the Camp David Accords and the Egyptian-Israeli peace treaty.

As a result of these disruptive activities, which caused widespread restiveness on the West Bank, Israel deported Milhem and Kawasmeh in 1981, and in Feb. 1982 formally banned their Committee. Some of the other mayors were dismissed from office.

Israel also undertook two major moves in this period to bolster efforts for autonomy on the West Bank and Gaza, as envisioned in the Camp David Accords: It replaced the military government with a civilian Israeli administrator, and it permitted creation of village councils in the rural areas and villages where 70% of the West Bank population lives. These councils in turn established regional Village Leagues as rural cooperative organizations in the Nablus, Ramallah, Tulkarm, Hebron, Bethlehem and Jenin regions.

These Leagues, representative of the majority of the Arab population, emerged as competition for the radicalized urban mayors as a political force on the West Bank—as a potential counter-force, in short, to the PLO.

Attacks on League officials, their relatives and supporters—including assassination—crippled the organizations and intimidated would-be supporters. PLO propaganda, based on the group's totalitarian impulse to monopolize Palestinian Arab representation, painted League participants as collaborators with Israel. In the spring of 1982, a wave of rioting featured PLO incitement of Palestinian Arab youngsters to throw rocks and Molotov cocktails at Israeli vehicles and soldiers, burning tires to disrupt traffic, and forced commercial strikes. Daily life was disrupted, and a number of Arabs were killed, and Arabs and Israelis wounded, as a result of the PLO's effort to block the emergence of an alternative leadership and to undermine ties between the residents of the territories and the civil administration.

One of the mayors appointed in 1986—presumably with the tacit approval of both King Hussein and Yasir Arafat—was Zafer al-Masri of Nablus, the largest West Bank city. According to Israel's Defense Minister, Yitzhak Rabin, al-Masri "represented to the terrorist organizations a real threat of authentic [Palestinian] representation, a leader who cares about the people." Al-Masri was assassinated soon after taking office. The PLO's own Popular Front for the Liberation of Palestine was later found to have been responsible.

In late 1987 and early 1988 the clandestine leaflets of "The PLO/Unified Command for the Uprising in the Occupied Territories" demanded the resignations of the thousands of Palestinian Arabs, including police and civil servants, who worked for the Israeli civil administration in the West Bank and Gaza Strip. These included the Palestinian Arab mayors who, in 1986, had replaced Israelis in office as a result of the earlier expulsions and had begun to rule over the major West Bank cities again.

As leaflet 17 put it, "We have issued our warning and are not responsible for the consequences" (Baghdad Voice of the PLO, May 22, 1988). Two weeks later, the Palestinian Arab mayor of El-Birch was stabbed.

MYTH

"The West Bank and Gaza Strip have suffered economically from Israel's occupation."

178

FACT

The 1982 State Department human rights report stated, "It is obvious that living standards have risen steadily throughout the period of Israeli control." According to *Judea, Samaria and the Gaza District, 1967-1987: Twenty Years of Civil Administration*, published by Israel's Defense Ministry, Jordan discriminated against the West Bank economically from 1949 to 1967; unemployment stood at 10% when Israel took control. But under Israel the gross national product in the West Bank and Gaza rose by 400% and 430%, respectively, in real terms, and resulted in what, by American standards, constitutes nearly full employment: a 4% unemployment rate in Judea and Samaria in 1985, 1.2% in Gaza.

Some 100,000 West Bank and Gaza Strip Arabs are employed all over Israel. Those recruited through the network of official employment offices set up by Israel enjoy equal pay and the same social benefits that the Histadrut (the Israel Labor Federation) has negotiated for Israeli citizens. Hundreds, over the age of 65, now receive old-age pensions. A retail and building boom on the West Bank has created a demand for better homes, furnishing and clothes. The increased income of West Bank workers has resulted in an expansion of local industry.

The agricultural produce of the West Bank has been moving across the bridges into Jordan and beyond into the wider Arab world, adding to the per capita income of the territory. Under an agreement concluded in 1985, produce from the West Bank has been air-shipped to Europe through Israel's marketing agent, Agrexco.

MYTH

"The United Nations confirms that Israel destroys hundreds of Arab homes on the West Bank and Gaza every year."

FACT

Israeli authorities have destroyed houses of individuals involved in acts of terrorism in accordance with emergency regulations promulgated by the British mandatory power, maintained by Jordan (but which the Jordanians say they did not use) and carried over in Israeli law. Both the State Department and United Nations noted that only a handful of houses were destroyed for this reason in the early 1980's.

But in 1985, as part of a crackdown on increased terrorism in Judea, Samaria and the Gaza Strip—and inside "Israel proper"—the Defense Ministry increased the use of demolitions, as well as measures such as preventative detentions and deportations. From mid-1985 through mid-1988, several scores of houses, or rooms of houses, were demolished.

Israel's Supreme Court upheld the practice in a 1986 case and reaffirmed it a year later. The court cited a deterrent effect because a prospective terrorist "should know that his criminal acts will not only hurt him, but are apt to cause great suffering to his family" *(Washington Post,* June 19, 1987). A spokesman for the civil administration noted that demolitions were carried out "only on very, very hard cases where blood was involved [terrorist attacks in which people were killed or wounded] . . . we think that this is another way to make people understand that terrorism is not the way."

The 1981 report of the Commissioner General of the United Nations Relief and Works Agency stated that Israel indeed destroyed hundreds of refugee homes—after the refugees were moved "into new housing in projects developed by the Israeli authorities . . . [or] purchased plots of land in these developments and built their own homes." The UNRWA director explained that Israel requires the demolition of refugee hovels after the refugees move in order to alleviate the camps' terrible congestion. Pro-PLO publicists (for example, Columbia University's Prof. Edward Said on ABC-TV's "This Week with David Brinkley" Jan. 3, 1988) have consistently misrepresented Israel's refugee housing construction and resettlement program. Said criticized a 1971 program in Gaza in which "thousands of people were moved out of their territory and put in refugee camps." In fact, in that year Israel introduced a voluntary program to move Palestinian Arab refugees out of camps into new housing. Approximately 10,000 families—about 50,000 people—took advantage of the offer before PLO opposition and intimidation reduced resettlement to a trickle.

Not long after, the UN General Assembly, in response to the Arab and "non-aligned" states, began passing annual resolutions condemning Israel for such programs. The latest of these—Resolution 42/69E—was approved on Dec. 2, 1987, six days before the uprising began and outside attention again was focused on the deplorable housing conditions in many of the camps. But their own and other Arab leaders—not Israel—have kept three generations of Palestinian Arabs penned in the camps, using them as political pawns.

MYTH

"The Israeli occupation of the West Bank has split families, violated international guarantees for reunification of families, and sealed off the West Bank from Jordan and the Arab world."

FACT

Immediately after the 1967 war, the Israeli authorities permitted over 9,000 family reunions. In 1968, almost 7,000 persons were permitted to rejoin their families. By 1981, such family reunions totalled over 50,000.

Millions of visitors from Arab states—even those at war with Israel—have crossed the Jordan River bridges or landed at Ben Gurion airport to visit their families in Israel and the occupied territories.

In the mid-1980's approximately one million people crossed the Jordan River bridges each year to visit relatives, conduct business, even tour and shop in Israel. Some 50,000 tons of West Bank agricultural produce are exported across the bridges annually.

Elections held under Israeli administration were conducted in conformity with Jordanian law—with two exceptions: Women and non-landowners, two groups which had been denied voting rights by Jordan, could participate in municipal elections.

The status of women in the West Bank and Gaza has improved in other ways as well. The State Department's 1979 human rights account reported, "Changes are taking place [due to] . . . exposure to education, to a basically egalitarian attitude toward women by Israelis."

According to State Department figures, female enrollment in primary and secondary schools grew 6.3% annually from 1969 to 1977 in the West Bank. By 1987, 45% of the total student body was female.

As the 1987 *Country Reports* noted, "there are no legal or administrative prohibitions on the employment of women in the occupied territories, although traditional cultural mores and family commitments restrict most to homemaking . . . . Although women legally have equal access to public education, custom and family pressures limit the number of women in West Bank schools. Even so, female school enrollment is quite high by Middle Eastern standards .... There is a wide range of women's cooperative groups for health care, child care, handicraft production, vocational training, and other services."

MYTH

"Israel seeks to take over West Bank farms. To this end it is disrupting the traditional Arab farming methods."

FACT

There is no question that Israeli farming techniques have changed farming methods. In fact, the primitive, pre-1967 methods have been revolutionized. As a world leader in modern agriculture, Israel has brought new farming methods to Arab farmers through its agricultural extension service. Israel has helped introduce West Bank farmers to new irrigation methods, high-yield strains and high-income crops.

For example, in 1968 there were 120 tractors in the West Bank. By 1986, the number had grown to over 3,700. Overall, the proportion of the territories' work force engaged in agriculture dropped from 45% in 1967 to 24.4% in 1985.

Agricultural produce increased at an annual rate of about 10%, continuing into the late 1980's after dipping in 1985 and 1986.

MYTH

"Israel is pushing Palestinian Arabs out of the West Bank by stealing water from them, drying up their farms. Israel has allowed Jews to drill wells but has not allowed Arabs to drill new wells."

FACT

In the years immediately after the 1967 war, water resources for the West Bank improved considerably. The water system in the southern Hebron region, for instance, grew in supply from 140 cubic meters per hour in 1967 to over 700 cubic meters per hour in 1977. New wells were drilled in the Hebron region, near Jenin, near Nablus and in Tulkarm. Over 60 towns on the West Bank were given new water supply systems or had antiquated ones improved.

And in some regions of Judea and Samaria, water systems were linked with Israeli water systems as insurance against mishap. In 1967, about 50 villages were linked to the region's water systems. By 1985, 150 villages were hooked into the system and another 50 were in the process of being integrated into the network.

In the late 1970's and the early 1980's, however, the Middle East suffered from one of the worst droughts in modern history. Water in the Dead Sea, Jordan River and Sea of Galilee dropped to critical levels.

Under these conditions, the Israeli government restricted the drilling of new wells on the West Bank. These measures were vital, for the West Bank and Israel share the same water table, and the drawing off of fresh water resources could promote saline water seepage. Israel's water commissioner, Meir Ben-Meir, reported in Sept. 1979, "The drought has hurt everyone equally . . . . All the water resources of the region are down."

Arab farmers on the West Bank are served by approximately 100 springs and 300 wells—many dug decades ago and now over-utilized. Restrictions on over-exploitation of shallow wells are in effect to prevent seepage of saline water or total depletion.

Some deep-bore wells were dug for Jewish villages to tap new, deep aquifers never before used. These water pools as a rule do not draw from the shallower Arab sources. In one location, near Bardalah, it was determined that deep bore wells at the Israeli village of Mehola may have caused deterioration of shallow wells and springs. Arab residents of the region were provided with water from the new wells.

In 1987, the government seriously considered a proposal for major new deep wells near the Herodian, east of Bethlehem in Judea. The wells were to increase the supply for Jerusalem and some Jewish settlements while continuing to provide a water source for nearby Arab municipalities. However, protests by local Arab officials helped lead to reconsideration and indefinite postponement of the project.

The severity of Israel's water problem and the need to restrict drilling can be seen in the fact that only the country's successful program of cloud-seeding—which went from experimental to operational in 1975—helped it keep pace, increasing annual rainfall approximately 15%. Nevertheless, according to Hebrew University Prof. Abraham Gagin, the project's chief, by 1987 Israel was "overdrafting," consuming more than 100% of its annual potential and thereby depleting reserves including groundwater.

MYTH

"The Israelis have closed Arab schools on the West Bank in an attempt to stamp out Arab cultural identity."

FACT

On several occasions, particularly following violent student riots, Israeli authorities temporarily closed some of the universities on the West Bank. But those universities' very existence testifies to the liberal intentions of Israel's administration. No institutions of higher education existed on the West Bank prior to 1967.

Today, in the West Bank and Gaza Strip, there are 17,000 young Arabs studying at 20 post-high school educational institutions. This total includes four universities on the West Bank, with over 7,800 students and approximately 600 lecturers. The four institutions are the Islamic Center in Hebron, An-Najah University in Nablus, Freres University in Bethlehem, and Bir Zeit University near Ramallah. All were founded or expanded into schools of higher education under Israeli administration.

Bir Zeit, well-known for its radicalism, has become a focal point for complaints against Israeli measures on the West Bank. The history of Bir Zeit, however, belies those charges.

In 1967, when Israel took over the West Bank, there were 100 students at Bir Zeit, which was equivalent to an American junior college. In 1972, the school requested and was granted permission by Israeli authorities to upgrade its academic status to university level and to issue Bachelor of Arts degrees. By 1978, the university had 600 students, new facilities, more lecturers and new financial sources. In 1987, the student body numbered almost 2,600.

All this was permitted despite the fact that Bir Zeit's school board was directed *in absentia* by Hana Nasir, a member of the PLO National Council.

In Dec. 1986, demonstrations erupted in the territories centered in the West Bank universities. After a PLO offensive against Shi'ite Amal militiamen in Lebanon, Arafat loyalists on the campuses mobilized supporters with leaf-

184

lets urging that "all Palestine is yours, go there with your blood." At Bir Zeit, students harassed Israeli troops at a lightly-manned checkpoint. A faculty member known for extremist views refused to move a car he drove into the checkpoint and began inciting students. Rocks were thrown and tear gas was fired.

Using pre-positioned junk cars, abandoned refrigerators and boulders, rioters established their own roadblock. The troops called for reinforcements. They fired rubber bullets and live rounds into the air but could not stop the youths throwing rocks and iron bars. The soldiers then opened fire on the crowd, killing two. Two other Palestinian Arabs were killed elsewhere in the territories.

The Dec. 1986 violence proved a test run for that of the following year: The UN Security Council voted to "deplore" Israel's actions, 14-0, with the United States abstaining, while the UN said nothing about the deaths of more than 500 people in Palestinian-Shi'ite fighting. Zimbabwe introduced the UN resolution on behalf of the PLO.

At the time, the PLO wanted to derail a tacit Jordanian-Israeli accommodation, which had just witnessed the appointment of Arab mayors to all the West Bank and Gaza municipalities, Jordan's announcement of a five-year investment plan for the territories and the long-awaited reopening of the Cairo-Amman Bank in Nablus. At the same time, the PLO dropped two relative moderates, journalist Hanna Siniora and lawyer Fayez Abu Rahmah, from its proposed joint negotiating team with Jordan.

Early in 1988, at a peak of violence during the "uprising" by Palestinian Arabs, Israeli authorities closed all primary and secondary schools and all colleges and universities in the territories. Some of the schools had become centers of incitement and organization for the waves of rioting— mostly by young people—which disrupted daily life. Closure was aimed not at Palestinian Arab culture, but at one of the sources of disorder.

By June, all schools were permitted to reopen, under the condition that they would remain peaceful and would concentrate on their primary task, education.

That Palestinian Arab identity was not Israel's target in shutting down the schools could be seen, for example, in the continued tenure of nationalists like Hanan Mikail-Asharawi, Dean of Arts at Bir Zeit. On ABC-TV's "Nightline" in April she described the violence of the uprising as only "symbolic" and asserted that a "foreign, alien occupation" stole Palestinian Arab rights. She justified terrorism as a "symptom" of that theft; neither she nor her colleagues on the program, broadcast from Jerusalem, were censored.

MYTH

"Israel has instituted a 'loyalty oath' in order to ban foreign instructors from teaching in West Bank universities."

FACT

Israel requires of foreigners entering Israel and the West Bank to have a work permit. A condition of the work permit is that the bearer refrain from aiding politically hostile organizations—such as the PLO.

The work permit condition states:

"During the period in which the permit is in force, the recipient of the permit will refrain from any act which is harmful to security and public order, and will observe the law and the security regulations prohibiting any action, and the rendering of any service, of a collaborative or helpful nature—to the PLO or any other hostile organization."

Such a condition is not rare. Other countries have similar visa regulations. In the United States, for instance, a visa can be denied to "aliens who seek to enter the United States to engage in prejudicial activities or unlawful activities of a subversive nature. . . ."

MYTH

"Israeli mistreatment of Arabs in the administered territories has been confirmed in a report of the UN Commission on Human Rights."

FACT

There was such a study made, but the members of that commission were from Yugoslavia, Sri Lanka and Senegal, none of which had relations with Israel, and none of whose representatives bothered to visit Israel to investigate charges. All three states voted to equate Zionism with racism in the UN General Assembly.

Arab states and their allies in the UN have often secured adoption of resolutions scoring Israeli policies, even though these resolutions are based on hearsay, distortion and propaganda.

Because of the politicized nature of some international organizations, Israel, according to the U.S. *Human Rights Report*, "has not been disposed to respond favorably to requests for international investigations. On the other hand, its decision to permit the International Committee of the Red Cross access to prisoners during the interrogation period is indicative of a willingness to cooperate with international bodies it regards as responsible." The 1982 human rights report added that Israel "has cooperated with recent visits by representatives of the World Health Organization, the International Labor Organization, and the United Nations Educational, Scientific and Cultural Organization (UNESCO).

MYTH

"The World Health Organization (WHO) has found that the health of residents in the territories has been affected by Israel's occupation."

FACT

Arab and Third World delegates rammed through the World Health Organization Assembly, on May 23, 1975, a resolution condemning Israeli health care in the administered territories. The resolution ignored a first-hand report submitted by Dr. A. Bellerive, special representative of the WHO director general. In his report, Bellerive said he "saw nothing that would suggest that standards of medical care have declined. . . . In some areas, there were manifest improvements."

According to the State Department's 1978 *Country Reports on Human Rights Practices*, Israel admitted an informal experts group from WHO in 1976 "to conduct an investigation of health conditions in the occupied territories. When the group produced a report that reflected favorably on Israel's administration, the report was rejected by the WHO Assembly on political grounds, without references to the merits of the report."

In fact, there are marked improvements in health care on the West Bank and Gaza regions. The following statistics show conditions in 1967, when Israel took over the regions, and in 1984-1985.

187

West Bank	1967/1968	1986
Population	582,000	813,400
Percent of hospital births	13.5%	55.2%
Maternal/child health centers	24	137
Doctors	80	250
	(West Bank & Gaza)	(1987 West Bank & Gaza)
Electric refrigerators	4.8% of homes	66% of homes
Cars/Trucks	2925	43,024
Classrooms	4401	8647

Gaza	1967/1968	1984
Population	355,900	525,000
Percent of hospital births	13.1%	56.8%
Electric refrigerators	2.5% of homes	77% of homes
Cars/Trucks	1737	20,743
Classrooms	1746	3940

In addition, malaria is now completely absent from the West Bank, and there has been a sharp drop in deaths from measles and poliomyelitis—factors which have drastically cut the infant mortality rate. A comprehensive health insurance plan was established on the West Bank in 1973 and expanded in 1978. Master plans in effect in 1987 called for an increase in bed space at most government hospitals of 50%. Meanwhile, immunization programs now cover more than 90% of the West Bank population, greatly reducing childhood mortality and morbidity. Basic sanitation and health education have been improved.

Technical advances continue, with open heart surgery performed for the first time in Judea-Samaria in 1986 and neurosurgery introduced in 1987. In Gaza, Shifa Hospital completed an expanded obstetrics department in 1986; a new radiology department was opened in 1987. At Khan Yunis Hospital, a renovated surgical suite was scheduled for completion in 1987. In addition, health care professionals from the territories studied in Israel with Israeli colleagues, and thousands of patients from the territories received care in Israeli hospitals.

MYTH

"Israel denies political leadership to the Arabs on the West Bank and Gaza. Two mayors and one religious leader were illegally deported in 1980."

FACT

On May 3, 1980, Mayors Fahd Kawasmeh of Hebron and Mohammed Milhem of Halhoul and religious leader Sheik Rajeb Buyud Tamimi were deported from the West Bank. The previous day, PLO terrorists opened fire on Jews walking through Hebron from Sabbath services; six were killed and 20 were wounded. Israeli military authorities accused Kawasmeh, Milhem and Tamimi of fanning tensions in Hebron prior to the terrorist outrage. Statements by the three men prior and subsequent to the terrorist attack uphold the Israeli authorities' accusation. The statements also serve as evidence of close ties between the mayors and the PLO. Both mayors had served on the "National Guidance Committee," a PLO front group on the West Bank.

Kawasmeh, on May 7, addressed a PLO rally in Beirut, saying:

"They have removed us from southern Palestine but we shall return to it from southern Lebanon. We shall return to it by the force of your arms, by the force of your guns, on the strength of the blood of the innocent fallen, by the force of the struggle, the struggle for the liberation of the land. We shall return in spite of the enemies, in spite of Sadat and in spite of the American imperialists, to Jaffa, Haifa and Hebron. . . . The whole Palestinian people is obedient to the PLO, to its commanders and its supreme command."

Two months before his expulsion, Tamimi called for attacks against Jews in his sermons in Hebron's mosques. He

189

called for a *jihad* to free "Jaffa, Haifa, Acre and Palestine. The way to achieve this aim is simply to carry out the divine commandment and use force.

In an interview two weeks after his expulsion, Milhem told *el-Wahda* (Abu Dhabi), "There is no room for the existence of the Zionists under a situation of true peace. They are only capable of existing in a situation of tension and war. . . and that goes for all the parties . . . [they are] neither doves nor hawks, only pigs."

Despite the mayors' identification with the PLO and anti-Israel incitement, they were allowed to return to the West Bank in Dec. 1980 to appeal their expulsion. The deportation order was upheld by a military tribunal and the Israeli Supreme Court.

The example of Kawasmeh illustrates how the violent nature of Arab politics—not Israeli meddling—deprives West Bankers and Gazans of leadership:

After being expelled from Israel, Kawasmeh in 1984 was named to the PLO's executive committee. An Arafat protege, he was considered an organizational "moderate," notwithstanding his rhetoric. Late in 1984 someone assassinated Kawasmeh in Amman. Syria—perhaps acting through Abu Nidal—was considered a likely suspect, a view reinforced by Arafat's funeral oration. Murdering Kawasmeh might have been a signal from Damascus to Arafat and King Hussein to slow down efforts at a PLO-Jordanian rapprochment. Regardless, Kawasmeh's case showed once more how Palestinian Arab politics incline toward and are held hostage by violence.

MYTH

"Continued use of deportations 'inflames passions, is counterproductive and violates the Fourth Geneva Conventions.'"

FACT

The United States used such language to condemn Israel's April 11, 1988 deportation of eight Palestinian Arabs to Lebanon after Israel charged that they were "leading organizers and instigators of the recent violent public disturbances." But Israel was not acting summarily—five of the eight had been ordered deported in Jan., the other three unsuccessfully had appealed earlier deportation orders. The violence itself showed that passions already had been inflamed; among those deported were Abed Aziz Odeh, a leader of the underground Islamic Jihad in Gaza, responsible for several assassinations and violent assaults in recent years in Gaza, and Jemayel Shatti Hindi, described as a major PLO operative in the Nablus area.

Also refuting the claim that the deportations—by removing potential participants for Israeli-Palestinian negotiations from the scene—were counterproductive, was the example of the Jan. 13 expulsion of four others accused of fomenting unrest in the territories. They were: Jabril Mahmoud Rujub, who was freed after serving 15 years of a life term for membership in a terrorist PLO cell and author of *Cell No. 704*, a West Bank best-seller; Jamal Mohammed Jibara, also released in the 1985 mass prisoner exchange after serving six years for PLO recruiting and planning of terrorist attacks; Bashir Ahmed Al Kheiri, a lawyer who had spent 15 years in prison for setting a bomb which killed several people; and Hussam Abdul Rahman Khader, who spent 18 months in jail for PLO recruiting, was freed and then rearrested after leading repeated disturbances at Kalkiliya.

Article 49 of the Fourth Geneva Convention, 1949, states: "Individual or mass forcible transfers, as well as deportations of protected persons from occupied territory to the territory of the occupying power or to that of any other country, occupied or not, are prohibited, regardless of motive. Nevertheless, the occupying power may undertake total or partial evacuation of a given area if the security of the population or imperative military reasons so demand . . . ."

Citing the 1969 Vienna Convention on the Law of Treaties, and legal scholars such as Prof. Julius Stone, Israel has held that the purpose of Article 49 was to protect citizens against arbitrary action by the army of the occupier in order to prevent atrocities such as those perpetrated by the Nazis during World War II, including forcible transfers for slave labor and extermination. Construing Article 49 absolutely, without consideration of the circumstances it addressed in 1949, would, for example, prohibit extradition of suspected murderers from the territories. According to a majority opinion in a 1987 Israeli Supreme Court case, persons in the occupied territories may be deported legally if their presence is liable to damage the security of the state or public order, on condition that, in the particular case, there is no other way to protect the population.

Foreign Minister Shimon Peres, after the April deportations, noted that "we don't expel residents, only inciters and extremists. Expulsion is one of the most effective deterrents we have. We also try not to use it too much." In fact, from early December 1987 through mid-May 1988, only a score of expulsions occurred, while the number of Palestinian Arabs arrested had reached 7,500.

In the first 21 years it controlled Judea, Samaria and the Gaza Strip, Israel deported some 1,000 Palestinian Arabs (Associated Press, April 11, 1988). By contrast, Kuwait deported approximately 27,000 non-Kuwaitis suspected of being security risks—including many Palestinian Arabs—in 1985 and 1986. This came after a series of terrorist attacks, presumably instigated by Iran and which included an attempted assassination of the ruling Emir.

MYTH

"Israel deported Palestinian leader, Mubarak Awad, head of the Palestinian Center for the Study of Non-Violence, in June 1988. Awad espouses non-violence and reconciliation between Palestinians and Israelis. He clearly is no terrorist or security threat."

FACT

Mubarak Awad, a Palestinian Arab who became an American citizen, claims to be a disciple of Mahatma Gandhi and Martin Luther King. Non-violent civil disobedience, however, is not Awad's tool for achieving his goals. He was a leader and instigator of the lengthy disturbances that wracked the West Bank and Gaza in the first half of 1988. On March 22, 1988, he stated in Jerusalem, "The PLO wants the entire Palestine and I agree. Palestine is for me the Galilee, Akko, Ashdod—everything. This is Palestine for me."

According to Israeli officials, Awad participated in the writing of at least one leaflet that called for violence. "Strike painful blows at the fascist entity," the leaflet stated, "in order to induce the collapse of the economic and social structure of the Zionist entity."

If his radical activities were not sufficient to warrant deportation, Awad had been living illegally in Israel on an expired visa.

192

MYTH

"Palestinian Arab despair at the unbearable Israeli occupation spawned the uprising."

FACT

In a special Feb. 1988 report of the American Academic Association for Peace in the Middle East's *Middle East Review* Rutgers University Professor Michael Curtis wrote:

[This] "extravagant rhetoric . . . disregards the ineptness of Palestinian representatives who refuse to renounce the goal of destroying Israel and enter into direct negotiations with Israel, whose legitimacy would be unconditionally recognized. It ignores [Palestinian Arab] rage and frustration over the indifference of the Arab states and the Palestine Liberation Organization, whose only triumph has been to prevent the emergence of a moderate Palestinian leadership . . . . It does injustice to the significant improvement in the quality of life in the territories since they were occupied by Israel . . . and it neglects to account for the growing provocation of the Islamic Jihad and other religious fundamentalist organizations in the West Bank and Gaza.

"The recent riots were not the result of manifest economic and social injustice brought on by a brutal occupation. Neither were they civil rights demonstrations following the classic model of Martin Luther King, Jr. The underlying problem is not the occupation, in fact, but the refusal of those claiming to speak for the Palestinians to recognize the legitimacy of Israel. The present territorial status arose because of the 1967 war provoked by [Egypt's Gamal Abdel] Nasser, and continues because of this refusal."

PLO Chairman Yasir Arafat himself was quoted by Reuters on June 2, 1988 as saying, "Our people in the occupied areas revolted in response to the insult at Amman [the Nov. 1987 Arab League summit which focused on the Iraq-Iran war] against them and their representative, the PLO." Apparently referring to plans for Arab-Israeli talks with a joint Jordanian-Palestinian delegation which would not include PLO members, Arafat added, "they tried [at the summit] to implement a U.S.-Israeli scheme and draw some of our Arab brothers into it."

Two days earlier the same wire service cited Daoud Kuttab, a Palestinian Arab writer, on the Arab League to the effect that "the Arabs should design an effective and realistic strategy to liberate the occupied areas rather than trying to beg Israel to negotiate." An unidentified "leading radical" told Reuter that "the Arab countries are impotent militarily and don't even understand what the intifadah is. The closest contact Arab states have with our uprising is when they suppress by force demonstrations in their countries in sympathy with our martyrs. We know of demonstrations brutally dispersed in Egypt, Morocco, Kuwait, Jordan, Syria and elsewhere."

MYTH

"The uprising erupted when it did because of intensified Israeli repression."

FACT

Although no people wants to live under the military control of another, Israel's administration of the West Bank (Judea and Samaria) and the Gaza Strip was recognized as comparatively benign. The steady rise in the standard of living in the territories while under Israeli control—including a jump in life expectancy from 48 in 1967 to 62 in early 1988—testified to the real nature of the occupation.

In fact, one reason Israeli police and the military, the Israel Defense Forces (IDF), had difficulty controlling the initial outbursts of rioting was due to the fact that they traditionally patrolled in small groups, with relatively few personnel assigned to police the territories. This was done to avoid unnecessary friction with the local population.

But when the violence began, small foot patrols found themselves easily surrounded. Tear gas, rubber bullets and warning shots (required by IDF regulations before live ammunition could be used) oftened failed to restore order. Soldiers were only allowed to use live ammunition if attacks with stones, iron bars, Molotov cocktails knives and sling shot-fired ballbearings continued and they felt their lives in danger.

By mid-May, 176 Palestinian Arabs had been killed, according to Defense Minister Rabin, and more than 1,400 wounded. A few died in unclear circumstances; at least two were killed as collaborators with Israel. In addition, three

Israelis (one soldier murdered by gunmen and a teen-age girl hiker shot by accident during a melee between armed Jewish escorts and Palestinian Arabs in the village of Beita) died in the violence and 98 soldiers were injured.

In March 28, 1988 testimony before the House Foreign Affairs Subcommittee on International Organizations and Human Rights, Assistant Secretary of State for Human Rights and Humanitarian Affairs Richard Schifter pointed out that the root of the difficulty Israel faced in dealing with the uprising "does not lie in the area of human rights." He said "the underlying problem is the state of war which has existed in this area [the Middle East] for close to 40 years, which has caused the shedding of blood across the decades, and which continues to have this sad result."

Although he expressed concern about the "brutalization of Palestinian prisoners immediately after they have been taken into custody and . . . beatings administered to persons who were not taken into custody and who were not suspected of or known to have been engaged in any conduct in breach of civil peace," Schifter added: "In our view Israel clearly has not only the right, but the obligation, to preserve or restore order in the occupied territories and to use appropriate levels of force to accomplish that end . . . " He said that Israel "has made a significant effort" to use non-lethal equipment including tear gas, rubber bullets and water cannons "and similar items which will allow for a more measured response to situations that are not inherently or imminently life-threatening." In April and May, more reliance was placed on administrative measures, including requiring payment of withheld taxes before drivers' licenses would be renewed, and curtailing the amount of currency which could be brought in from abroad (and used to support those observing the commercial and labor strike calls).

As to timing of the uprising:

• In mid-Nov. 1987 the Arab League summit in Amman spurned the Palestinian Arabs, focusing instead on the Iraq-Iran war. It informally opened the way for numerous Arab states to restore ties with Egypt, regardless of the Egyptian-Israeli peace treaty. And it was seen to virtually ignore Arafat and the PLO;

• About the same time four escaped terrorists were killed by Israeli forces in a Gaza shoot-out, and residents protested the expulsion of a terrorist suspect;

• After the stabbing deaths of several Israeli civilians, four Arabs died in a Gaza traffic collision involving an Israeli truck. Rumors spread that the accident was in reprisal for the terrorist murders;

• At the end of Nov. an assault by a hang-glider borne guerrilla from the Popular Front for the Liberation of Palestine-General Command, a pro-Syrian PLO subgroup, on an IDF base in northern Israel left six soldiers and the attacker dead—and inspired Palestinian Arabs in the territories.

These events *triggered*, but did not *cause*, the uprising.

MYTH

"Israeli troops were out of control when dealing with rioters during the uprising."

FACT

The cases often mentioned to prove Israeli wanton actions were the Feb. 1988 incidents in the West Bank village of Kfar Salem, when Israeli soldiers used a bulldozer to bury four villagers up to their heads in dirt, and in Nablus where CBS-TV News videotape showed four soldiers beating two Palestinian Arabs caught throwing stones.

In the first case, all four soldiers were punished in military court, receiving demotions, jail terms or both. The master sergeant in charge received the most severe punishment: four months in prison and demotion to private.

In the second, one soldier was sentenced to one-and-a-half months in jail and reduced in rank from corporal to private, and given an additional three-and-a-half months probation; two others received five months probation each. West Bank commander, Gen. Amram Mitzna, said he had been "shocked" by the episode; military police found that the quartet knew they were acting against orders, "but, they said during questioning, after being hit by rocks and seeing their comrades injured, they became fed up and 'exploded'"(*Jerusalem Post International Edition*, March 12, 1988).

Later the army decided to use the CBS videotape as an educational tool to demonstrate intolerable behavior, and the IDF education branch distributed a letter outlining proper use of force to suppress violent demonstrations.

Army Chief of Staff Dan Shomron already had gone on IDF Radio to reiterate standing orders that protesters were not to be beaten after being caught.

At the same time, Brig. Gen. Nehemia Dagan, chief of the education branch, said that brutal behavior by troops was the exception, not the norm, and that soldiers were taught not to be brutal. "They [rioters] throw stones at them, they spit at them, they are doing everything to make the soldiers lose their temper." But, he said, instructions call on troops to "reduce violence and stop violence using the minimum power."

Dagan noted that Israel could not behave like other Middle Eastern countries such as Syria—which killed between 5,000 and 30,000 of its own citizens in Hama in 1982 to put down the Moslem Brotherhood—or Iraq—which levels scores of Kurdish villages and kills or removes the population: "We have to keep democracy and our moral standards high because we and the other side are human beings. We are going to be making peace with them in the future, there's no question about that."

"We must remember, however, that Israel has shown far more restraint towards violent demonstrations than any hostile neighboring Arab state has ever shown toward peaceful demonstrations against government policy. Israel remains the only country in the entire Middle East in which Arabs can enjoy any measure of political freedom." Sen. Daniel Patrick Moynihan, in a May 3, 1988 letter to a constitutent.

MYTH

"Self-determination for the Palestinian Arabs is the answer to the problems on the West Bank and Gaza Strip."

FACT

As the Reagan Administration recognized when it refused to use the word in discussing its 1982 plan, self-determination in the Arab-Israeli context has come to mean a West Bank and Gaza Strip state, a state likely to be controlled by the PLO and heavily influenced by both the Soviet Union and Islamic extremists. Such a state would threaten Jewish self-determination inside the pre-1967 green line.

No authoritative leaders arose from the uprising who demanded such self-determination in the territories. Instead, the underground leaflets, the broadcasts from the clandestine *Al-Quds* (Jerusalem) radio—presumably of the PFLP-GC—in Syria and from Arafat's own Voice of the PLO in Baghdad hailed Palestinian Arab solidarity not only in the territories but in the Galilee, the coastal plain, Jerusalem and the Negev. In short, praising not a limited self-determination but an unrestrained revanchism.

By habitually giving equal emphasis to "right-of-return" as well as "self-determination," the PLO makes clear its real goals. Even "moderates" like Jordanian Prime Minister Zaid al-Rifai put these dual demands on the table. Al-Rifai, himself a Palestinian Arab from Nablus, pointed out during Secretary of State George Shultz's spring 1988 Middle East shuttle: "There is more to the Palestinian cause than the occupation of the West Bank and Gaza Strip. The Palestinian people had rights before 1967, including the right of return. We have reminded the United States that a great number of Palestinians [from pre-1948 Palestine] form the biggest refugee camps now in the West Bank and Gaza."

Almost two months into the uprising Salah Khalaf (Abu Iyad), a top Arafat aide, said "the establishment of an independent Palestinian state on the West Bank and the Gaza Strip does not contradict our ultimate strategic aim, which is the establishment of a democratic state in the entire territory of Palestine, but rather is a step in that direction."

And if the poll which appeared in the pro-Arafat east Jerusalem newspaper *Al-Fajr* 18 months before the uprising is any guide, Palestinian Arabs do not want even a "secular, democratic state." Nearly 60% said they wanted a state founded on Islamic law or a mixture of Islamic law and Arab nationalism. Seventy-eight percent want their state "in all of Palestine." Only 17% favored a so-called two-state solution—a West Bank and Gaza Arab state alongside a Jewish Israel. (In fact, that would be a three-state solution, Jordan already being an Arab state occupying more than 75% of mandatory Palestine.)

Former IDF military intelligence chief Brig. Gen. (Res.) Shlomo Gazit—now head of Ben Gurion University—said early in 1988 that self-determination based on land-for-peace (Israeli withdrawal from most of the territories) required the Arabs "to give up the claim for the right of return. There is no sense to make peace and yet have 1.5 million Palestinian Arab refugees who say they still want to go home to Haifa, Jaffa, and Ramle." But that is what they were saying—and what the uprising was demanding.

MYTH

"Israel's press restrictions during the uprising revealed anti-democratic tendencies."

FACT

The press, foreign and Israeli, was generally free to go where it wanted and report as it saw best during the intifadah—just as it had been previously, subject only to military censorship.

Israel did seal the entire West Bank and Gaza for several consecutive days when it anticipated greatly heightened tensions—but afterward reopened the areas to coverage. Local commanders did exercise their authority to declare certain neighborhoods closed military areas during some violent incidents or in anticipation of them, but these closures also were of limited duration.

Two U.S. correspondents, Martin Fletcher of NBC-TV and Glenn Frankel of the *Washington Post*, had their credentials temporarily suspended for not clearing reports—not confirmed by Israel—that in April 1988 Israeli agents assassinated Khalil al-Wazir (Abu Jihad), the PLO's top "military" commander and a man responsible for many fatal terrorists attacks throughout the 1970's and 1980's. The suspension did not mean they could not work in Israel, only that they would not receive the services of the Government Press Office. Submitting potentially problematic stories to the censors—who considered security matters only, not political commentary—was generally up to the discretion of the journalist, and, as some of them noted, routinely bypassed.

If anything, Israel's remarkable openness to the world's news media—unlike any country in the Arab-Islamic Middle East—reaffirmed its democratic nature. (At the same time Fletcher was suspended in Israel, NBC's Rick Davis was booted out of Jordan. Before his expulsion he was the only American television network correspondent stationed in an Arab country, according to NBC News president Lawrence Grossman.) Israel's general openness continued even as Palestinian Arabs exulted that they were winning the propaganda battle, thanks to international news coverage.

In fact, coverage of the uprising tended to confirm critics' indictments of television news in particular. For example, although the violence typically was the work of 200 to 300 people in four or five locations at the most on any given day, in Jan. all three American networks made it the top story on their evening news—ahead of such developments as the 1988 American presidential campaign, the Soviets' looming withdrawal from Afghanistan, and the Central American peace plan, among others. A.D.T. Research, a New York City media analysis firm, noted that 23% of the time given to the top 30 news stories went to the violence in the territories.

At issue was not importance but proportion, the lack of which can make Israel seem the center of the world's bad news, the cause of the problem. During Jan., approximately 7,000 reporters covered 50,000 Israeli troops in the territories, roughly one reporter for every seven soldiers; at such a ratio the news media themselves become actors, not just observers. And when major media, including television and the wire services, must condense complicated stories to simple action pictures and short paragraphs, distortion by omission occurs.

Something similar happened in 1985 during the hijacking of TWA flight 847. According to a study by George Washington University professor William Adams, the evening news shows on ABC and CBS during the 16-day hijacking showed the networks giving 68% and 62% of their total time, respectively, to the story.

ABC alloted 37% of its hijacking coverage to the hostages, 15% to spokesmen for U.S. government officials, 7% to non-government experts, 6% each to Israeli spokesmen and ex-U.S. officials, and only 4% to released hostages. CBS' breakdown was similar.

That meant that while one of the kidnappers' demands was the release of terrorist suspects held in Israel, "Israel really got very little time devoted to defending its position," Adams noted. "Television hates a story requiring you to understand" complicated issues, he added.

MYTH

"Israel used poison gas to quell the uprising; many Palestinian Arabs were killed or injured by it, and many miscarriages resulted."

FACT

Israel did use CS gas, a standard form of tear gas, in putting down the riots. In April 1988, a group frequently involved in anti-Israel activities, the American Arab Anti-Discrimination Committee, successfully lobbied the gas' U.S. maker to halt sales to Israel. By the end of May the group was alleging that use of the gas had caused 41 deaths.

The Washington Post reported on May 31 that "Palestinian doctors and officials working for the UN Relief and Works Agency (UNRWA)"—the organization for and largely staffed by Palestinian Arabs—"contend there have been . . . dozens of miscarriages and at least 11 deaths from tear gas since the uprising began Dec. 9." But the paper added that "they concede they lack hard data and autopsy results to verify many of their claims . . ." "There is until now no solid scientific proof, but certainly the accumulated evidence is strongly incriminating," said Dr. Samir Badri, a Palestinian who is UNRWA's chief health officer in the Gaza Strip.

Israeli officials did not accept the partisan allegation resting on claimed circumstantial evidence. "We have not seen any cases where it could be proven by a coroner that anybody has been killed due to exposure to tear gas," the *Post* quoted Brig. Gen. Yehuda Doron, the Israel Army surgeon general, as saying, "and we have no scientific evidence that there have been more miscarriages following the use" of tear gas.

Further, the newspaper noted that while misuse of the gas—in closed rooms or small courtyards—could be harmful, especially to small children, the elderly, pregnant women and people with heart or lung problems—"health conditions in the squalid, overcrowded refugee camps of Gaza have deteriorated dramatically in recent months due to disruptions of medical services and child feeding programs caused both by Palestinian violence and Israeli military restrictions. As a result, the population is more vulnerable to many kinds of health hazards, one of which is exposure to tear gas.

"Upon close examination, some of the UN and Palestinian claims appear groundless."

And the *Post* added that a Boston-based group of physicians who charged that the harmful effects of CS gas were being drastically underestimated, visited the West Bank and Gaza Strip in Feb. The group "could not substantiate claims of an increase in the incidence of miscarriages due to tear gas."

18

Jerusalem

MYTH

"Jerusalem is an Arab city."

FACT

Jerusalem was the ancient capital of Israel, and Jews have always lived there. They have constituted the largest single group of inhabitants since the 1840's.

Jerusalem was never an imperial or provincial capital under the Moslems. No Islamic school of note was ever established there, although it is the site of Moslem holy places. Jerusalem is the physical and spiritual crown of Judaism.

JERUSALEM'S POPULATION

Year	Jews	Moslems	Christians	(Source)
1844	7,120	5,000	3,390	*Encyclopaedia Britannica, quoting Turkish census.*
1876	12,000	7,560	5,470	*The Living Guide Indicator de la Terre-Sainte, (France—1876)*
1896	28,112	8,560	8,748	*Calendar of Palestine (1895-1896)*
1922	33,971	13,413	14,699	*Reports and General Abstracts of the Census of 1922 by British Mandate (Jerusalem, Government Printer, 1922)*
1931	51,222	19,894	19,335	*E. Mills, Census of Palestine 1931 (Jerusalem, 1932)*
1948	100,000	40,000	25,000	*Z. Vilnay, Jerusalem—The Old City (1962)*
1967	195,700	54,963	12,646	*Israel Central Bureau of Statistics*
1970	215,000	61,600	11,500	*Jerusalem Municipality*
1985	306,000	108,500	13,700	*Israel Central Bureau of Statistics*
1987	340,000	121,000	14,000	*Israel Central Bureau of Statistics*

MYTH

"Jerusalem need not be the capital of Israel."

FACT

Jerusalem has always played a central role in Jewish religious and political life. Jerusalem was a fortified Jebusite ridge when King David made it his capital 3,000 years ago, and it has been the home of Jews ever since. The Western Wall in Jerusalem, part of the Jewish Temple complex built by Herod over 2,000 years ago, has been the object of Jewish veneration and the focus of Jewish prayer. Jerusalem, Zion, and Israel are synonymous in Jewish prayer. The entire city is central to the Jewish people's religious faith and tradition, and to its historic culture.

MYTH

"The Arabs accepted the internationalization of Jerusalem."

FACT

When the UN took up the Palestine question in 1947, it recommended that the entire city of Jerusalem be internationalized.

The Jewish Agency in 1947 was willing to accept the plan in the hope that internationalization might preserve the historic city from conflict. The Arab states were as bitterly opposed to internationalization of Jerusalem as they were to partition.

The UN Trusteeship Council was directed to write a statute for Jerusalem. Israel's representatives cooperated. But, just as the UN Palestine Commission failed to implement the overall partition resolution, so the Trusteeship Council defaulted.

Notwithstanding the 1948 failure, the UN again directed the Trusteeship Council to arrange for the internationalization of Jerusalem and its environs in Dec. 1949. The United States opposed this unworkable plan, which was supported by a combination of Soviet, Latin American and Arab states.

MYTH

"Internationalization is still the best solution."

FACT

Ironically, the cry for the internationalization of Jerusalem has been much louder during the 21 years that Israel has ruled, allowing free access to the holy places of all three faiths, than it was when Jordan ruled the Old City, barring Jews and Israeli Moslems from their holy sites.

Theoretically, internationalization may sound reasonable in a discussion of Jerusalem. But in fact, it has never worked anywhere. Divided Berlin is a glaring example of the failure of internationalization despite solemn Four Power guarantees.

Since 1967, Israel's administration of Jerusalem has shown that the holy places can be protected and access assured for all faiths without attempting to turn Jerusalem into an unrealistic territorial *corpus separatum*.

MYTH

"Jordan accepted internationalization."

FACT

The Arab states revised their position following Israel's military victory. The Arabs had previously opposed internationalization because they claimed Jerusalem as an all-Arab city. Following defeat in the 1948 war, however, the Arabs found it expedient to proclaim their willingness to accept international rule. There was one significant exception among the Arab states.

Jordan, the only Arab state which controlled the Old City—where almost all the holy places are located—was opposed. Jordan's delegate, Fawzi Pasha Mulki, bluntly told the UN Ad Hoc Political Committee on Dec. 6, 1949:

> "My delegation believes that no form of internationalization . . . serves any purpose, as the holy places under the protection and control of my government are safe and secure, without any necessity for a special regime."

When the Trusteeship Council met in Geneva early in 1950 to draw up a new statute for Jerusalem, Jordan refused to permit UN supervision of any nature—functional or territorial. Jordan even declined to appear before the Council. Israel again submitted her proposal for functional internationalization.

Later, at the 1950 session of the General Assembly, the Trusteeship Council reported its inability to carry out the 1949 resolution. It transmitted Jordan's refusal and Israel's offer (*Special Report of the Trusteeship Council*, June 14, 1950).

MYTH

"Israel sought to annex the Arab sections of Jerusalem during the War of Independence."

FACT

When the British left Palestine, Jerusalem was besieged by Arab forces which cut off the roads and blocked food and water in an attempt to isolate and starve its people.

Jerusalem was rescued by the Jews, who carved a new road through mountains to bring food and water to its inhabitants. In six weeks, 1,490 men, women and children—1.5% of the Jewish population—were killed in the defense of the city, many by indiscriminate shelling of the Transjordan Arab Legion and by Egyptian and Iraqi artillery batteries.

Arab Legion forces seized the Old City, and the Jewish population of the ancient quarter was driven out or captured. The Old City and its holy places became part of Jordan, under Moslem control.

The New City, however, expanded by the Jewish development of the previous century, withstood attack and became the capital of Israel, linked with the rest of the country by a narrow corridor.

MYTH

"From 1948 to 1967, Jordan protected the holy places and the free exercise of religion."

FACT

Under Jordanian rule, Jordan violated holy places sacred to the Jews—the Western Wall and the Mount of Olives in Jerusalem. The Tomb of Rachel near Bethlehem and the Tomb of the Patriarchs near Hebron were closed to Jews, although the 1949 UN armistice assured free access.

Under paragraph eight of the agreement, Jordan and Israel had agreed to the immediate establishment of a special four-man committee, consisting of representatives from each government, to arrange free movement of traffic on vital roads, including the Bethlehem and Latrun-Jerusalem roads; resumption of the normal functioning of the cultural and humanitarian institutions on Mount Scopus and free access thereto; free access to the holy places and cultural institutions; use of the cemetery on the Mount of Olives; and resumption of the operation of the railroad to Jerusalem.

The Jordanian Government reneged. No Jews were allowed to worship at the Wall or to visit the Mount of Olives Cemetery, where Jews have buried their dead for 2,500 years.

Hussein made a concession to Christians from Israel. They were allowed to enter the Old City for Christmas and Easter, but Israeli Moslems were not permitted to cross into the Old City.

MYTH

"Jordan took proper care of Jewish holy places."

FACT

Jordan desecrated Jewish holy places.

To promote tourism, King Hussein permitted the construction of a road to the Intercontinental Hotel across the Mount of Olives Cemetery. Hundreds of Jewish graves were destroyed by a highway that could easily have been built elsewhere. The gravestones, honoring the memory of rabbis and sages, were used by the engineer corps of the Jordan Arab Legion to construct the foundation, walls, pavements and latrines of a military camp. (Inscriptions on the stones are still visible.) Some were used to build the garden wall of the hotel, and a small mosque was built over the graves.

Similarly, the Jewish cemetery at Hebron was destroyed. The ancient Jewish Quarter of Jerusalem was ravaged. Also destroyed were 34 Jerusalem synagogues, some of which were centuries old. Arab squatters arrived from Hebron and converted the Jewish Quarter into a slum. The Western Wall was desecrated by slum dwellings and latrines.

Two great institutions—Hadassah Hospital and the Hebrew University—remained idle on the top of Mount Scopus for 20 years.

MYTH

"Israel attacked religious shrines in 1967."

FACT

On the second day of the Six-Day War, Hussein ignored Israeli appeals to stay out of the war. Eventually he fired the opening shots on Jerusalem and lost the Old City to Israel's counter-attack. The barriers and barbed wire that had been erected in 1948 were ripped away. Sensational and malicious reports from Beirut, Cairo, and Damascus charged that shrines were desecrated. On-the-spot observers in Jerusalem repudiated these lies.

In fact, the holy places suffered very little damage in the fighting. In order to protect the holy places from damage, the Israeli army refrained from bombing or artillery shelling and resorted to hand-to-hand fighting to capture the Old City, sustaining heavy casualties as a consequence. As a further precaution, the Israelis stationed guards around the shrines. Damage done to the Church of the Dormition was caused by indiscriminate Jordanian shelling.

MYTH

"Israeli authorities bulldozed hundreds of Arab homes in Jerusalem, leaving thousands of Arab residents homeless."

FACT

After the capture of the Old City in 1967, Israeli authorities found more than wanton destruction of synagogues in the Jewish Quarter: hundreds of squatters had made their homes in the district, living amongst the ruins in makeshift hovels. Israeli civil engineers cleared the ruins in order to reconstruct the quarter, but only after offering compensation or alternate housing to the squatters.

Ironically, Israeli officials were not the first to see the need to relocate the quarter's squatters. On July 17, 1966, the Prime Minister of Jordan ordered "that the refugees living in the el-Musaker [Jewish] quarter be transferred to the new place allotted to them for residence. . . . The Jerusalem Municipality shall demolish all the tumbledown dwellings of the said quarter after their evacuation."

MYTH

"Under Israeli rule, religious freedom has been curbed in Jerusalem."

FACT

The UN's fact-finding representative, Ambassador Ernesto Thalmann, a Swiss diplomat, visited Jerusalem in Sept. 1967, three months after the war. The various religious representatives told him that Israeli authorities had conformed to the "principles which had been laid down with respect to the holy places and that there was no ground for complaint."

Sheik Toufiq Assiliya, the Moslem Kadi of Jaffa, said this in 1967:

> "We prayed today with our Moslem brethren of Jerusalem in the blessed Al Aksa Mosque. This is a great day for us to be able to pray at the site for which we were yearning for many years. I pray to the Almighty that He may bestow peace upon our region."

The Patriarch of the Church of Ethiopia, His Beatitude Theophilos, sent the following letter to Israel's ambassador in Addis Ababa in July 1967:

> "The Patriarchate of the Ethiopian Orthodox Church would like to express its appreciation to the Israeli Government for the proper care with which it handled the sanctuaries in the Holy Land in general and the Ethiopian convent in particular."

Les Filles de la Charité de l'Hospice Saint Vincent de Paul of Jerusalem wrote a letter repudiating attacks on Israel's conduct in Jerusalem. (*Catholic Herald of London*, Oct. 6, 1967):

> "We do not know the source from which those who are hawking such rumors are drawing their inspiration, but they fill us with profound grief. There is no question for us of 'taking sides'. . . . But we owe it to truth to put on record that our work here has been made especially happy and its path smoother by the goodwill of the Israeli authorities—in peace and in war alike—smoother, that is, not only for ourselves but (more important) for the Arabs in our care. . . . The recent war, moreover, has revealed them to us—both the soldiers and the civilians—as deserving of our deepest admiration."

The Greek Orthodox Patriarch of Jerusalem, Benedictos, said on April 12, 1968:

"It is true, and we would like to stress it again, that the Holy Places in general, monasteries and churches, were given full respect and protection by the Israelis before the war, during the war and afterwards. . . . "

The National Coalition of American Nuns, an autonomous Roman Catholic organization founded in 1969 to study, speak and work for social justice, called for the continuation of Israeli rule in Jerusalem on Sept. 10, 1971:

"The National Coalition of American Nuns expresses strong support for the current status of Jerusalem under Israeli control. We oppose any possible internationalization of the Holy City. Jews have always been in Jerusalem. . . . It is their spiritual home, and the daily prayer of the Jewish people voices their enduring historic relation to the city. Further, Israel has rebuilt Jerusalem pouring into it millions of dollars, and more especially, untold human resources. Jerusalem is now available to all faiths and never before have the holy places been so protected and maintained."

C. Witton-Davies, Archdeacon of Christ Church in Oxford, England, wrote, in a letter published in *The Guardian* (London) on Sept. 30, 1979:

"Jerusalem has been now for 12 years a city of freedom and friendship with free movement throughout the city and free access to the holy sites of the three main religions for everyone in the world. . . . From my own personal conversations and observations, I testify that Jerusalem has never been so fairly administered, or made so accessible to adherents of all three monotheisms, as well as to the general tourist, sightseer, or visitor, whether Jew, Christian, or Moslem, or whatever, as has been the undoubted achievement of [Mayor] Teddy Kollek and his administration."

MYTH

"Israel prevents Moslems from free access to their holy sites."

FACT

According to Israeli law, "Whoever does anything that is likely to violate the freedom of access of the members of the various religions to the places sacred to them or their feelings with regard to those places shall be liable to imprisonment for a term of five years."

The holy places are administered by the religious bodies to which they belong. When a site is deemed holy to more than one religious group, suitable arrangments assure access to all.

MYTH

"Israel's excavations in the Old City have caused considerable damage to Moslem buildings and threaten the historical character of Jerusalem. The 1974 UNESCO condemnation confirmed this."

FACT

The UNESCO declaration in Nov. 1974 was a crude political act. The resolution disregarded the reports on Israel's archeological work submitted by UNESCO's own experts. Prof. Raymond Lemaire, appointed by the director-general of UNESCO, reported:

"Criticisms that have been leveled at the methods used in the excavations are groundless. The excavations are being carried out by a perfectly well-qualified team of experts . . . who are extremely attentive to all aspects and to all the periods of which remains have been found on the site. The same care is expended on the preservation of remains of the Umayad palaces as on those of the Herodian period."

According to Lemaire, excavations south of the Temple Mount caused no damage to any building, including the Al Aksa Mosque. Tunnels north of the Western Wall comply with Lemaire's suggestions on shoring.

If any country altered the historical character of Jerusalem, it was Jordan. Besides destroying ancient Jewish buildings and sites, Jordan hindered excavations of known Christian and Jewish sites. The ancient City of David, a barren area south of the Temple Mount, for example, was covered with dwellings during Jordan's 19-year administration, preventing archeological study of the area.

In one instance, when excavations by Dame Katherine Kenyon appeared to have uncovered an ancient Christian church, Jordanian officials halted the digging. In an apparent attempt to prevent the uncovering of Jerusalem's non-

Islamic history, the Jordanians built a police station over the archeological site. After the 1967 war, Israeli archeologists resumed excavations and discovered, ironically, that the ruins were those of an ancient Arab Umayad palace.

In early 1981, Israeli archeologists uncovered paving stones dating from the Herodian period near the Third Station of the Cross, the spot where, according to the Gospels, Jesus fell for the first time under the weight of the cross. The Herodian pavement was reinstalled along the Via Dolorosa, so that pilgrims can retrace Jesus' steps on the same ancient paving stones that he walked.

In reaction to the restoration, an Irish priest living in East Jerusalem told *The Times* of London in 1981: "Nothing has been unnecessarily rushed, and from the outset the Israelis have worked in harmony with the churches along the route. It is hard to have anything but good words for a restoration project which has been carried out at Jewish expense."

MYTH

"Israeli policy encourages attacks by Jewish fanatics against Moslem and Christian holy sites."

FACT

Israeli authorities have consistently attempted to stop fanatics—of all faiths—from perpetrating their violent or desecrating acts. If the acts cannot be thwarted, Israel punishes the perpetrators. Allan Goodman, who in April 1982 shot up the Temple Mount, was sentenced to life imprisonment.

In 1984, Israeli authorities infiltrated a Jewish terrorist group which planned acts of violence against non-Jewish sites and civilians. The terrorists were indicted, tried and imprisoned. This treatment of would-be anti-Arab terrorists by Israeli authorities clearly contrasts with the handling of far more common anti-Jewish terrorists by Arab governments. In the Arab world such terrorists are praised.

Relations between Moslems and Christians are also carefully monitored. Following the Goodman incident, Moslems in Jerusalem declared a general strike which prompted one Christian resident of Jerusalem to write to the editor of *The Economist*. The published letter explained that the strike coincided with Holy Week, reflecting "the hatred and con-

212

tempt of local Moslems and Christians . . . . Moslems regularly accuse Christians of achieving their greater relative prosperity through collaborating with the Israeli authorities. Christians are emigrating in large numbers, not merely because of the current problems, but because of fear of the alternative: a Palestinian state dominated by Moslems."

The writer continued, "Even if their shop windows are sometimes smashed by Moslems and the tiny band of Jewish fanatics sometimes manages to cause trouble, that is all that can happen to Christians."

New York Times reporter Thomas Friedman highlighted Israel's—and Mayor Kollek's—success in transforming a united Jerusalem, with its volatile population mix, into something other than Berlin or Belfast, in an Aug. 4, 1985 story: "Jerusalem has become one of the world's most beautiful cities, where every major intersection seems to be painted with roses and oleander, and strict zoning laws insure that every new building is faced with Jerusalem's native pinkish-white stone [the light reflection of which gives the city its 'Jerusalem of gold' look]. Even for those who hate the political order, Jerusalem the city has become hard to resist."

There were those, both Arab and Jewish extremists, who hated what Kollek and the municipal and national governments accomplished: turning a war-torn, provincial backwater into a major, and surprisingly civil, international capital in two decades. Even the violence of early 1988, in which special police units were deployed in east Jerusalem in large numbers, did not change the success of Jerusalem's thoughtful modernization or the fact that residents and visitors were safer there than in most major American cities.

MYTH

"Under UN Resolution 242, east Jerusalem is considered 'occupied territory.' Israeli annexation of Jerusalem, therefore, violates the UN resolution."

FACT

One of the drafters of the UN Resolution, Arthur J. Goldberg, served as United States Ambassador to the United Nations. According to Goldberg, "Resolution 242 in no way refers to Jerusalem, and this omission was deliberate. . . . Jerusalem was a discrete matter, not linked to the West Bank."

"In a number of speeches at the UN in 1967," Goldberg continued in a 1980 letter to *The New York Times*, "I repeatedly stated that the armistice lines of 1948 were intended to be temporary. This, of course, was particularly true of Jerusalem. At no time in these many speeches did I refer to east Jerusalem as occupied territory."

MYTH

"The illegality of Israeli actions in Jerusalem is the reason no country recognizes Jerusalem as Israel's capital."

FACT

Thirteen nations maintained embassies in Jerusalem until 1980 when Arab states threatened oil blackmail against them.

In April 1980, the Egyptian parliament decreed that Jerusalem was "an integral part of the West Bank," challenging Israel's sovereignty over the city and the measures taken to unify the city, which had been split for 19 years. The United Nations had previously labelled the reunification and measures taken by Israel—including those which opened holy sites to all faiths—as "illegal, null and void, and nonbinding."

In response, in May 1980, an opposition member of the Israeli parliament introduced a bill entitled "Basic Law: Jerusalem" which reiterated Israeli policy since 1967. The bill, which was passed on July 30, 1980, declared that Jerusalem, "united in its entirety, is the capital of Israel" and the seat of Israel's government. The law reiterated Israel's policy of protecting *all* religious sites of *all* religions.

Arab states then rammed through the UN General Assembly a condemnation of Israel. *The Los Angeles Times*, commenting on the UN action, declared that the General Assembly, "in most political matters generally, and those affecting Israel particularly, has long ceased being a morally credible source committed to conciliation or even honesty in the conduct of international affairs." Even the usually pro-Arab *Christian Science Monitor* found the Arab-sponsored resolution on Jerusalem "so one-sided and so deficient that the United States had no choice but to oppose it."

214

> In Sept. 1980 and again in Nov. 1981, Ronald Reagan expressed his desire for Jerusalem to remain under Israeli administration. "American policy toward Jerusalem is that it should remain undivided, with free access to the holy sites," an official White House statement said. "The President said that he preferred for Jerusalem to remain under Israel's sovereignty."

Iraq and Saudi Arabia led the campaign to nullify diplomatic recognition of Jerusalem by threatening to cut diplomatic, economic and petroleum ties to any nation with an embassy in Jerusalem. The threats forced these nations to move their diplomatic offices: Bolivia, Chile, Colombia, Costa Rica, The Dominican Republic, Ecuador, El Salvador, Guatemala, Haiti, the Netherlands, Panama, Uruguay and Venezuela.

By 1983, however, Costa Rica had reestablished its embassy in Jerusalem. El Salvador moved its embassy to Jerusalem one year later. In 1986 the Ivory Coast reestablished full diplomatic relations with Israel and opened its embassy in Jerusalem; after months of pressure from Arab countries, the African nation moved its embassy to Tel Aviv.

It should be noted that while the U.S. embassy has always been in Tel Aviv, both the 1984 Democratic and Republican Party Platforms supported an undivided Jerusalem with free and unimpeded access to all holy places for people of all faiths. The Democratic platform of 1984 also reiterated the 1972, 1976, and 1980 position that the U.S. embassy should be moved from Tel Aviv to Jerusalem.

Responding to the assertion that the embassy location issue is "only symbolic," Pulitzer Prize-winning columnist George Will said, in an April 25, 1988 speech in Baltimore: "It is one symbolic measure that all political candidates should be pressed on. It is a scandal that the U.S. Embassy is located in Tel Aviv. Some things are not negotiable, including the location of the Israeli capital in Jerusalem."

19

U.S. Policy in the Middle East

MYTH

"The United States alone is responsible for the creation of Israel."

FACT

The United States was not the prime mover in gaining adoption of the 1947 UN partition resolution. It was not a member of the 11-nation commission which recommended partition, and it was but one of 33 countries which approved it.

Declassified State Department documents contained in *Foreign Relations of the United States, 1947—The Near East, Volume 5,* demonstrate unequivocally that neither the State Department nor President Truman put pressure on any nation to vote for partition.

Yet Arabs single out the United States for hostility, ostensibly because of its 1947 stand. On the other hand, many Arabs applaud the Soviet Union even though it also supported partition and speedily recognized Israel. To compound the inconsistency, the Arabs have always scorned the United Kingdom which resisted partition and supported them in the UN debates.

Ironically, the United States abandoned support for the partition resolution and proposed trusteeship in 1948, while the Russians continued to advocate the partition plan.

MYTH

"The United States favored Israel over the Arabs in 1948 because of the pressures of the Jewish lobby."

FACT

Contrary to Arab claims, most Americans—not just American Jews—favored the creation of the State of Israel, although the Department of State was reluctant to support it.

American support for the redemption of Zion began generations ago, with early colonists influenced by the Bible, long before there was a substantial Jewish population in the United States.

President John Adams wrote in 1818:

"I really wish the Jews again in Judea an independent nation for, as I believe, the most enlightened men of it have participated in the amelioration of the philosophy of the age."

Persecution of the Jews in Europe focused attention on the need for a Jewish homeland.

The present-day Zionist movement was not established until 1897. But six years earlier, on March 5, 1891, the Rev. William E. Blackstone presented a memorial to President Benjamin Harrison, appealing for an international conference "to consider the Israelite claim to Palestine as their ancient home." It said in part:

"Why not give Palestine back to them again? According to God's distribution of nations, it is their home—an inalienable possession from which they were expelled by force. . . ."

This petition was signed by many leaders in public life, in the church, the press and in the business world.

Sympathetic views were expressed by Presidents McKinley, Roosevelt and Taft. President Wilson endorsed the Balfour Declaration.

The intelligence section of the American delegation to the 1919 Paris Peace Conference recommended "that the Jews be invited to return to Palestine and settle there . . . that it will be the policy of the League of Nations to recognize Palestine as a Jewish state as soon as it is a Jewish state in fact."

In 1922, Congress adopted a resolution approving the Balfour Declaration. Both national political parties called for the restoration of the Jewish Commonwealth in 1944, and a similar resolution was adopted by Congress in 1945.

This does not mean that American policy always flowed smoothly. At times, antagonistic interests deflected and reversed its course.

Traditional isolationism inhibited any positive U.S. initiative after President Wilson's original commitment, especially since the United States regarded the Middle East as a sphere of British responsibility. After World War II, Washington was the scene of a sharp struggle over partition. But when the debate ended and President Truman recognized Israel in 1948, he was doing what most Americans favored.

It is true that American Jews spearheaded the campaign for a Jewish state. It is also true that some high U.S. officials were opposed to that state and encouraged the Arabs to believe that it would not be established. Indeed, in his memoirs, Truman wrote that the diplomats "continue to be more concerned about the Arab reaction than the sufferings of the Jews."

But the contemporary public opinion polls and historians of 1948 confirmed that the overwhelming majority of the people of the United States—Christians and Jews, Zionists and non-Zionists—supported Israel's cause. The polls after the Six-Day War, the Yom Kippur War, the Lebanon War and the 1987-1988 uprising confirmed that they continued to do so.

A Harris poll released in March 1987, based on a national cross-section of Americans, showed that 68% considered Israel either a close ally or a country friendly to the United States, while only 18% saw it as an enemy or unfriendly— this after months of news headlines about the Jonathan Pollard espionage case and Israel's tie to the Reagan Administration's Iranian arms-for-hostages scheme. The Harris poll found that 79% of the respondents agreed with the description of Israel as "a small, courageous, democratic nation which is trying to preserve its independence," while only 12% disagreed.

A Gallup poll conducted in Oct. and Nov. 1986, and updated in Jan. 1987 to take account of the Iran-*Contra* affair, showed that the public placed Israel sixth when listing countries in which the United States has a vital interest.

Ahead of Israel, in order, were, Great Britain, Canada, Japan, West Germany and Saudi Arabia. Asked to rank countries for which respondents had "warm feelings," Israel again finished sixth — behind Canada, Great Britain, West Germany, Japan and Mexico. Saudi Arabia, the first Arab country on the list, ranked 15th.

In April 1988, a *Los Angeles Times* survey of more than 1,000 Americans indicated that 67% had not changed their views on the Middle East as a result of the rioting by Palestinian Arabs. Overall, 51% sympathized with Israel, only 12% with Arab countries. While one-third held a favorable impression of Palestinian Arabs as a group, 52% expressed negative opinions on the PLO.

Commenting on such surveys, Hebrew University Prof. Eytan Gilboa, author of *American Public Opinion Toward Israel and the Arab-Israeli Conflict*, explained that one-third of the public are "hard-core" supporters, and another third tend to be pro-Israel. He contended that basic support for strong U.S.-Israel relations is strong enough to "take quite a beating" in periodic crises, and will bounce back — especially if the U.S. administration stands by the relationship.

MYTH

"U.S. policy has always favored Israel."

FACT

Arab nationalism owes a debt to the United States which Arabs do not acknowledge: The United States helped the Arab states achieve independence.

President Wilson's stand for self-determination for all nations and the U.S. entry into World War I helped bring about the dissolution of the Ottoman Empire.

But from the beginning the Arabs presented Washington with an "either-or" ultimatum that it choose between Israel and the Arab states. The United States refused to accede and tried to be the impartial friend of all. At the same time, it tried to insulate the Middle East from communist penetration and to safeguard immense U.S. oil investments.

The Arab states bitterly blamed Israel's military victories and diplomatic gains on the United States. They demanded that the U.S. government force Israel to make concessions to its would-be destroyers.

While they always complain that the United States was the first country to recognize Israel, they overlook the arms embargo that was almost immediately imposed by the United States on the new state.

The United States feared the Soviet Union would make political, diplomatic and military gains in the Middle East and, accordingly, it always has tried to avoid decisions which might offend the Arabs and polarize the region.

The Arab position has enjoyed total support from the Soviet Union, and Arab propaganda tends to put the United States at the opposite pole, even though the United States offers many Arab countries aid, arms, and friendship.

MYTH

"The United States has supported Israel automatically ever since 1948."

FACT

Many aspects of U.S. policy favored the Arabs.

In 1948, the United States reversed its stand in favor of partition.

The United States was long reluctant to challenge Arab violations of the UN charter and of UN resolutions: the blockade of the Suez Canal; the Arab boycott; warlike threats; terrorism. Again and again, American spokesmen tended to dismiss belligerent Arab speeches as rhetoric intended for "local consumption" and not to be taken seriously.

The United States failed to insist on projects to resettle the Arab refugees.

The U.S. government did not adequately protect American businessmen from the Arab boycott. Its UN delegation has frequently gone along with one-sided resolutions which censure Israeli replies to Arab provocations, but not the provocations themselves. The United States did not use its Security Council veto to block an anti-Israel resolution until 1972.

The United States pressured Israel to withdraw from Sinai in 1957 without a peace settlement, relying on insubstantial and illusory guarantees, thereby helping set the stage for Arab aggression and the 1967 war.

It condoned Arab aggression against other Arabs, like the brutal Egyptian invasion of Yemen in 1963, and recognized the Yemeni puppet regime set up by the Egyptians, thereby rewarding aggression and strengthening Nasser's hand against other Arab regimes—a blunder which harmed U.S. interests.

"In the period from 1948 to 1963, Israel received deep sympathy and was the object of a sense of moral responsibility [from the United States], but official Washington was very interested in evenhandedness" with regard to Israel and the Arabs, according to Rep. Les Aspin (D-Wis.), chairman of the House Armed Services Committee and a former top aide to Defense Secretary Robert McNamara, who served in both the Kennedy and Johnson cabinets. In a May 18, 1988 speech in Washington, Aspin noted that because the United States "did not want to offend the Arabs," arms sales to Israel in that period were out of the question. Israeli port calls by U.S. Navy ships, let alone exchanges of state visits, were similarly off limits. Nevertheless, beginning in those early years, the intelligence services of both countries "found they had . . . common interests."

Gradually, Aspin said, "a relationship of the head [as well as the heart] developed. It was not something the United States would like to do, but something that was in U.S. interests." Only after France under De Gaulle turned on Israel in 1967 to help resolve the French war in Algeria did the United States move into the arms sales gap. Only then, two decades after Israel's founding, did an American president—Lyndon Johnson—meet with an Israeli Prime Minister—Levi Eshkol.

Under Nixon and Ford, with Secretary of State Henry Kissinger's era of "realpolitik," regular official meetings between ranking American and Israelis became routine, and in 1978 under Carter the U.S. Navy began making port calls in Israel, Aspin said. State Department concerns that Arab countries would be alienated proved groundless. "We were simply too cautious [concerning developing ties with Israel] and imagined Arab sensitivities which didn't exist. If we're going to have imaginative policies with regard to the Arab countries, we've got to do better than that."

Finally, under the Reagan Administration, a number of factors helped cement a strategic relationship between Washington and Jerusalem. These included, Aspin said, U.S. interest in blocking Soviet influence in the Middle East, the loss of Iran to the Islamic revolutionaries of Khomeini, growing international terrorism and Israel's ability to conduct effective counter-terrorism, closer U.S.-Israel ties as a by-product of the Egyptian-Israeli peace, and the president's own sympathies.

Such a review showed a policy that was evolutionary, not automatically supportive of Israel, let alone dominated by the "Zionist lobby."

MYTH

"U.S. aid in the Middle East has always been one-sided, with the Arabs getting practically nothing."

FACT

Israel has received more direct aid from the United States in the post-World War II period than the Arab states have but the figures, from the Library of Congress' Congressional Research Service, are closer than most people realize. From fiscal 1946 through fiscal 1988, Israel obtained $40.911 billion; the Arab states—not including Mauritania, Somalia and Djibouti—got $38.279 billion in American aid. Both totals were in 1988 current dollars. This comparison does not reflect the fact that, unlike Israel, Arab states also receive aid—especially modern weaponry—from Communist bloc countries and Western Europe.

Moreover, since the 1979 signing of the Camp David peace accords, Egypt and Israel have been the recipients of almost equal amounts of military and economic assistance from the United States.

Two factors led to the notion that Israel gets all of Washington's attention when it comes to dispensing aid in the Middle East. Starting in the 1950's many Arab countries adamantly refused to accept American assistance. Later, for propaganda value or out of ignorance, many critics lumped private contributions and Israeli arms *purchases* with U.S. grants to Israel.

In 1951, Congress voted to help Israel cope with the economic burdens imposed by the influx of Jewish refugees from the refugee camps in Europe and from the ghettos of the Arab countries.

Arabs then complained that the United States was giving more aid to Israel than to them. But Arab states had no interest in or use for U.S. aid at that time. Syria rejected U.S. aid in 1951. Oil-rich Iraq and Saudi Arabia never needed U.S. economic aid. Jordan, for a long time, was the ward of Great Britain.

To curtail U.S. aid to Israel because its Arab neighbors did not want it for themselves would have been to join their boycott of Israel. U.S. assistance generally has been allocated on the basis of need and on the capacity of the beneficiary to make effective use of it.

After 1957, when the United States assumed responsibility for the budget of Jordan and resumed economic aid to Egypt, economic assistance to the Arab states soared. Meanwhile, U.S. economic grants to Israel ended in 1959. U.S. aid to Israel from then until the early 1980's consisted largely of loans, which Israel repaid, and surplus commodities, which Israel bought. In fact, Israel has averaged over $1 billion a year in imports from the United States since 1978, the figure reaching nearly $1.9 billion by 1985.

Israel began buying arms from the United States in 1962 but, until the 1973 Yom Kippur War, Israel never received grant military assistance.

As a result, Israel had to go deeply into debt to finance its economic development and arms procurement. In 1971, Israel appealed to the U.S. Government to include Israel in the grant economic assistance program. The administration refused but, as in 1951, Congress took the initiative and a $50 million grant for economic support assistance for Israel was included in the Foreign Assistance Act approved for fiscal year 1972. In 1985 all economic aid, like military assistance, was converted to grants. In 1986 and 1987, economic aid stood at $1.2 billion annually. An emergency grant of $1.5 billion, spread over 18 months, helped Israel's national unity government reform the country's budget in 1985, bringing an annual inflation rate of 400% to under 20% and leading to the first real economic growth in more than a decade.

Congress recognized the burden Israel's defense needs place on its economy—almost 25% of the gross national product (GNP)—during the mid-1980's, compared to about 6% of GNP for the United States *after* Reagan's first term defense buildup; most NATO countries spend proportionately less on defense than either country. In 1986 and 1987, Israel's $1.2 billion in annual U.S. economic aid roughly equalled the amount of interest Israel repaid the United States each year on older, high interest military loans. The loans were taken out to rebuild the Israel Defense Force (IDF) after the 1973 Yom Kippur War and to relocate much of the IDF infrastructure and continue modernization after the 1979 peace with Egypt, when the other Arab states, meeting in Baghdad, announced creation of the "rejectionist" front.

So Congress authorized conversion of military aid from loans to grants in 1985, acknowledging that without a strong Israel, war in the Middle East was more, not less, likely, and that the United States would face higher direct expenditures. (For example, the deployment of several dozen U.S. Navy ships in and around the Persian Gulf after the reflagging of 11 Kuwaiti oil tankers in 1987 cost an additional $1 million a day. With any significant introduction of army and air force units—as would be necessary in the event of a larger deployment—the cost would have skyrocketed.)

Figures on private American aid to Israel have been wildly exaggerated. They often include inflated estimates of donations by private citizens to the United Jewish Appeal and purchases of Israel bonds.

Since 1951, Israel bonds sales in the United States have totalled about $5 billion. The total amount contributed by the United Jewish Appeal from 1939 to the present was approximately $6.5 billion. These monies help provide educational and social services in the Jewish state.

These totals include the emergency funds which were raised by Americans to help Israel when its economy was battered and its survival threatened by catastrophic wars.

It is worth noting that bond purchasers pay substantial taxes to the U.S. Treasury on the interest they receive. Finally, it must be emphasized that funds contributed by private citizens to the UJA are used to help resettle Jewish refugees and that bond funds assist in developing Israel's economy—not to procure arms.

MYTH

"The United States has provided Israel with economic and military assistance far beyond its needs."

FACT

Israel's population of 4.4 million has borne the major burden of its own defense. Israel's taxation rates, even after the economic reform program of 1985-1986, were among the highest in the free world.

U.S. assistance to Israel had never been more than $300 million a year until the 1973 Yom Kippur War. By 1973, Israel's defense costs had risen to 49% of the state budget of $8.5 billion. U.S. economic and military assistance to Israel in 1973 was $417 million, of which $366 million was in the form of a loan.

An erosion of purchasing power in the average Israeli wage of 20% to 25% during the 1985-1986 economic recovery program testified to its austerity. After years of announced cuts, real government expenditure dropped by 3% to 4%, and more efficient collections boosted income tax revenue. The mid-1980's oil price plunge also helped, saving the country between $300 million and $400 million, according to Bank of Israel researchers. (Israel relinquished the Alma oilfields—which it had developed—to Egypt when it returned the Sinai in keeping with the Camp David Accords. The fields supplied more than half of Israel's energy needs.)

Secretary of State George Shultz, who put together a team of American economists to help advise Israel during the reform program, noted in March 1986, as wage and price controls were gradually being lifted, that Israel's economic situation was "radically different" from what it was during the inflationary climb two years before. "The problems aren't over," he said, "but great progress had been made."

An often overlooked aspect of U.S.-Israel economic relations are Israeli imports from the United States. Despite its small size—its $25 billion GNP in the mid-1980's was roughly equivalent to the economic activity of greater Philadelphia—Israel is one of the largest U.S. trade partners in the Middle East. In 1987, under the precedent-setting Free Trade Area Agreement between the two countries (which proved a catalyst for a similar agreement between the United States and Canada) Israel's civilian imports from the United States totaled $3.1 billion. Its exports to the United States reached $2.7 billion, giving America a $400 million trade surplus.

MYTH

"Israel always received all the arms it wanted free of charge."

FACT

Although about 80% of all worldwide U.S. military assistance since 1946 has been in the form of grants, Israel never received military aid on a grant basis until the 1973 Yom Kippur War. It has, therefore, gone deeply into debt to pay for its security. Israel's foreign debt was $23.1 billion at the end of 1987, of which $10.4 billion was owed to the United States. Israel's defense expeditures already consume 25% of the country's GNP, compared with 6% in the United States.

A significant portion of the U.S. aid to Israel has been in the form of loans paid with interest, and Israel, unlike many other nations, pays its debts—and on time. In 1987 alone, Israel repaid the United States over $1 billion in interest and principal on previous years' military and non-military loans.

MYTH

"Israel is a strategic burden to the United States."

FACT

In a region wracked by upheaval in the last decade, Israel remains one of the few stable U.S. allies in the Middle East. The inherent instability of the Middle East can be seen in the revolution in Iran; the Iraq-Iran war; the Soviet war in Afghanistan; Iranian-inspired terrorism in Kuwait and the 1987 Mecca pilgrimage riots in Saudi Arabia; factional strife in Lebanon; and the reluctance of several Arab Persian Gulf states to be seen aiding the U.S. reflagging policy for Kuwaiti tankers in 1987-1988. Israel remains one of the few stable, reliable democracies in the world upon which the United States can rely to uphold Western interests. Difficult, sometimes unsatisfactory renegotiations on base rights with formal NATO allies like Portugal, Spain and Greece in 1987 and 1988 also illustrated, by contrast, Israel's dependability, serving as NATO's *de facto* anchor for the eastern Mediterranean basin. Israel's reliability as an ally, coupled with a proven military-intelligence capability, makes it an important strategic asset to the United States.

Israel supplies the United States with a constant stream of information on the performance of the latest U.S. weapons systems. And it has not hesitated to share with the United States valuable intelligence on sophisticated Soviet equipment captured from the Arab states—thus providing the U.S. defense establishment with otherwise unobtainable information. During the 1982 Lebanon war, for instance, Israeli planes downed 85 late-model Syrian MiG's, destroyed Soviet-supplied surface-to-air missiles, and knocked out the much-vaunted T-72 tank. This was not just a blow to the Syrians; it was a severe blow to Soviet prestige, technology, and military planning for central Europe.

The list of Soviet equipment captured by Israel and turned over to the United States represents almost a total Soviet tactical order of battle. The arms include MiG-21's which now are used in U.S. Air Force training programs; a whole range of tanks, including the late-model T-62; armored personnel carriers; chemical warfare items; artillery systems; aerospace electronic systems; anti-tank missiles; radar systems; anti-aircraft guns; and a full range of surface-to-air missiles.

There are other ways in which Israel serves as a key intelligence partner to the United States. In 1978, Israeli intelligence provided the CIA with assessments predicting upheaval in Iran. In 1976, its intelligence alerted Egypt and Saudi Arabia, through the United States, of conspiracies and planned coup attempts. Israeli intelligence also remains in the forefront in the battle against international terrorism. With the loss in recent years of U.S. intelligence outposts throughout the Mediterranean and Asia, Israel is one of the few potential points for monitoring Soviet activities through operation of surveillance aircraft and electronic intelligence facilities. The ongoing nature of the bilateral intelligence relationship was highlighted by Rep. Aspin in the 1988 speech noted above.

Israeli armed forces have proven themselves capable of direct action in support of U.S. interests. In 1970, Soviet-backed Syrian forces threatened the pro-Western government of Jordan. Only the massing of Israeli forces (at the request of the United States) on the Jordanian and Syrian borders deterred the Syrians from aiding the PLO in its "Black September" civil war against King Hussein. In both U.S. and Soviet strategic military planning for the eastern Mediterranean and Middle East, Israeli forces constitute a major asset in the U.S. column.

The rapid growth of Soviet naval power highlights the potential importance to the United States of Israel's naval, air, and ground-support facilities. Israel could provide the

United States with a staging area, a land route for supplies, combat-proven hospitals, a communications center, a refueling base, and a tactical-support and maintenance facility.

By 1988, the United States and Israel had concluded agreements on the prepositioning of American military supplies in Israel. Israel stands ready to provide the United States with access to militarily secure, deep-water ports and some of the most modern airbases in the world. U.S. Sixth Fleet aircraft, in need of land target practice ranges, have practiced over Israeli ranges in the Negev desert. Some 25,000 U.S. Naval personnel visited Israel in 1987 alone on Sixth Fleet visits to the ports of Haifa and Ashdod.

In addition, private Israeli firms already provide maintenance and repair services for the United States. Since the two countries share many of the same weapons systems, Israel is capable of providing full-scale repair and overhaul services for U.S. armed forces—on either a regular or emergency basis.

In 1988, Congress voted to spend tens of millions of dollars for procurement of several advanced Israeli-designed weapons systems, including the Popeye air-to-ground missile and 120-mm mortars and ammunition. The acquisition and use of Israeli-built drones as spotters was increasing dramatically the accuracy of artillery-fire from recommissioned U.S. battleships. As Defense Secretary Frank Carlucci noted in May of that year, such cooperation "testifies to the advanced state of Israel's technological base, and its ability to employ technological advances to strengthen its defenses." Carlucci added that America benefitted as "Israeli defense sales to the U.S. have risen from just $9 million in 1983 to at least $250 million in 1987.

"As the United States continues to explore cost-effective ways to acquire the weapons systems it needs, there is little doubt purchases from Israel will continue to grow. Even with severe fiscal pressures on U.S. defense spending, Israel will remain an important source of systems that are proven and ready, in some cases saving the United States the time and expense of developing its own."

In addition, Israel was one of just four nations willing and able to work with the United States on a government-to-government basis on Strategic Defense Initiative (SDI) research. It also joined with the United States in the experimental Arrow anti-tactical ballistic missile system, which military experts said held great promise. Not only was this important for Israel—threatened by Soviet-built SS-21's in Syria, Chinese-built CSS-2 East Wind missiles in Saudi Arabia, and other missile systems in Iraq and elsewhere in the region—but an anti-tactical missile defense could greatly improve the position of NATO versus Warsaw Pact forces in Europe. (The danger of chemical warheads, primarily but not exclusively from Syria, was such that in 1986 and 1987 Israeli civilians, including school children—as well as IDF forces—began practicing defensive steps, including gas-mask drills.)

"Our relationship with Israel is in our mutual self-interest. But a narrow calculation of interest is not the sole basis of the bond between our nations. At its heart is a moral obligation on our part to do whatever is necessary to defend and protect Israel." President Ronald Reagan, in a May 13, 1988 letter.

In 1987, Israel agreed to construction of a major Voice of America (VOA) transmitter in the Arava region of the Negev desert, to enable VOA, Radio Free Europe and Radio Liberty to improve broadcasts to the central Soviet Union, South Asia and Africa. President Reagan said the decision meant that "our special relationship will be given a new dimension. We could not be happier with this partnership with Israel because it will result in the broader dissemination of those values we have in common." Israel accepted the VOA project after several other generally pro-U.S. countries, including Egypt, refused.

Attesting to the broad and deep relationship, in 1987 Israel was designated, along with a handful of other countries, a major non-NATO ally of the United States, entitling it, among other things, to some special benefits in military trade.

MYTH

"Nevertheless, the cost of the U.S.-Israel alliance is too high, especially given U.S. budget deficits and pressure to cut defense spending."

229

FACT

Of the $1.8 billion in U.S. military aid—Foreign Military Sales (FMS) funds—granted to Israel annually in recent years, only $300 million is not spent in the United States. As UCLA Professor Steven Spiegel pointed out in a 1988 study for the Los Angeles-based Council for Foreign Policy Options, the close relationship has produced concrete military benefits for both countries. Especially since the fall of the Shah of Iran in 1979 and the U.S. debacle in Lebanon in 1983, American reliance on a strong Israel has grown.

The graph below, from Spiegel's paper, puts aid to Israel in perspective with costs incurred in the United States defense budget as a result of various international commitments.

Earlier in the decade, another analyst, Joseph Churba, a former top Air Force intelligence official and head of the Washington-based Center for International Security, estimated that it would cost the United States $100 billion or more in additional spending—and the deployment of more than 200,000 of its own troops—to replace Israel's pro-U.S. strategic weight in the Middle East.

MYTH

"The fact that Israel is not an ally of the United States can be seen in Israel's use of spies against the United States. The employment of Jonathan Pollard to spy on the United States is proof that Israel works against U.S. interests."

FACT

In Nov. 1985, the FBI arrested Jonathan Jay Pollard, a U.S. Navy intelligence analyst, on charges of selling classified material to Israel. Pollard was subsequently sentenced to life imprisonment. His wife, Anne, was sentenced to five years in prison for assisting her husband.

Immediately upon Pollard's arrest, the government of Israel apologized and explained that the Pollard operation was unauthorized. "It is Israel's policy to refrain from any intelligence activity related to the United States," an official government statement declared, "in view of the close and special relationship of friendship" between two countries. Prime Minister Shimon Peres stated, "Spying on the United States stands in total contradiction to our policy."

The United States and Israel worked together to investi-

Table I:

Aid to Israel Compared to Major International Costs

(Figures based on FY 1987 expenditures)

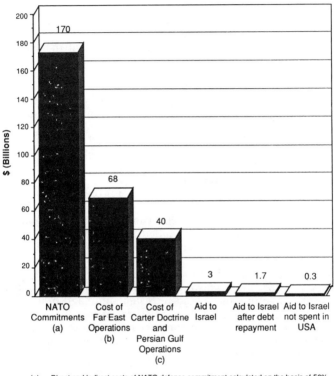

(a) Direct and Indirect costs of NATO defense commitment calculated on the basis of 56% of defense budget (this percentage based on figures in "Reduction in U.S. Costs to Station Forces in FRG and UK Are Unlikely," General Accounting Office, July 31, 1984).

(b) Direct and Indirect costs of Far East commitments based on number of troops stationed in Asia (114,000) compared to number of troops stationed in NATO countries (290,000).

(c) John Lehman, "Carter Doctrine Is No Longer Adequate in Gulf," The Wall Street Journal, August 5, 1987, page 22.

gate the Pollard affair. By Feb. 1986, Attorney General Edwin Meese said, "The Israeli government has cooperated with us in providing necessary evidence that was available in that country."

231

Israeli investigations revealed that Pollard was not working for the Israeli military intelligence nor for the Mossad, Israel's vaunted intelligence service. Pollard was directed by a small, independent scientific intelligence unit, headed by Rafi Eitan. His first contact with an Israeli was with an Israeli air force officer studying on sabbatical in the United States. It was initiated by Pollard.

Perhaps the most thorough investigation of the Pollard affair was carried out by a parliamentary body in Israel's Knesset. The Subcommittee of the Defense and Foreign Affairs Committee on Intelligence and Security Services had access to all files and interviewed all Israeli officials involved. The committee concluded, "beyond all doubt . . . that the operational echelons (namely: the Scientific Liaison Unit headed by Rafi Eitan) decided to recruit and handle Pollard without any check or consultation with the political echelon or receiving its direct or indirect approval." The Knesset committee took to task the upper echelon of Israel's government for not properly supervising the scientific unit.

As promised to the U.S. government, the spy unit which directed Pollard was disbanded, his handlers were punished, and the stolen documents were returned. Rafi Eitan was fired, barred from engaging further in intelligence matters, and was given a job in a non-security-related government corporation. The air force officer was denied a promised promotion and forced to resign command of a major air base. The officer was a much-decorated pilot, yet, according to the Knesset committee report, "a large question mark hangs over the future of his career in the air force." Israel's return of the documents, legal authorities suggest, provided vital evidence for the U.S. Justice Department's case against Pollard.

According to published reports, Pollard provided Israel with information on Soviet arms shipments to Syria, including SS-21 surface-to-surface missiles; on Iraqi and Syrian chemical warfare production and capabilities; on the Pakistani atomic bomb project; on the PLO headquarters in Tunisia; and on the Libyan air defense system. For his part, Pollard denied that he was spying "against" the United States, according to an interview published in *The Washington Post*. "I was neither engaged in nor directed to conduct any activities against the United States, and I will never admit to that fact."

MYTH

"Until Israel cancelled its program to develop the Lavi fighter plane it wasted billions of dollars of American aid. The plane was designed to compete with American aircraft exports."

FACT

In Aug. 1987, the government of Israel decided to cancel the Lavi project. The decision was based on *economic* and not technical grounds.

Israel embarked on the Lavi program after assessing the general role of aircraft in the 1973 Yom Kippur War. In that war, Arab States' dense anti-aircraft missile coverage gave protection to their offensive ground attacks against Israel and threatened to push Israel's combat aircraft from the battle theater. In response to that missile threat, Israel faced several options: It could continue to use outdated Skyhawk and Kfir aircraft (with its 1960's technology), it could use the American-made F-16 in conjunction with the air-superiority F-15 fighter (1970's technology), or it could develop for the 1990's its own multi-mission, close ground-support aircraft capable of overcoming the missile threat.

For five years, the U.S. Congress supported the Lavi project and appropriated aid for its development. "The Lavi is going to be the leading edge of the western aerospace curve," said Rep. Charles Wilson (D-Tex.). "The roll-out of the Lavi," Rep. Jack Kemp (R-N.Y.) reported, "was a real and visible expression of the partnership of the Israeli democracy and the United States." Approximately 50% of the aircraft's systems were to be manufactured in the United States, employing an estimated 20,000 workers.

The aircraft was a uniquely well-planned aircraft, incorporating the requirements of the Israel Air Force (IAF), the engineering of Israel Aircraft Industries, and the experience of IAF fighter pilots. The Lavi made its first test flight in Dec. 1986. In almost all tests the aircraft surpassed its planners' expectations. Yet, several factors were already at play that were to ground the Lavi.

With the falling value of the dollar on the world market in the mid-1980's, the cost of producing the plane rose substantially. Pentagon analysts projected the Lavi's cost to be higher than expected. And most importantly, Israeli military planners had concluded that the plane's mission was capable of being met by other efficient and less expensive technological developments.

The Lavi was never meant to compete with American-manufactured aircraft. The production schedule and Israel's own requirements provided aircraft only for Israel's use for at least the first 5-10 years of production.

The cancellation of a weapons system is certainly not rare in the arms industry. After many years of development, Britain cancelled the Nimrod aircraft surveillance system. In recent years, Northrop Corp. cancelled the F-20 Tigershark aircraft, and the Pentagon cancelled the multi-billion dollar DIVAD system when it failed to meet the operational specifications. In the case of the Lavi, however, the system met all specifications. Indeed, the United States and Israel will continue to benefit from the Lavi project as subsystems of the aircraft are studied and produced, particularly in the fields of avionics, radars, composites, construction and human engineering.

MYTH

"Israel tricked the United States into selling arms to Iran in exchange for hostages, and then attempted to cover up Jerusalem's involvement in the scheme."

FACT

According to the Report of the Congressional Committees Investigating the Iran-*Contra* Affair issued in Nov. 1987, the sale of U.S. arms to Iran through Israel began in the summer of 1985, after receiving the approval of President Reagan. The report shows that Israel's involvement was stimulated by separate overtures in 1985 from Iranian arms merchant Manucher Ghorbanifar and U.S. National Security Council (NSC) consultant Michael Ledeen working for National Security Adviser Robert McFarlane. When Ledeen asked Prime Minister Shimon Peres for assistance, the Israeli leader agreed to sell weapons to Iran at America's behest, providing the sale had high-level U.S. approval.

Before the Israelis would participate, says the report, they demanded "a clear, express, and binding consent by the U.S. Government." McFarlane told the congressional committee that he first received President Reagan's approval in July 1985. In Aug., Reagan again orally authorized the first sale of weapons to Iran, over the objections of

Defense Secretary Caspar Weinberger and Secretary of State George Shultz. As a result of that deal Rev. Benjamin Weir, held captive in Lebanon for 16 months, was released.

When a shipment of Hawk missiles was proposed in Nov., Israeli Defense Minister Yitzhak Rabin again demanded specific U.S. approval. According to McFarlane, the president agreed.

By Dec. 1985, the president had decided that future sales to the Iranians would come directly from U.S. supplies.

According to the committees' report, NSC aide Lt. Col. Oliver North first used money from the Iran operation to fund the Nicaraguan resistance in Nov. 1985. He later testified, however, that the diversion of funds to the contras was proposed to him by Ghorbanifar, whom he labeled an Israeli intelligence operative, during a meeting in Jan. 1986.

The Joint House-Senate Committee praised the Israeli government for providing detailed chronologies of events based on relevant documents and interviews with key participants in the operation. The committees' report concluded: "[We] received unprecedented cooperation from the State of Israel."

The joint committees' report corroborated an earlier study by the president's special review board under the chairmanship of former Sen. John Tower. The Tower Commission report demonstrated that U.S. officials were cognizant of the risks involved in selling arms to Iran and concluded: "U.S. decision-makers made their own decisions and must bear responsibility for the consequences."

20

The Peace Process: 1985-1988

MYTH

"American officials saw 'a new momentum to the search for peace' in the Middle East, as Assistant Secretary of State Richard Murphy put it. But positive developments on the Arab side were stymied by Israel."

FACT

On Feb. 11, 1985, Jordan's King Hussein and PLO Chairman Yasir Arafat announced that they had "reached agreement on the formula of the joint Jordanian-Palestinian move for attaining a just and peaceful solution" to the issue of the West Bank (Judea and Samaria) and the Gaza Strip. At the time Jordan hoped for a major U.S. arms sale. But the move echoed a similar effort two years earlier. Then Arafat, under pressure from Syria and Syrian-backed PLO rebels in Lebanon, looked to Hussein as an ally of convenience. But when he felt strong enough, he bolted Hussein's embrace.

The 1985 announcement contained little new. The PLO still did not endorse UN Security Council Resolution 242—the basis for U.S. Middle East diplomacy and for those successful Arab-Israeli negotiations which have occurred since 1967. Neither did the PLO recognize Israel nor renounce the use of terrorism. And neither Hussein nor Arafat indicated they were ready to enter direct, bilateral negotiations with Israel. By insisting that their joint initiative be given an Arab League seal of approval (meaning acceptance by Syria and the other rejectionists) they assured that their maneuver was virtually stillborn.

Although Hussein told the Americans that the PLO had agreed to self-determination in a West Bank and Gaza entity federated with Jordan, this did not turn out to be the case.

Meanwhile Israel, far from blocking intra-Arab development, again stated its willingness to talk. For example, on March 31 then-Prime Minister Shimon Peres told the east Jerusalem Arabic-language daily *Al-Quds* that "we are prepared to negotiate unconditionally with a joint Jordanian-Palestinian delegation, a Jordanian delegation, or a Palestinian delegation in our efforts toward an immediate peaceful solution or a solution in stages." But no non-PLO Palestinian Arab or joint-Jordanian-Palestinian delegation was permitted by the PLO to materialize.

MYTH

"U.S. rejection of three specific PLO peace proposals caused the Arafat-Hussein agreement to collapse."

FACT

In Feb. 1986, Hussein, exasperated with PLO intrigues, broke off the joint effort. He concluded that he was "unable to coordinate politically with the PLO leadership until such time as their word becomes their bond, characterized by commitment, credibility, and consistency."

Arafat launched a propaganda blitz meant to shift the blame to Washington. But in March, the State Department said King Hussein's remarks made "clear where the responsibility lies for the state of the peace process . . . . The PLO leadership has failed to seize the opportunity offered."

More was offered, apparently, than was public knowledge at the time. Weeks later news reports stated that the Reagan Administration, encouraged by Hussein, had informed the PLO through intermediaries that the United States would accept the organization in talks if it accepted Resolution 242, agreed to negotiate with Israel and renounced terrorism. When the PLO said no, Hussein made his public cancellation.

Arafat—pressured by the Soviets, by those in the PLO more extreme than he, and yielding to his own inclinations—"kicked it away," in the words of a Feb. 23, 1986 *Washington Post* editorial. Arafat, "foolishly" demanded that the United States accept Palestinian Arab self-determination—a PLO state—*before* any international Middle East peace conference would be held, the paper stated.

The PLO had no choice but to reject the U.S. offer. "Political department" head Farouk Kaddoumi—with Arafat a founder of Fatah, the PLO's major component—explained why in March. He told a newspaper in the United Arab Emirates that in accepting 242 "we would have been recognizing Israel's right to exist without getting anything in

237

return. It would mean accepting the 1967 boundaries as Israel's boundaries, which we don't." Asked if most Palestinian Arabs would accept Israel within the pre-1967 lines, Kaddoumi added, "I don't think so."

Meanwhile, the war would continue on all fronts: "the diplomatic front, the political front, the armed struggle." Asked about Arafat's 1985 Cairo declaration, in which the PLO chairman abjured terrorism outside the "occupied territories," Kaddoumi said, "that's right, but all Palestine is occupied, and this means that we continue our struggle in the occupied territories, and this is something exactly right." Asked about settling for less than "the whole of Palestine," Kaddoumi replied: "Whole rights. Self-determination, the independent state of Palestine, and return to Palestine."

Israeli Defense Minister Yitzhak Rabin noted that Hussein's break with the PLO presented "an historic opportunity" for the residents of the territories. If they "understand that this is the hour of truth, and they take the initiative to get together with Hussein, then this may be the opening for a renewed chance for a dialogue." But they did not.

MYTH

"The 1988 Shultz initiative, with its call for an international conference, was the best hope for Arab-Israeli peace. But Israel's national unity government sabotaged the Secretary's efforts."

FACT

In early 1988, after making several trips between Middle East capitals, U.S. Secretary of State George Shultz sent letters to Jordan's King Hussein and Israeli Prime Minister Yitzhak Shamir in which he outlined a process which might lead to Arab-Israeli talks. Explaining his plan, Shultz said, "In the Arab-Israeli conflict, negotiations work. [Experience shows] they provide the means for parties to learn to deal with each other. They produce durable and realistic agreements that meet the fundamental concerns of the parties."

Shultz based his plan on U.N. Security Council Resolutions 242 and 338 and proposed: a two-staged, interlocked set of talks over the West Bank and Gaza Strip, first for a short period of interim autonomy, then leading to negotiations on the final status of the territories; an international conference because "the Arabs require a conference to launch negotiations"; and, growing out of the conference, direct, bilateral talks between Israel and each of the parties. Shultz and President Reagan said the proposal was designed with the various parties in mind and could not be amended. "In particular, we will not permit a conference to become authoritative or plenipotentiary, or to pass judgments on the negotiations, or to exceed its jurisdiction as agreed by the parties," the Secretary stated.

Israel's Foreign Minister, Shimon Peres, head of the Labor Party half of Israel's national unity government, endorsed Shultz's effort. Reports said it echoed an agreement reached between Peres and Hussein in secret talks in London in the spring of 1987.

Shamir and his Likud bloc half of the Israeli government objected to parts of the plan, fearing a "runaway" international conference, despite U.S. pledges to the contrary. They noted that the Arabs, including Hussein, insisted on a conference convened by the five permanent members of the U.N. Security Council—including the Soviet Union and China, neither of which had diplomatic relations with Israel at the time. Despite overt Soviet moves to warm relations (dispatching a consular delegation to Israel in 1987 and a moderate increase in Soviet Jewish emigration) and covert Chinese moves (increased commercial and military trade) both Security Council members almost automatically backed Arab positions.

In addition, Hussein stepped away from the reported London agreement, insisting on a separate PLO delegation instead of a joint Jordanian-Palestinian delegation without official PLO representation. And Shamir worried that condensing the transitional autonomy period to a matter of months (Camp David called for a five-year transition), and making it dependent on prior agreement on the permanent status of the territories, would not allow for any evolutionary improvement or confidence-building between the two sides as Israeli military control was scaled back.

While supporters of Israel and Israelis themselves differed over the Shultz initiative—Henry Kissinger cautioning against it, Abba Eban urging that it be tried, for example—Jordan waffled not only over the PLO's role but the nature of the conference itself, asserting that it must be "more than a photo opportunity" and hinting that the conference *would* have the power to resolve disputes [impose a settlement] arising from bilateral talks. Syria rejected the U.S. effort, calling it "a fig leaf" for Israeli expansionism. The Soviets issued contradictory statements regarding their understanding of the power of the proposed conference and the participation of the PLO. And the PLO itself—and the pamphlets issued in the name of the uprising—ordered Palestinian Arabs to spurn U.S. invitations to meet with Shultz and to defeat his "imperialistic" scheme.

MYTH

"Shamir was insincere about wanting peace; he had no plan of his own."

FACT

Yitzhak Shamir held fast to Revisionist Zionist ideology which asserted the Jewish claim to all of *Eretz Yisrael*—the land of Israel promised by God to the Jewish people in the covenants of the Hebrew Bible. (This was not out of the Zionist mainstream philosophically; Ben-Gurion told the Peel Commission before World War II that the Bible was the Jews' mandate or deed to a homeland in Palestine.) Yet Shamir's Herut Party—the major element in Likud and the

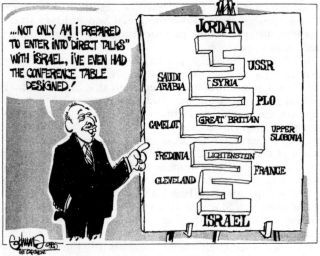

"King Hussein's Offer"

240

heir to Revisionism—had given up the claim to the East Bank of the Jordan, suggested as part of the future Jewish national home during the early period of British control, after the first partition of Palestine and the creation of Transjordan.

Although Shamir himself did not vote for the Egyptian-Israeli peace treaty, as Prime Minister he came to see the Camp David autonomy provisions as a key to achieving peace. He repeatedly stressed his desire to meet and negotiate with Jordan's King Hussein, publicly or privately, and to talk with non-PLO Palestinian Arab leaders. Shamir noted that in such talks each side would be free to put its claims on the table *for negotiations.* He offered, through the United States, to resume the peace process by meeting with Hussein and Egyptian President Hosni Mubarak in Washington on the sidelines of the Reagan-Gorbachev summit in Dec. 1987 and to negotiate under the auspices of the superpowers alone. Hussein rejected this offer; he rejected it a second time when Shamir said he was still interested in the idea as an offshoot to the May 1988 Moscow superpower summit.

In Feb. 1988, Shamir drafted a position paper focusing on: solving the Palestinian Arab refugee problem through the construction of 30,000 housing units in the Gaza Strip and 11,000 in Judea and Samaria (the West Bank) for the 280,000 refugees still living in camps (one-third of the Gaza population and 10% of that on the West Bank); a comprehensive peace with Jordan; and an autonomy plan involving a three-year period leading to a permanent resolution of the status of the territories. The autonomy negotiations were to resume where they had ended with Egypt in 1982. Shultz had said, after reviewing the record of the autonomy talks, that people would be surprised to learn how much progress had been made. (The earlier autonomy negotiations were halted partly because the Palestinian Arabs would not put forth participants without terrorist connections.)

Little attention was given to the Prime Minister's proposals by either the Arabs or the United States. Critics charged that Shamir's peace rhetoric was solely a mask for annexationist desires. But as Ambassador Moshe Arad told the *Washington Jewish Week* for its April 21, 1988 issue: "Those who doubt the sincerity and the willingness of Israel to make sacrifices . . . to achieve peace should put Israel to the test . . . . Did this government or any other government [of Israel] ever get put to the test and then not live up to its responsibility?"

MYTH

"The PLO did accept Resolution 242; Israel and the United States are the real rejectionists, refusing to take the organization at its word."

FACT

Over the years occasional press accounts report that the PLO indeed is almost ready to endorse 242, is about to recognize Israel, has just renounced violence or otherwise qualified for diplomatic acceptance. Close examination always shows otherwise. For example:

On Sept. 7, 1987, Arafat met with Communist Knesset members Charlie Biton and Tawfik Zayyad, and Gen. Matti Peled (Ret.) and Muhammad Miari of the far-left but non-Communist Progressive List for Peace. According to one Israeli news report, Arafat supposedly called for a UN-sponsored conference on the Middle East "on the basis of international legality as well as the international resolutions approved by the UN relevant to the Palestinian cause and the Middle East crisis, including Resolutions 242 and 338."

But when the PLO says *all* relevant U.N. resolutions, it means more than 242 and 338. Such comprehensiveness opens the door to General Assembly resolutions which virtually negate the two Security Council resolutions and to measures which call for UN members to sever ties with Israel, which brand Zionism itself an outlaw ideology and Israel a pariah state.

As just one example among many, there is General Assembly Resolution 3236, of Nov. 22, 1974, which, among other things, "reaffirms the inalienable rights of the Palestinian people in Palestine, including: the right to self-determination without external interference; . . . the inalienable right of Palestinians to return to their homes and property from which they have been displaced and uprooted, and calls for their return; [and] emphasizes that full respect for and the realization of these inalienable rights of the Palestinian people are indispensable for the solution of the question of Palestine . . . "

Of course, in UN General Assembly parlance, the "question of Palestine" is the question of Israel; Resolution 3236, totally unbalanced, ignores the inalienable rights of the Jewish people, accepts the Arab rejectionist view of the origins of the conflict, and, in essence, calls for the dismantling of Israel.

And when the PLO cites international legality, it can mean the 1947 UN partition plan, calling for a Jewish statelet in only eastern Galilee, the coastal plain and the Negev, or even the PLO charter, which describes the creation of Israel as "fundamentally null and void, whatever time as elapsed . . ."

At one point Arafat's Sept. 1987 "offer" was referred to as a three-point document, at another, as only spoken remarks. Biton said Arafat wanted an end to hostilities, mutual recognition, and a suspension of the building of Jewish settlements in the territories. But at the time Israel already recognized, in the Camp David Accords, the "legitimate rights" of Palestinian Arabs; it did not recognize the legitimacy of the PLO. Likewise, it was not engaged in hostilities against the Palestinian Arabs, but was defending itself against PLO terrorism. And since the settlements are not illegal *per se* under international law, Arafat, as usual, was offering nothing.

The adventure of Biton et al. resembled that of former Rep. Paul McCloskey (R-Calif.), who in a 1982 Beirut encounter with Arafat, emerged waving a scrap of paper. McCloskey said that Arafat had signed a statement accepting "all UN resolutions relevant to the Palestinian question." Then Arafat's headquarters was under siege by Israeli troops. When McCloskey met with Biton and the other Knesset members, he may have been trying to thwart U.S. efforts to close down the two PLO offices in the United States.

Israeli Foreign Minister Peres noted that "Arafat loves to play word games occasionally, especially when he sees some Israeli leftists and wants to give them something for the road." *Ma'ariv* described the affair this way: "The message is not credible, the messengers are unimportant and the sender is . . . a mass murderer."

MYTH

"Arafat and the mainstream PLO are relative moderates. Israel and the United States should do business with them."

FACT

A report by veteran correspondent Daniel Schorr on National Public Radio's "All Things Considered," on Oct. 17, 1985, provides a case study refuting such claims:

"According to intelligence sources, Yasir Arafat was overheard ordering leaders of his delegation in London to renege on a statement renouncing violence. He also justified the plan that went awry in the hijacking of the Italian cruise liner. And he indicated a decision to return to a policy of armed struggle.

"Partial transcripts of telephone conversations last weekend between Arafat and two Palestinians in London, Mohammed Milhem and Anglican Bishop Elias Khoury, are understood to be in the hands of the Reagan Administration.

"A statement recognizing Israel's right to exist and supporting a peaceful settlement had been agreed upon and was supposed to be signed before a meeting between a joint Jordanian-Palestinian delegation and British officials headed by Foreign Secretary Geoffrey Howe.

"On the telephone, according to our sources, the leaders of the Palestinian delegation appeared to be astounded when Arafat ordered them not to sign the statement. Bishop Khoury said this would jeopardize the meeting with Howe. Arafat replied that there was no need to worry—that sooner or later the British would be obliged to deal with the PLO.

"Arafat then said that the PLO was going back to its policy of armed struggle that had been pursued in the early 1970's. [That was the period after the PLO's expulsion from Jordan, a particularly violent time that included the assault of the so-called "Black September" on the Israeli team at the Munich Olympic Games.]

"Then Arafat referred to the botched attempt to infiltrate armed men into an Israeli port aboard the Achille Lauro. He is quoted as saying, 'This act was important. Its objective was to make the world tremble before the PLO fighters. I predicted that if our aspirations were ignored, the volcano would erupt. And that has happened.'

"This is the first information directly linking Arafat to the hijacking episode, and it suggests that it was part of a basic policy shift.

"Also intercepted, intelligence sources say, was a message in Arafat's name ordering PLO offices around the world to say that cancellation of the London meeting had resulted from British efforts to make last-minute changes in the working of the agreed statement. That has been flatly denied by King Hussein, to whom Prime Minister Thatcher originally suggested such a meeting during her visit to Jordan a month ago."

MYTH

"Israel's deportation of some Palestinian Arabs during the uprising showed it did not want to talk to anyone on the other side."

FACT

Over the past decade Israeli leaders from both the Likud bloc and the Labor Party made it clear that they were ready to talk to any Palestinian Arab leaders who were not members of the PLO or otherwise advocates of violence against Israel. Even during the height of the uprising, top military officials, including Defense Minister Yitzhak Rabin, in charge of the territories, and Gen. Amram Mitzna, commander of the West Bank, insisted that only a political solution would suffice in the long run.

But as journalist Lally Weymouth noted in the *Washington Post*, May 29, 1988: "If there is ever to be a peace settlement, the Palestinians will have to be clear—more than during the *intifada*—what the fighting is about. If it's about the existence of Israel, then there will be nothing to talk about. If it's about the size of the Israeli state, then both sides will have to compromise, as neither can impose a solution on the other.

"The present deadlock was spelled out in a story told by an Israeli official about the *intifada*: 'A 17-year-old Palestinian boy climbed on a high-voltage wire to put up a PLO flag and was electrocuted. He's brave enough to go on the high voltage and hang the flag, but he's not brave enough to talk to us. This is their tragedy. They are not afraid of our bullets but of the PLO leadership that doesn't allow them to talk to us.'"

An episode seen by many Americans illustrated the problem. Three Palestinian Arab intellectuals participated in a debate broadcast live from Jerusalem on ABC Television's "Nightline" program in late April 1988. They insisted that a low but symbolic wall be placed between them and the four

Israeli Knesset members on the stage. The wall, the avoidance by the Palestinian panelists of eye contact with the Israelis, and their refusal to shake hands with panelist Chaim Ramon, a Labor Party Knesset member, epitomized the difficulty facing Israel—and the United States—in finding Palestinian Arab interlocutors.

MYTH

"Israel hoped the peace process would fail. It really wanted to expel all the Palestinan Arabs from the West Bank to Jordan."

FACT

Top officials in the coalition government—from both the Labor Party and the Likud bloc—insisted repeatedly that the real solution had to be political, not military. They stated publicly, as did leading military officers, that until a political settlement was reached, the potential for more demonstrations and riots would continue to exist. But they also pointed out that they could not make peace unilaterally. An Arab negotiating partner or partners—Palestinian, Jordanian or Syrian—was necessary which would recognize Israel, its legitimacy and national, religious and security claims.

It did appear that the prolonged 1988 uprising drove Israeli public opinion to a harder line; in the circumstances, that was to be expected. Yet at the same time that one public opinion poll showed sentiment for a mass population transfer topping 50%, a second indicated that more than 60% still favored a trade of at least some of the territories for peace. The point was that Israeli public opinion in the first half of 1988 was still in flux, responding as in any democratic society to events, and, like the Israeli body politic in 1977 on the eve of Anwar Sadat's visit, still ready to react positively to a positive offer from the other side.

Meanwhile, uprising leaflet number 18, the first to put forward a political program, appeared at the end of May. It demanded the withdrawal of the Israeli army, the release of Palestinian Arab detainees, the return of deported Palestinians, cancellation of special military and civil regulations issued during the uprising, the end of certain economic restrictions and free elections in the territories. These steps would lead to "the right of return, to self-determination and the right to establish our independent state." In essence, leaflet 18 was restating the basic PLO program as enshrined by UN General Assembly Resolution 3236 (1974). As noted previously, the right to return pertained to Israel inside the pre-1967 green line; the leaflet did not address itself to Israel at all.

In its 1948 Declaration of Independence, Israel had tried to initiate a peace process: "We extend our hand to all neighboring states and their peoples in an offer of peace and good neighborliness, and appeal to them to establish bonds of cooperation and mutual help with the sovereign Jewish people settled in its own land. The State of Israel is prepared to do its share in a common effort for the advancement of the entire Middle East." In 1948 the Arabs chose war. Forty years later only Egypt had chosen peace; Israel, each of whose successive governments reiterated the offer of the Declaration, was still waiting for the rest of its neighbors.

21

Oil and Saudi Arabia

MYTH

"The United States is critically dependent on Saudi Arabia for oil."

FACT

In 1987, 11% of all U.S. oil imports originated in Saudi Arabia. This figure represented less than 1.5% of total energy consumption in the United States.

In that year Saudi Arabia was third on the list of countries from which the United States imported oil, behind non-OPEC Canada and non-Arab OPEC member Venezuela. In 1980, the Saudis ranked first among America's suppliers of imported oil; they dropped to ninth in 1984 before creeping back up the list.

MYTH

"The United States must accommodate Saudi Arabia to guarantee the supply of oil on which it depends so heavily."

FACT

Saudi Arabia is more dependent on the United States than the United States is on Saudi Arabia. U.S. sales of arms, military construction and non-military goods; markets for Saudi oil; and repositories for Saudi investments and American diplomatic and military backing in the face of Iranian threats make the Washington connection more important to Riyadh than the Riyadh connection is to Washington.

In 1981, Saudi Arabia purchased almost $16 billion worth of U.S. arms and military construction, including the $8.5 billion AWACS package. That total made it America's single largest military customer. In 1986, the Saudis purchased $730.5 million and in 1987, $636.5 million worth of U.S. weapons and military construction.

Some 15,000 Americans are living and working in Saudi Arabia, according to what the State Department calls a "very rough" estimate. The number is down considerably from the boom years of the early 1980's.

The Saudis put much of their petrodollar profits into the United States—not out of friendship but out of recognition that America is a stable place for investments.

As noted above, Americans depend on the kingdom for less than 1.5% of their total energy needs. Diversification of imports, conservation measures and more use of alternative sources of energy have helped decrease U.S. reliance on Saudi oil.

RANK ORDER OF OIL EXPORTERS

1980	Average hundred of thousands b/d	1987	Average hundreds of thousands b/d
1) Saudi Arabia*	1,261	1) Canada	837
2) Nigeria*	857	2) Venezuela*	768
3) Libya*	554	3) Saudi Arabia*	747
4) Mexico	533	4) Mexico	645
5) Algeria*	488	5) Nigeria*	530
6) Venezuela*	481	6) United Kingdom	349
7) Canada	455	7) Algeria*	284
8) Virgin Islands	388	8) Indonesia*	277
9) Indonesia*	348	9) Virgin Islands	272
10) Netherlands Antilles	225	10) Other OPEC**	231

*OPEC members
b/d = barrels per day
**Educador, Gabon, Iraq, Kuwait, and Qatar.
(Source: Dept. of Energy, Energy Information Adm.)

MYTH

"OPEC pricing policies were related to the Arab-Israeli conflict and the eightfold increase in prices after 1973 was a direct result of the Yom Kippur War."

FACT

The process by which OPEC was able to dramatically increase prices began in 1971, when Libya insisted on re-negotiating contracts with American oil companies. The 1973 oil embargo merely provided the pretext for the price explosion. At that time the effort to increase prices was pressed vigorously by Venezuela and Iran, two non-Arab OPEC producers. Indeed, approximately half of OPEC's members are non-Arab with little direct interest in the Arab-Israel conflict.

Following the 1973-1974 Arab oil embargo, it was discovered that two of the most radical Arab nations, Iraq and Libya, had never ceased selling oil to the West.

SOURCES OF UNITED STATES ENERGY

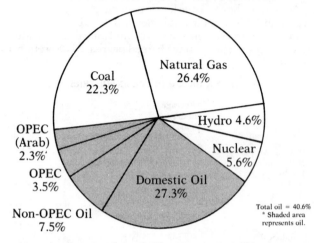

Total oil = 40.6%
* Shaded area represents oil.

Figures represent estimated percentage of sources for U.S. energy consumption in 1986.

Source: U.S. Department of Energy

MYTH

"Saudi Arabia is a close ally of the United States and vital to U.S. plans for the defense of the Persian Gulf."

FACT

Saudi Arabia itself denies the appearance of a close alliance with the United States, afraid that anything resembling a public embrace would undermine either its Arab nationalist or Islamic leadership credentials. In 1987 and 1988 it did not openly support the large U.S. naval presence in the Persian Gulf region.

Reagan Administration officials, asked by Congress to outline Saudi helpfulness with the reflagging of Kuwaiti tankers and their protection by the U.S. Navy, were reduced to generalities about "behind-the-scenes" assistance as requested in certain instances. Although it is by far the largest and most important country in the six-nation Gulf Cooperation Council (GCC), Saudi Arabia trailed both Bahrain and Oman in its willingness to assist publicly the United States.

In 1980, then Crown Prince Fahd told *Al Hawadess*, "We are not compelled to be friends of the Americans. There are many doors wide open to us, be it on the military, technological or economic level. . . . We can easily replace the Americans."

In Sept. 1981, Prince Khaled ibn Sultan, the director of planning of the Saudi Air Defense Command, told the Los Angeles World Affairs Council that Saudi Arabia would consider purchasing arms from the Soviet Union. "To protect ourselves, our lands and our heritage," the prince said, "we are willing to deal with the devil himself if it is in our best national interests."

Saudi "national interests" have led in the past decade to threats against the United States for attempting to fill the U.S. Strategic Petroleum Reserve; pressure against Oman to reverse a decision permitting U.S. use of a base on the Arabian Peninsula; attempts to sabotage U.S. peace efforts as embodied in the Camp David Accords; expulsion of the CIA station chief in Saudi Arabia; spurning an American request to donate $300 million to Afghan refugees in Pakistan; pressure on Washington to recall Ambassador Hume Horan in 1988, apparently, in part, because he spoke Arabic too well and had non-official sources of information in the Kingdom; the secret acquisition the same year of Chinese-built East Wind intermediate-range ballistic missiles and refusal to grant U.S. officials permission to inspect the missile sites after pledging that the missiles would not carry nuclear warheads; refusal to dispatch its own minesweepers to help in the U.S.-Western European patrols of the Persian Gulf; and lavish subsidies to the PLO. (Officially Saudi Arabia gives the PLO $96 million annually. But with reported private, direct payments by members of the royal family to individual PLO faction leaders, the total probably is much more.) The Saudis continued to rely on air defense information from American-built and supported AWACS planes, and continued to deny America bases or support facilities.

MYTH

"Saudi Arabia is an Arab moderate, interested in peace with Israel."

251

FACT

Saudi Arabia has always been, in word and deed, one of the most dedicated foes of Israel's existence. In 1948 and again in 1973, Saudi Arabia contributed troops to front-line Arab states at war with Israel. Saudi leaders have frequently pledged their wealth, arms and soldiers to Arab efforts to eradicate Israel.

The late Saudi King Khalid proclaimed on Jan. 28, 1981, "The Moslem nation has asserted anew that the liberation of holy Jerusalem from the claws of Zionism is a must."

Saudi King Fahd, speaking as Crown Prince, stated on May 18, 1979, "We would spare no effort to force Egypt's President Anwar Sadat to renounce his newly signed peace treaty with Israel."

"We will never recognize Israel," Fahd vowed to *Al Hawadess* in 1977. "We don't have to recognize anyone we don't want to recognize."

In a 1977 interview, Foreign Minister Saud ibn Faisal warned, "Not only will Saudi Arabia sacrifice its oil and financial resources, but also the blood of its sons."

This theme was repeated by then-Saudi Oil Minister

Anwar Sadat is portrayed stabbing the Arab world. His sword says "Camp David." —From the Saudi newspaper *Al Riyadh*, August 30, 1980

252

Sheik Yamani, usually perceived in the Western world as urbane and moderate. He vowed in Feb. 1981, "We are prepared to use all that we have, even to fight and shed our blood, in order to liberate Jerusalem and Palestine."

According to Saudi state television on Oct. 19, 1985, Defense Minister Sultan Abd al-Aziz asserted that "the truth is that anything praised by the Jews is despised, and anything that is abused by the Jews and their organizations is precious." A few months earlier the Saudi's U.N. representative, Samir Shihabi, stated that "Hitler preceded [Israelis] with his Nazi destructive machinery in the ways of brutality and murder, collectively and individually, and even though they have surpassed them now, his end was inevitable and their end will be inevitable, if the world does not stop them before it is too late" (*New York Times*, March 13, 1985).

In 1987 Saudi Arabia spent between $17 billion to $18 billion on military expansion—a sum equal to about 75% of Israel's gross national product. It faced a real threat from Iran and a potential one from Iraq which, before its invasion of Iran in 1980, had glanced acquisitively at Kuwait, on the border between Saudi Arabia and Iraq. Yet in Feb. of that year the *Washington Post* reported that Saudi officials publicly insisted the main target of their strategic planning was Israel; also in 1987 some Saudi officials echoed King Fahd's 1986 exhortation to "the Moslems to launch *jihad* and to use all their capabilities to restore Moslem Palestine and the holy al-Aqsa mosque from the Zionist usurpers and aggressors": they lamented the Mecca riots, averring that Muslims instead should join together to "liberate" Jerusalem.

Meanwhile, Saudi Arabia has allowed the PLO to fight Israel on its behalf. And some American-made explosives, ammunition and small arms supplied to the kingdom were seized by Israeli forces in Lebanon in 1982. (Transfer of American-provided weapons from a second party to a terrorist organization violates U.S. law.)

MYTH

"The Saudi call for jihad (holy war) against Israel should not be taken literally as 'armed combat.' The term has a broader meaning and is used to put maximum emotional emphasis on the Saudi demand for Israeli withdrawal."

FACT

The above definition of *jihad* actually was offered by the Department of State during the 1981 AWACS debate.

Unfortunately, Saudi Arabia's own leaders dispute that interpretation. On Sept. 17, 1980, King Fahd told the Riyadh Radio: "What is meant by a *jihad* is a united, comprehensive, integrated Arab-Islamic confrontation in which we place all our resources and our spiritual, cultural, political, material and *military potentials* in a long and untiring *jihad*." (Emphasis added.)

MYTH

"Saudi Arabia devotes a high percentage of its budget to foreign assistance, particularly to pro-Western countries like Morocco, Sudan and Jordan."

FACT

Foreign assistance from Saudi Arabia—and from Arab oil producers in general—barely compensated poor third world nations for the exorbitant oil prices they were forced to pay before the 1985 price collapse. As reported by the London *Times* (June 24, 1981), many African delegations at the Organization of African Unity meeting complained that "they have suffered the economic effects of soaring oil prices with what they regard as only meager compensatory aid from the Arab states." Arab oil producers pledged $1.46 billion to African countries at the 1977 Afro-Arab summit meeting in Cairo. Saudi Arabia was to provide the lion's share. But in 1983, for example, only $62 million had been deposited in the African Development Fund or the Arab Bank for Economic Development in Africa.

Saudi Arabia also gives billions of dollars to pro-Soviet Syria, radical Iraq and the PLO terrorists. Saudi assistance to Egypt was vitally important to that poor country but was cut off after Anwar Sadat journeyed to Jerusalem to make peace with Israel. Saudi Arabia has played a pivotal role in funding and sustaining the "rejectionist front" of Arab nations opposed to peace with Israel.

Saudi Arabian "foreign aid" apparently can take other forms. Saudi billionaire oil and arms trader Adnan Khashoggi said in an interview on ABC TV on Dec. 11, 1986 that he advanced $1 million to help finance the first arms shipment in the U.S.-Iran-*Contra* arms scandal and put up $4

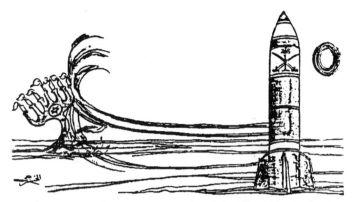

Saudi sentiment—This cartoon appeared in the Saudi Arabian newspaper Al-Jazira and was reprinted in the Apr. 27, 1988 edition of Yediot Achronot, an Israelli daily. It shows the "wind" from a Saudi Chinese-built "East Wind" intermediate-range ballistic missile blowing over a menorah bearing the Star of David.

million for the second shipment. According to the Tower Commission, which investigated the affair, a foreign official [reportedly Saudi King Fahd] donated $1 million to $2 million monthly from July 1984 to April 1985 for covert financing for the *Contras*. Saudi Arabia denied aiding the Nicaraguan rebels. But the *New York Times* reported on Feb. 4, 1987 that the contribution may have been part of a 1981 secret agreement between Riyadh and Washington "to aid anti-communist resistance groups around the world as part of the arrangement allowing them [the Saudis] to buy sophisticated American AWACS radar planes, according to United States officials and others familiar with the deal."

MYTH

"The major American oil companies take no position on the Arab-Israel conflict."

FACT

Egypt's President Sadat was able to persuade the late Saudi King Faisal to threaten to withhold oil from the West, in order to exploit for political advantage the growing dependence of the industrialized West on Arab oil. The tactic was effective: soon the major American oil companies—

255

ARAMCO partners—threw their support to the Arab cause in public and private efforts to weaken U.S. support for Israel.

According to a 1974 report of the Senate Foreign Relations Subcommittee on Multinational Corporations, the ARAMCO consortium—Exxon, Mobil, Texaco and SOCAL—attempted to block America's emergency airlift to Israel. During the war the companies cooperated closely with Saudi Arabia to deny oil and fuel to the U.S. Navy.

On other occasions, the major oil firms have advocated the positions of the Arab countries, particularly Saudi Arabia. The major oil companies vigorously lobbied Congress on behalf of the sale of F-15 fighter-bombers in 1978 and AWACS aircraft in 1981. Together with Saudi foreign agents, these corporations enlisted many other American corporations to lobby on the Saudis' behalf.

According to author Hoag Levins (*Arab Reach: The Secret War Against Israel*), Saudi Arabia has a powerful lobby in the United States. "In 1981, more than 700 of America's largest corporations in 42 states held contracts for approximately $35 billion worth of business with Saudi Arabia," Levins wrote. "And each of these corporations . . . had hundreds of subcontractors and vendors equally dependent on maintaining the good graces of Moslem leaders whose countries now collectively represent the single richest market in the world."

Both SOCAL and Mobil corporations placed advertisements in major American newspapers urging a more pro-Arab U.S. foreign policy.

The Saudis often attack what they claim is the excessive influence of Israel's supporters in the United States. But in his 1985 book, *The American House of Saud: The Secret Petrodollar Connection*, investigative journalist Steve Emerson turned that claim upside down. After detailing many of the ties between Saudi Arabia and U.S. businesses, universities, lobbyists and former high-ranking government officials, he concluded: "The breadth and scope of the petrodollar impact is beyond any legal remedy. With so many corporations, institutions, and individuals thirsting after—and receiving—oil money, petrodollar influence is ubiquitous in American society. The result is the appearance of widespread, spontaneous support for the policies of Saudi Arabia and other Arab oil producers by American institutions ranging from universities to the Congress. The

256

proliferation of vested ties has allowed special interests to be confused with national interests.

"Never before in American history has any foreign economic power been as successful as Saudi Arabia in reaching and cultivating powerful supporters all across the country. The Saudis have discovered that one quintessential American weakness, the love of money, and the petrodollar connection has become diffused throughout the United States."

MYTH

"Saudi Arabia has been a price moderate within OPEC. It has priced its crude oil well below the general OPEC level in order to protect Western economies. This explains why Saudi Arabia engineered the glut in the world oil market in the first half of 1982."

FACT

Saudi oil price and production policies have been motivated by only one factor: Saudi Arabia's own economic interest. Saudi Arabia's long-term interests are based on the steady but slow sale of its vast oil reserves. If the price of oil were to rise too high, it would force energy consumers to develop alternate sources of fuel.

This economic fact of life was articulated by Saudi Arabia's own Petroleum Minister Ahmed Zaki Yamani in a lecture to the Saudi University of Petroleum and Minerals in early 1981.

In 1981, Saudi Arabia's Petroleum Minister, Ahmed Zaki Yamani told a Saudi university audience:

"If we were to force the Western countries to invest large sums of money in alternative energy resources, it would take seven to 10 years to bring about some results of these investments, which would reduce oil demand to a level that would affect Saudi Arabia, which at that time would not find enough markets to sell its oil to meet its economic demands. . . .

"Other countries have a clear interest in obtaining the largest possible income in dollars for each barrel for the short period it can sell for. . . . The interest of the Kingdom of Saudi Arabia is that we extend the life of oil to the largest extent possible . . ."

Yamani's efforts to arrange production cutbacks among OPEC members to stem falling world oil prices in Oct., 1984 highlighted Saudi Arabia's self-interest at work. "We are prepared to reduce [production] considerably from where we are now. We will make sure that the price goes back up," he stated.

Support by the kingdom for a tighter version of production quotas for 1986 petroleum markets stemmed from the same calculation of Saudi self-interest. Uncharacteristically, cartel members stuck to the newer quotas—more or less. They succeeded, at least temporarily. They manipulated world spot market prices for crude oil—which had plunged to $10 a barrel briefly in 1985—to $16.77 in Jan. 1988.

Yamani himself fell victim to calculations of national interest. In 1985, Saudi Arabia, worried about Khomeini's Islamic revolution and Iranian attacks on Arab tankers, tried to improve relations with Iran. The Iranians—in need of cash for the war with Iraq—were among the leaders of an OPEC faction which demanded both higher prices and larger production quotas. The *Wall Street Journal* reported on Dec. 29, 1986 that after direct talks between Saudi King Fahd and the Iranian oil minister, Yamani—engineer of an earlier price war—was fired. The paper quoted "a well-placed Saudi official" as summing up Saudi actions this way: "As usual, our policy was appeasement. Whenever we are called upon to show strength, we do it in such a way that it dilutes the impact of our action."

22

The Arms Balance

MYTH

"The threat from Israel and the withdrawal of the United States' offer to build the Aswan Dam drove Egypt to seek arms from the Soviet Union in 1955. This started the Middle East arms race."

FACT

Nasser turned to the Soviet Union in 1955 in anger because the United States had armed Iraq, Egypt's hated rival, and promoted the Baghdad Pact. Nasser always opposed any defense alliance with the West.

Egypt began to get Soviet arms in 1955. The United States, hoping to maintain a degree of influence in Egypt and to induce Nasser to reduce his arms acquisitions, offered to build the Aswan Dam. But Nasser increased his arms orders and spurned a U.S. peace initiative. Egypt had embarked on a policy of "neutralism," which meant that Nasser intended to get aid from both East and West if he could, while maintaining his freedom to attack the West and assist Soviet efforts to penetrate the Arab and Afro-Asian worlds. For this, and because Nasser became increasingly hostile to the West, the United States withdrew the Aswan offer. Egypt then nationalized the Suez Canal.

Immediately after Nasser made his 1955 arms deal, Israel appealed to the United States—not for a *gift* of arms, but for their *purchase*.

The United States recognized the need to maintain an arms balance, but it referred Israel to France and other European suppliers. It was not until 1962 that the United States agreed to sell Israel its first American equipment, the Hawk anti-aircraft missile.

MYTH

"The Arab states have had to keep pace with an Israeli-led arms race."

FACT

Egypt got the Soviet IL-28 bomber in 1955. It was not until 1958 that France provided Israel with a squadron of comparable Sud Vautour twin-jet tactical bombers.

Egypt got the MiG-17 in 1957. Israel received the comparable Super Mystere in 1959. Egypt had submarines in 1957; Israel in 1959. After the Egyptians obtained the MiG-21, the Israelis ordered the Dassault Mirage III supersonic interceptor and fighter-bomber.

Egypt received ground-to-air missiles—the SA-2—two years before Israel obtained Hawk missiles from the United States in 1962. Later, and reluctantly, Washington agreed to sell Israel Patton tanks—at first via West Germany. And in 1966, the United States approved the sale of 48 A-4 Skyhawk bombers.

Between 1955 and 1967, it was estimated that Egypt received more than $1 billion worth of Soviet arms, another $1 billion in Soviet economic aid and more than $650 million in economic assistance from Eastern Europe and China.

The arms were supplied at knock-down prices—$600,000 per MiG—in exchange for cotton and with long-term, cheap-money credits. Israel had to pay much more, plus interest, for comparable planes.

MYTH

"Israel enjoys military superiority over the Arab states and the gap is widening in its favor."

FACT

Israel cannot seek quantitative military superiority over its Arab neighbors. Rather, it strives for deterrence against future Arab aggression and, if deterrence fails, to be able to defend itself. While Israel has been able to defend itself, the long-range trend may favor the Arab states.

Israel's adversaries continue to purchase massive quantities of sophisticated armaments from the Soviet Union as well as from the United States, Great Britain, France and other Western nations. Since 1973, there have been major arms sales to Arab countries from the West and the Soviet Union. Conservative estimates have placed the value of these sales at more than $154 billion (see chart). Most of these sales have been financed by the Arab oil-producing states, which had raised oil prices eight-fold from the 1973 war to 1984.

Major Military Acquisitions by the Arab States Since 1973
(Delivered or on order)

Country	Amount	Military Items
Syria	$22 billion	MiG-21 and MiG-23 fighter-bombers; MiG-25 interceptors; Su-7, Su-17 and Su-20 attack aircraft; MiG-27 fighter-bombers, MiG-29 advanced fighter-bombers; Sepal SS-C-3 shore-to-shore missiles; T-55, T-62, T-72, and T-80 tanks; SA-2, SA-3, SA-5, SA-6, SA-7, SA-8, SA-9, SA-11, and SA-13 surface-to-air missiles; ZSU-23-4 anti-aircraft missiles; Mi-6, Mi-8, Mi-24, Ka-25, Gazelle, Super Frelon, and AB-212 helicopters; BTR-50, BTR-60, and BMP armored personnel carriers; FROG, SCUD, and SS-21 surface-to-surface missiles; AT-3 Sagger, AT-4 Spigot, Milan, and HOT anti-tank missiles; SAU-122 and SAU-152 self-propelled artillery; OSA and KOMAR missile patrol boats; Petya class frigates; Nanuchka II corvettes, ROMEO class submarines.
Iraq	$48 billion +	Mirage F-1, MiG-21, MiG-23, and MiG-27 fighter-bombers; F-6, F-7, and MiG-25 interceptors; Super Etendard, Su-7, and Su-20 attack planes; Tu-22 bombers; MPS air-to-ground missiles; Alouette III, Super Frelon, Gazelle, Lynx, Puma, Mi-6, Mi-8, Mi-24, AS-61TS, AB-212, and BO-105 helicopters; SA-8 surface-to-air missiles; T-55, T-62, T-72, Type-69, and AMX-30 tanks; BTR-60, BMP, Panhard M-3, and EE-11 Urutu armored personnel carriers; BRDM, JPz SK-105, VCR-TH, EE-3 Jaraca, EE-9 Cascavel, ERC-90, and FUG-70 light armored vehicles; HOT, Swingfire, SS-11, and Sagger anti-tank missiles; SCUD and FROG surface-to-surface missiles; Al-Hussein and Al-Abbas surface-to-surface missiles; SAU-122, SAU-152, and GCT 155 self-propelled artillery; Astros II rocket launchers; OSA-2 missile patrol boats; Lupo frigates; Wadi class corvettes; Exocet anti-ship missiles
Jordan	$ 5.4 billion	Mirage F-1, F-5E/F, F-5A/B, and Mirage 2000 fighter-bombers; Tornado fighter-bombers; SA-8, Redeye, and Hawk surface-to-air missiles; Vulcan and ZSU-23-4 self-propelled anti-aircraft guns; AH-1 Cobra, S-76, helicopters; M-48, M-60, and Khalid tanks; M-113 armored personnel carriers; GHN-45, M-110, and M-109 self-propelled artillery; TOW and DRAGON anti-tank missiles

Kuwait	$ 3.0 billion	Mirage F-1 fighter-bombers; A-4 Skyhawk attack planes; Super Puma, Puma, and Gazelle helicopters; Amoun anti-aircraft systems; Hawkeye missiles; SA-7 and Improved HAWK surface-to-air missiles; Vickers and Chieftain tanks; M-901 and Scorpion light armored vehicles; M-113 armored personnel carriers; HOT and TOW anti-tank missiles; FROG surface-to-surface missiles; TNC-47 and FPB-57 missile patrol boats; SRN-6 hovercraft; Exocet anti-ship missiles
Libya	$24.3 billion	Mirage F-1, MiG-21, MiG-23, and MiG-25 interceptors and fighter-bombers; Tu-22 bombers; Su-20 and J-1 Jastreb attack aircraft; L-29 Albatros aircraft; A-109, CH-47, Mi-8, Mi-14, and Mi-24 helicopters; Crotale, SA-2, SA-3, SA-6, and SA-9 surface-to-air missiles; ZSU-23-4 anti-aircraft guns; T-55, T-62, T-72, and OF-40 tanks; BRDM-2 and EE-9 Cascavel armored cars; M-113A1, BMP, EE-11 Urutu, Fiat 6614, BTR-50, BTR-60, OT-62, and OT-64 armored personnel carriers; SAU-122, SAU-152, Palmaria 155mm, and M-109 self-propelled artillery; Assad and Nanuchka corvettes; OSA-2 and La Combattante II missile patrol boats; patrol boats; Foxtrot-class submarines; SS-N-2 Styx and OTOMAT anti-ship missiles
Saudi Arabia	$34 billion	F-15 and F-5E fighter-bombers; Tornado IDS and ADU fighter-bombers; E-3A Sentry & Airborne Warning and Control System (AWACS); RF-5E reconnaissance aircraft; Atlantic NG maritime patrol aircraft; M-2/M-3 Bradley IFV's; Osario tanks; Astros II rocket launchers; Maverick air-to-ground missiles; AMX-30SA self-propelled anti-aircraft guns; Redeye, Shahine, Improved HAWK surface-to-air missiles; Stinger surface-to-air missiles; KV-107, AB-212, Dauphine 2 helicopters; AMX-30 and M-60 tanks; M-113, Panhard M-3, and AMX-10 armored personnel carriers; V-150, JPz SK-105, and VCC-1 light armored vehicles; TOW, Dragon, and HOT anti-tank missiles; FH-70 and GCT self-propelled artillery; M-992 artillery vehicles; F-2000 frigates; PCG-1 corvettes; GCC-1 class missile patrol boats; SRN-6 hovercraft; MSC 232 minsweepers; OTOMAT, AS-15 and Harpoon anti-ship missiles; East wind surface-to-surface missiles
Morocco	$ 2.4 billion	Mirage F-1 and F-5E fighter-bombers; OV-10 Bronco; Highes 500D, A-109, Gazelle, AB-206, Puma helicopters; C-130 transports; Maverick air-to-ground missiles; Aspide, Chaparral, SA-7, and Crotale surface-to-air missiles; AMX-13 DCA self-propelled anti-aircraft guns; M-60 tanks; M-48 tanks; T-55 tanks; EBR-75, AMX-10RC, RAM V1 armored cars; UR-416, Ratel, and Steyr 4K-7FA armored personnel carriers; Dragon, Milan, and TOW

262

		anti-tank missiles; Descubierta frigate; Lazaga class and PR-72 missile patrol boat; Exocet anti-ship missiles
Oman	$ 1.3 million	Jaguar and Hunter attack planes; Tornado fighter-bombers; Bell 214ST helicopters; Blowpipe surface-to-air missiles; M-60 and Chieftain tanks; TOW anti-tank missiles; Palmaria 155mm self-propelled artillery; Dhofar class missile patrol boats; Province class fast attack craft; logistics support ship; Exocet anti-ship missiles
United Arab Emirates	$ 3.6 billion	Mirage 2000 and Mirage 5 fighter-bombers; Alpha Jet and MB-326 attack planes; Super Puma, Gazelle, Lynx, and Puma helicopters; Skyguard anti-aircraft system; Rapier, Crotale, RBS-70, and Improved HAWK surface-to-air missiles; OF-40 and AMX-30 tanks; AMX-10 APC's; AML-90 armored cars; Scorpion light tanks; TOW anti-tank missiles; TNC-45 missile patrol boats; Exocet anti-ship missiles
TOTAL:	$144 billion	(Without Egypt. See following.)
Egypt	$10.8 billion	F-16, Mirage 2000, Mirage 5, MiG-23 fighter-bombers; MiG-21, F-7, and F-6 interceptors; F-4 fighters; ALPHA JET strike aircraft; E-2C Hawkeye airborne early warning aircraft; AS-61, helicopters; M-60, T-55, T-62, tanks; M-1 tanks; M-113 armored personnel carriers; TOW, Swingfire anti-tank missiles; Descubierta class frigates; ROMEO class submarines; Ramadan, October, and Cormoran class missile patrol boats; OTOMAT anti-ship missiles; Sakr 80 and Condor 3 surface-to-surface missiles.

Reagan Administration officials repeatedly pledged themselves to maintaining Israel's military "qualitative edge" over any likely combination of Arab enemies—even while attempting to justify new U.S. arms sales to Arab countries. But technical superiority is difficult to measure and dependent on a host of interrelated elements, including which countries are purchasing what quantities of certain weapons systems, how well their troops are trained to handle them, whether funds are available for maintenance and upgrading, whether such countries could operate in concert, morale, and so on. Further, most analysts agree that at some point quantitative superiority begins to cancel any qualitative edge.

In Aug., 1987 for example, senior administration officials told the Senate Foreign Relations Committee, in a closed door session, that not only did Israel hold a military edge over potential Arab enemies, but that the gap was growing in Israel's favor. However, a former intelligence analyst familiar with the testimony told reporters afterward that the administration's claim rested on the "extrapolation fallacy." That is, projecting current trends indefinitely into an unchanging future. Such extrapolation, minimizing developments like Syria's acquisition of Soviet SCUD-B and SS-21 missiles, chemical weapons, and top-of-the-line MiG-29 fighter-bombers, always would show Israel's forces superior to Syria's, regardless of changing realities. Such a fallacy pointed to the Shah of Iran retaining power—less than two years before the return of Khomeini.

In fact, to maintain the military edge presumed to exist in 1987, Israel hoped to build a close-air-support fighter, the Lavi, but could not afford it. It needed to replace its three aging submarines—while Syria alone was acquiring six— and needed to modernize its missile and patrol boats, upgrade its armor corps, and restore cuts made in training, procurement and other areas because of the fight against inflation in the mid-1980's. Israel, the only country in the region to decrease military spending in real terms in the middle of the decade, must keep pace with Arab states which in recent years continued to buy tens of billions of dollars worth of advanced weaponry from both the communist bloc and Western nations.

MYTH

"In any future conflict, Israel will be facing only Syria. Other Arab involvement is of little or no consequence."

FACT

Even the seriousness of a "one-front" war against Syria should not be minimized. Since 1983, Syria has embarked on a massive Soviet-supplied military buildup, seeking what President Hafez Assad calls "strategic parity," the ability of his country to fight a war with Israel unassisted by other Arab states. The Syrian expansion has included not only a much larger, better equipped standing army, but the addition of highly accurate ground-to-ground missiles and a reported chemical weapons capability.

Yet it is unlikely that Israel will face only Syria in a future conflict. Nine Arab states gave their active support to Egypt and Syria during the Yom Kippur War, and many of them have vowed to support front-line states in the event of re-newed hostilities. And Egyptian Defense Minister Abdel Halim Abu Ghazallah has made contradictory statements about whether Egypt's inter-Arab defense commitments or its treaty with Israel would take precedence.

Jordan's King Hussein may be forced by other Arab states to commit his military in another war, and his forces have completed a post-1973 modernization and expansion. His army consists of at least four fully mechanized armored and infantry divisions equipped with late model M-60A3 and British-made Chieftain tanks, some of them transferred to Jordan from Iraq after their capture from Iran. Hussein has stepped up arms purchases, including mobile surface-to-air missiles (SAM's) from the Soviet Union. He also has ac-quired mobile anti-aircraft missiles, bridging equipment, and late model aircraft from European and Soviet sources.

Saudi Arabian pilots, flying U.S.-made F-5 interceptors, have participated in war games and aerial maneuvers in southern Syria on several occasions since the 1973 war. F-15 fighter-bombers, which Saudi Arabia began receiving in 1982, and AWACS received in 1986, also could be con-tributed to a new war effort. As a result, Saudi Arabia must be regarded as a direct military threat by Israel's military planners. In 1987, the Saudis themselves claimed that Is-rael remained their top strategic target.

In spring 1988, Israeli Defense Minister Yitzhak Rabin pointed out that if, after the Iraq-Iran war ended, the Iraqis sent half their tank corps to join Syria and Jordan, then Israel would face on its eastern front more tanks than NATO has deployed in Europe.

Israel has traditionally attempted to maintain a 1-to-3 balance of power *in favor* of the confrontation Arab states. Yet, it is likely that even this unfavorable ratio—which Israel can sustain only at a tremendous cost to its economy and society—will soon grow even larger. And, as the abso-lute number of Arab armaments increases, so does the magnitude of destruction which the Arab states are capable of inflicting on Israel. Even when weapons systems are re-placed on a one-to-one ratio, today's armaments are more accurate and several times more destructive than those of the 1967 Six-Day War.

To counter the imbalance, Israel had always been able to maintain a qualitative military advantage. In recent years, however, Western nations, particularly the United States, have been providing Arab states with the same state-of-the-art technology. Thus, today, Arab states have the same anti-aircraft missiles, guided munitions, tanks, radars, and aircraft that Israel possesses.

MYTH

"Israel will not make peace if the United States provides it with massive arms shipments."

FACT

It has been proven over the years that Arab states will not negotiate with a weakened Israel, but will rather maintain their military option. Similarly, Israel will never feel secure enough to make strategic concessions if it feels threatened. Thus, U.S. military aid to Israel promotes conditions in which peace can be discussed in the Middle East and is a vital ingredient of a successful American foreign policy. Just as the Soviet Union began serious talks with the United States over reducing intermediate-range ballistic missiles in Europe *after* NATO deployed such weapons, so are Arab countries prone to take a strong Israel seriously and consider negotiations with it.

MYTH

"The United States sale of F-15's, AWACS, M-60 battle tanks, Sidewinder and Maverick missiles to Saudi Arabia was justifiable as a reward for past moderation and an inducement for future moderation."

FACT

No justification exists for selling the Saudis the most sophisticated aircraft in the American arsenal. The least compelling reason is to reward Saudi moderation, since such moderation is illusory.

Despite predictions to the contrary, the Saudi government has yet to publicly endorse the peace treaty between Egypt and Israel or the Camp David peace frameworks. In fact, it joined radical Arab states in denouncing the accords and breaking relations with Egypt. The Saudis still refuse to recognize Israel's right to exist and acknowledge subsidizing the PLO at the rate of at least $96 million a year. The Saudis must also take primary responsibility for the

800% increase in oil prices from 1973 to 1982 which triggered world-wide inflation and recession.

Even if Saudi behavior were worthy of reward, other overriding considerations still make the sales unjustifiable. In addition to the threat which Saudi AWACS and F-15's represent to Israel, the planes could be a security problem for the United States as well. Security in Saudi Arabia is problematical; some of that country's aerospace technicians are Syrian, Iraqi and Palestinian aliens who could be Soviet sympathizers and who could facilitate the process of top secret technology's winding up in Russian hands. Radical forces in Saudi Arabia captured Mecca's Grand Mosque in Nov. 1979; they may be able to get their hands on U.S. arms.

More troublesome than unsympathetic ground technicians, however, is the prospect of the Saudi regime falling. According to London's *Economist,* (Dec. 9, 1978), "The stability of a pro-Western Saudi Arabia can no longer be taken for granted; for all the careful precautions the Saudi royal family has taken, a Saudi colonel as unknown as Libya's Colonel Qaddafi once was—and as geopolitically unstable as he now is—could emerge from the desert as suddenly as he did." Seven years later Saudi experts such as Dr. Jacob Goldberg of Tel Aviv University, then visiting Professor of Middle East studies at George Washington University, repeated warnings against taking Saudi internal stability for granted, noting that the ruling dynasty continued to feel the need to reassert its claims to legitimacy.

MYTH

"The Saudi AWACS will present no threat to Israel. AWACS close enough to Israel to monitor its aircraft would be vulnerable to being shot down by Israeli fighter aircraft."

FACT

Saudi leaders have vowed to use all their weapons— including AWACS—in the Arab struggle against Israel.

Saudi AWACS can be used to monitor all of Israel without unduly endangering themselves. The AWACS aircraft can fly well within Arab air space—accompanied by Arab fighter escort and protected by surface-to-air missiles deployed along the border—and still be able to detect any approaching interceptor. If the AWACS detected an Israeli aircraft, they could call on fighter support, turn away and fly at almost 600 miles per hour, or deploy electronic counter-measures.

AWACS in the Saudi arsenal may preclude Israel's ability to fight a preemptive war—still a vital option for a small country outgunned by the combined forces of its hostile neighbors. Special operations, such as the 1976 Entebbe rescue or the 1981 bombing of the Iraqi nuclear reactor, may become impossible.

MYTH

"Israeli arms supremacy does not guarantee stability. The bombing of Iraq's research reactor is proof that Israel seeks supremacy to terrorize other nations."

FACT

If there is an element of terror in the arms buildup in the Middle East, it is inherent in the development of nuclear, chemical and biological weapons by such nations as Libya, Syria and Iraq. Long before news photos in 1988 showed the corpses of Kurdish poison gas victims sprawled in Halabja—killed by Iraqi troops ostensibly fighting to defend the town against Iran—Israeli school children had begun to practice wearing gas masks in defensive drills.

Israeli nuclear policy is clear: it will never be the first nation to introduce nuclear weaponry into the region. But at the same time, Israel is determined to keep nuclear weaponry out of the hands of its sworn foes. Iraq, with its Ba'ath party radicalism and bloody record of aggression, represented a particularly dangerous threat to Israel as its nuclear reactor neared completion in June 1981.

There is little doubt among nuclear specialists that Iraq was embarked on a program to develop nuclear weapons. If any question existed, it was how soon Iraq's nuclear weapons could have been produced, with experts speculating that Iraq could have developed a nuclear bomb by 1983.

Oil-rich Iraq did not secure the nuclear facility for the generation of power. As explained by Dr. Don Trauger, associate director for Nuclear Engineering at the Oak Ridge, Tenn. nuclear center, "The Iraqi reactor was large enough to make weapons. The 70-megawatt research reactor was

268

larger than one would expect a country like Iraq would need." (*Associated Press*, June 11, 1981.)

Professor Kosta Tsipis of MIT told the *Los Angeles Times* on June 9, 1981, "You use a reactor like that either for metallurgical research or for making plutonium. Since there's no metallurgical industry in Iraq, it has to be for plutonium. . . . [This is] the cheapest way to produce plutonium. . . . This is a parsimonious way to make a bomb."

In June 1981, *Nucleonics Week* interviewed an unnamed "veteran non-partisan specialist intimately involved in international safeguard mechanisms . . . who has won widespread respect in the international nuclear community." According to the *Nucleonics Week* report, "Israel had reason not to be trusting of Iraq's [intentions]. The very idea that Iraq would engage in pure nuclear research on as grand a scale as indicated by its burgeoning nuclear complex is hard for this source to accept. Moreover, Iraq bought 300 tons of yellowcake, which has absolutely no capability to fabricate into any form for commercial use. In addition, Iraq is known to have purchased from Common Market countries about five tons of natural uranium processed for potential use as a breeding blanket and another five tons or so of depleted uranium also with blanket potential."

It should be recalled that the French government, spurred by the United States, attempted to replace weapons-grade uranium (93% enriched) with another fuel unsuitable for the production of weapons-grade material ("caramel"). Iraq rejected the substitute, demanding the weapons-grade fuel. The Socialist government which came to power in 1981 promised to rebuild the reactor, but the Iraq-Iran war and other problems prevented an agreement on doing so, the *Washington Post* reported on July 24, 1987.

The proliferation of ground-to-ground missiles throughout the region—in possession of Iraq and Iran, which used them against each other in the "war of the cities"; and in the possession of Syria, Saudi Arabia, Libya, Egypt—is in itself destabilizing. These newer missiles have greater range and accuracy. They necessitated Israel's reported development of the Jericho missile, not to achieve supremacy but to maintain deterrence if possible. The same is true of Israel's oft-reported nuclear weapons effort. Certainly a perceived lack of such capabilities on Israel's part would weaken deterrence and increase the likelihood of war by miscalculation on the Arab side.

269

MYTH

"Jordan requires new American military equipment for the formation of a rapid deployment force. Such a force will serve to protect U.S. interests in the Persian Gulf region."

FACT

For several years, the formation and funding of a Jordanian Rapid Deployment Force was a guarded secret in Washington. Made public in 1983, the plan would have established two brigades of elite Jordanian soldiers. They would have been provided by the United States with transport planes, shoulder-fired anti-aircraft missiles, communications equipment, tank transports, and infantry and river-crossing equipment.

Considering Jordan's repeated refusals to enter peace negotiations with Israel, the sale and others like it would have been reckless. Jordan's army twice used American equipment against Israel forces—in the 1967 and 1973 wars. Dozens of tanks sold by Washington to Amman by the Johnson Administration, on the promise they would remain east of the Jordan River, were captured by Israel in 1967. The bridging equipment and shoulder-fired missiles considered for sale in 1983 would have been particularly dangerous, giving Jordan the capability of launching a military operation against Israel across the Jordan River. Jordan later acquired such material from Britain, and by 1988 had reorganized its army into a small but well-armed, highly trained mobile force with great firepower.

MYTH

"Israel does not really want peace because its domestic arms industry is an important part of its economy. In fact, it is a leading weapons exporter, eager to sell to anyone."

FACT

The Iran-*Contra* scandal highlighted several U.S.-sanctioned Israeli shipments of arms to Iran (which apparently led to the 1985 release of Rev. Benjamin Weir). Afterwards, articles in major American newspapers picked up the Israel-as-merchant-of-death theme. Extravagant charges, some relying on pro-Arab sources, painted Israel as a major arms exporter.

In fact, the authoritative *World Military Expenditures and Arms Transfers, 1985* published by the U.S. Arms Control and Disarmament Agency, showed Israel's share of the global arms market as 0.77%. In comparison, the Soviet Union was first with 28.4% of all weapons exports from 1981 through 1984, the United States second with 24.6%, Great Britain third at 5.2%, West Germany fourth at 4.3% and Italy fifth with 2.9%.

The 1987 edition of the report ranked Israel 18th of 39 countries in arms exports, behind not only the traditional leaders but also Brazil, Sweden and Warsaw Pact countries among others. Despite allegations by some anti-Israel researchers that Israeli arms exports topped $2 billion, 1985 figures—the most recent available—put the total at $250 million.

Israel's arms industry, and its exports, grew from the imperative of survival, not from a commercial choice. Before the 1948 War of Independence, mandate-holder Great Britain slapped a weapons embargo on Palestine; another was imposed by the United States after the fighting broke out. These affected the beleaguered Jews much more than the attacking Arabs and put the survival of the new Jewish state in jeopardy.

In the late 1950's and early 1960's, responding to a Soviet decision to arm neighboring Arab states, Israel imported major weapons systems, including combat aircraft, from France. But in the wake of the 1967 war, De Gaulle, angry that Israel had complicated his diplomatic courtship of the Arabs and his efforts to settle the Algerian war, imposed a new embargo. He even refused to deliver material already paid for. Israel, still surrounded by hostile Arab states, determined to become as militarily self-sufficient as possible.

But in the 1970's and 1980's weapons systems jumped several generations in complexity, destructiveness, and cost. Selling Israeli-manufactured arms only to Israel's small military could not defray the expense of maintaining a technically advanced domestic arms production capability. Notwithstanding high levels of U.S. aid, Israeli arms exports became necessary. In one sense, such exports—to sustain Israel's own military production capacity—are a minor echo of the $150 billion-plus worth of arms the Arab world has imported from 1973 on (see chart above). For while its enemies can choose from many potential suppliers, Israel still faces a *de facto* embargo; only the United

States sells it any significant amount of military goods. The rest it must manufacture itself, or, in effect, unilaterally disarm.

Its domestic arms industry employs approximately 10% of Israel's work force. Israeli men must serve six weeks or more of active military duty a year into their 50's. And Israelis carry the highest tax rate in the free world. None of this is the result of a militaristic society.

It is because, as Conor Cruise O'Brien has written, "in Israel, the sense of siege, of an abiding threat to security, remains strong. Israelis felt, and with reason, that such acceptance as Israel had won—even from Egypt—was 'constrained acceptance.' Any serious weakening of Israel's military strength—whether due to domestic dissension, economic collapse, changes in military technology or the weakening of the tie with America—is thought of as likely to draw the whole Arab world in against Israel, and this time for Israel's destruction."

23

Arab Attitudes Toward Israel

With the *recent* exception of Egypt, the Arab states have never accepted Israel's right to exist. Statements by PLO leaders and other noteworthy Palestinian Arabs consistently have stressed maximalist demands. Despite occasional statements for Western consumption, the attitude of Arab leaders and officials from 1948 *to the present* has almost always demonstrated a commitment to the destruction of Israel:

"This will be a war of extermination and a momentous massacre which will be spoken of like the Mongolian massacres and the Crusades."
Arab League Sec. Gen. Azzam Pasha
May 15, 1948, the day five Arab armies
invaded the new state of Israel

"I declare a holy war, my Moslem brothers! Murder the Jews! Murder them all!"
Haj Amin al Husseini,
Mufti of Jerusalem, 1948

"The Arab nations should sacrifice up to 10 million of their 50 million people, if necessary to wipe out Israel. . . . Israel to the Arab world is like a cancer to the human body, and the only way of remedy is to uproot it, just like a cancer."
Saud ibn Abdul Aziz
King of Saudi Arabia
Associated Press, Jan. 9, 1954

"I announce from here, on behalf of the United Arab Republic people, that this time we will exterminate Israel."
President Gamal Abdel Nasser of Egypt
Speech in Alexandria, July 26, 1959

"Our basic objective will be the destruction of Israel."
President Gamal Abdel Nasser of Egypt
May 27, 1967, nine days before the
start of the Six-Day War

"The existence of Israel is an error which must be rectified. This is our opportunity to wipe out the ignominy which has

been with us since 1948. Our goal is clear—to wipe Israel off the map."

President Abdel Rahman Aref
of Iraq, May 31, 1967

"The goal of our struggle is the end of Israel, and there can be no compromise."

PLO Chairman Yasir Arafat
The Washington Post, March 29, 1970

"Israel's existence in the heart of the Arab people is an absurdity and ought to be got rid of by any means whatever."

Radio Amman (Jordan), Nov. 17, 1970

"All countries should wage war against the Zionists, who are there to destroy all human organizations and to destroy civilization and the work which good people are trying to do."

King Faisal of Saudi Arabia
Speech in Uganda.
Beirut Daily Star, Nov. 17, 1972

"Our forces continue to pressure the enemy and will continue to strike at him until we recover the occupied territory, and we will then continue until all the land is liberated."

President Hafez Assad of Syria
Radio Demascus, Oct. 16, 1973

"The battle with Israel must be such that, after it, Israel will cease to exist."

President Muammar Qaddafi of Libya
al-Usbu al-Arabi (Beirut)
quoted by *Algiers Radio*, Nov. 12, 1973

"After we perform our duty in liberating the West Bank and Jerusalem, our national duty is to liberate all the Arab occupied territories."

King Hussein of Jordan *Radio Amman*, Dec. 1, 1973

"... Palestine is not only a part of our Arab homeland, but a basic part of southern Syria."

President Hafez Assad of Syria
Radio Damascus, March 8, 1974

"If the rights of the Palestinian people are merely the establishment of a Palestinian state in the West Bank and the Gaza Strip, then what did we fight for as an Arab nation in 1967? ... We agreed on the presence of the delegation representing the PLO at the Geneva Conference ... to discuss the Palestinian people's rights, which go beyond the June 5 (1967) lines."

Zeid al-Rifai
Prime Minister of Jordan
Radio Amman, May 12, 1974

"You are the generation that will reach the sea and hoist the flag of Palestine over Tel Aviv."

PLO Chairman Yasir Arafat
Speech to guerrilla training camp
ANSA from Cairo, July 25, 1974

" . . . there is a minimal Palestinian national position. This minimum is the rejection of any recognition of the Zionist entity . . . our rejection of any settlement based on the continued existence of this foreign entity."

PFLP leader Dr. George Habash
Al-Bayrad, (Beirut), Feb. 4, 1975

"The Zionist existence in our homeland is one of those errors which human history is witness to. This error cannot continue and is bound toward demise."

Editorial in *Al-Ba'ath* (Damascus)
The official organ of the ruling
Ba'ath Party, May 2, 1975

"This racist entity in the Middle East must be destroyed and it will be destroyed one day."

Mansour Rashid Kikhia,
Libyan Ambassador to the UN
Statement to Security Council,
March 24, 1976

"The Arabs will not only demand the West Bank and the Gaza Strip, but all of the land conquered since 1948. . . . The slogan that the rights of the Palestinians be restored and Palestine liberated can have but one meaning—the elimination of Israel."

Radio Damascus, Dec. 22, 1976

"We cannot think of recognition [of Israel] because this would mean conceding a part of our lands. Our intermediate goal is the creation of an independent Palestinian state on all parts of our land that will be liberated. There have been similar developments in the world. In Vietnam for example, the Vietnamese decided on the creation of North Vietnam, and after ten years they liberated South Vietnam."

Farouk Kaddoumi, Head of the PLO's political department
Quoted on *Voice of Palestine*, July 2, 1977

"The right of self-determination in the Arab nationalist sense means the total liberation and return of all the national historical rights of the Palestinian nation in its land. . . . The right of the Palestinian nation to self-determination is expressed in the exposure and the destruction of the Zionist idea, and of Israel, which is the result of that idea."

Sami el-Atri, Secretary of the Palestinian Central Committee
Interview with Kuwaiti paper *Al-Kabas*, March 7, 1978

"Perhaps the worst result of the shameful visit [to Jerusalem] is that the 'faithful' president [Sadat] was mixed up in interpreting the word of God. . . . He praised the Jews in a manner that is contradictory to the Koran . . . The late King Faisal [of Saudi Arabia] said he has reviewed the Koran from the beginning to the end and could not find one single sentence praising the Jews. . . . Does Sadat know more about the interpretation of the Koran than King Faisal?

"I ask all sincere people in the Arab nation: Who is the man whose acrobatic policies and initiative have caused divisions in the Arab ranks? Let us tell Sadat to go to hell in order to restore Arab solidarity, stronger than ever."

Syrian Defense Minister Mustafa Tlas
Tishrin, Damascus, Feb. 6, 1978

"Sadat should understand that he will be struck down. It is his destiny. Anyone who betrays the Palestinian people will be struck down."

Yasir Arafat
Associated Press, Beirut, March 12, 1979

"Begin is in Cairo today. Do something, Egypt. Poison the Nile water that Begin will drink. Keep the grave of Abdel Nasser from Begin's sight, lest he die a second time upon seeing Begin in Cairo. Say something, Egypt. It is not important what, just do not show Begin that you are dead, that you were felled by the claws of Zionism as Palestine fell before you."

Radio Damascus, April 2, 1979

"I am confident that we shall eventually overrun Begin's own offices in both Jerusalem and Tel Aviv. Even if only one guerrilla cub survives the prolonged struggle, I am confident that he will raise the flag of Palestine over Jerusalem. . . . Jerusalem is destined to be the eternal capital of our sovereign, independent Palestinian state under the PLO leadership."

Yasir Arafat
Associated Press, Beirut, May 8, 1979

"The PLO will not become a political organization but will continue to be above all an organization for armed struggle. The PLO will not cease its attacks on Israel in favor of a diplomatic initiative."

Voice of Palestine
Lebanon, Oct. 8, 1979

"The partitioning of Palestine in 1947 and the establishment of Israel are fundamentally null and void . . . the liberation of Palestine will destroy the Zionist and imperialist presence. . . . "

The Palestine National Covenant (of the PLO)
Articles 19 and 22

"Peace for us means the destruction of Israel. We are preparing for an all-out war, a war which will last for generations. Since Jan. 1965, when Fatah was born, we have become the most dangerous enemy that Israel has. . . . We shall not rest until the day when we return to our home, and until we destroy Israel. . . ."

PLO Chairman Yasir Arafat
El Mundo, Caracas, Venezuela, Feb. 11, 1980

"Jerusalem's occupation is a deep wound bleeding in our hearts and souls. . . . We are determined to recover it and continue to pursue its recovery together with our beloved land Palestine. This, however, cannot be achieved by talking about it or by talking about peace, but through patience and sound planning and by efforts and *jihad,* and above all through unity of the word and the closing of ranks."

King Khalid of Saudi Arabia
Riyadh Domestic Service, March 8, 1980

"Machine guns and rifle bullets are the only way to reach an understanding with the Zionist enemy. Statements, protests and UN resolutions are of no avail. Only the massive use of bullets. . . . Our people cannot cease its struggle, which is carried out with bullets, machine guns and hand grenades."

Khalil al-Wazir (Abu Jihad)
Head of the military wing, Fatah
Voice of Palestine, Beirut, May 3, 1980

"The Fatah movement . . . aim is the liberation of Palestine in its entirety, and the extermination of the Zionist entity economically, politically, militarily, culturally and idealistically."

The Fourth Fatah Organization Convention
Damascus, Syria, May 31, 1980

"There has been no change whatsoever in the fundamental strategy of the PLO, which is based on the total liberation of Palestine and the destruction of the occupying country. . . . On no accounts will the Palestinians accept part of Palestine and call it the Palestinian state, while forfeiting the remaining areas which are called the State of Israel."

Rafiq Najshah, PLO Representative in Saudi Arabia
Saudi Arabian News Agency, June 9, 1980

"Do not believe that it is possible to regain Palestine and to return to Jerusalem by means of a political statement. You will not return to Palestine or raise the flag of the revolution over Jerusalem other than by means of the rifle. We will not achieve political victory so long as we do not achieve military victory. You must strengthen the iron fist around the rifle which will lead to victory."

PLO Chairman Yasir Arafat
Voice of Palestine, Beirut, June 16, 1980

"The removal of the Israeli occupation from our occupied land, Palestine, is the first and basic condition for just peace. . . . The Islamic nation and just believers in any religion or creed will not accept the situation of the land of the Prophet's flight to heaven and the cradle of prophets and divine messages being captive of Zionist occupation."

King Hussein of Jordan
Speech at the Islamic Conference
Amman Domestic Service, July 11, 1980

"The victory march will continue until the Palestinian flag flies in Jerusalem and in all of Palestine—from the Jordan River to the Mediterranean Sea and from Rosh Hanikra to Eilat."

PLO Chairman Yasir Arafat
Speech at the University of Beirut
Saut Falastin, Beirut, Dec. 7, 1980

"We shall not rest until our usurped land is liberated and until the Palestinian people return with dignity and pride to their independent state, with Jerusalem its capital."

King Fahd of Saudi Arabia
Saudi Press Agency, Riyadh, Jan. 21, 1981

"We are determined to wage a *jihad* by all the means at our disposal in order to liberate our occupied territories. . . . We assert our determination to confront aggression and pressures by all means and to make preparations for a *jihad* for the liberation of the occupied Palestinian and Arab territories."

Mecca Declaration of the Islamic Conference
Broadcast by *Riyadh Domestic Service*
Mecca, Saudi Arabia, Jan. 29, 1981

"Jordan feels the heartbeat of the Palestinian people on the occupied land. Jordan perceives Nablus and Hebron in the same manner as it perceives the Galilee and Nazareth."

Jordan's Crown Prince Hassan
Amman Radio, March 31, 1981

"I shall make it perfectly clear to you. We shall never recognize Israel, never accept the usurper, the colonialist, the imperialist. . . . We shall never allow Israel to live in peace. We shall never allow it total security. Every Israeli will feel that behind every wall there might be a guerrilla who is aiming at me. . . . "

Farouk Kaddoumi, Head of the PLO's political department
Interview in *Stern*, West Germany, July 30, 1981

"The liquidation of Israel is one of the means we adopt to achieve unity and freedom in the Arab world. We know that liberation is a long-term goal, but I am about to determine that, at the end of this year, a democratic Palestinian state will be established."

Hani al-Hassan, Political Adviser to Yasir Arafat
Speech at the American University, Beirut
An-Nahar, Beirut, Jan. 9, 1982

"**The Reagan Plan attempts to contain and to extinguish the Palestinian revolution. . . . Unfortunately, it does not deal with the refugees of 1948, and limits the right of return to the West Bank and Gaza, and not to their fundamental place in Jaffa, Haifa, and Safed. Our rights extend beyond the West Bank and Gaza . . . "**
Farouk Kaddoumi, head of the
PLO's Political Section
Al-Hadaf, Jan. 17, 1983

"**The war of attrition against the Zionist enemy will never cease. . . . It is in my interest to have a war in the region, because I believe that the only remedy for the ills of the Arab nation is a true war against the Zionist enemy.**"
PLO Chairman Yasir Arafat
Al-Destour (Lebanon)
Dec. 26, 1983

"**The truth is that anything praised by the Jews is despised, and anything that is abused by the Jews and their organizations is precious.**"
Prince Sultan, Saudi Defense Minister
Riyadh Television, Oct. 19, 1985

"**When we talk about an armed struggle, the legality of which has been acknowledged by the United Nations, we are talking about all the occupied areas of Palestine . . . It is our right to fight an enemy which occupies our land, whether this is a result of the conquest of 1967 or of the conquest of 1948.**"
Farouk Kaddoumi head of
the PLO's political section
Ouotidien de Paris, Nov. 11, 1985

"**The struggle with the Zionist enemy is not a struggle about Israel's borders, but about Israel's existence. We will never agree to anything less than the return of all our land and the establishment of the independent state.**"
Bassam Abu Sharif, a top Arafat aide
and PLO spokesman
Quoted by Kuwait News Agency, May 31, 1986

"**There are two different approaches in the Arab world: that Israel can be overwhelmed militarily or that a military victory is impossible. The power struggle between Israel and the Arabs is a long-term historical trial. Victory or defeat are for us questions of existence or annihilation, the outcome of an irreconcilable hatred.**"
Al-Riyadh, Saudi Arabia, July 11, 1986

"[I] urge the Muslims to launch jihad and to use all their capabilities to restore Muslim Palestine and the holy al-Aqsa mosque from the Zionist usurpers and aggressors. The Muslims must be united in the confrontation of the Jews and those who support them."

> King Fahd
> Quoted by the Saudi Press Agency, July 15, 1986

"...It is highly doubtful that there will be peace [in the Middle East], although there may be temporary cease-fires. As long as imperialism is there, and as long as Israel is there, it is highly doubtful that there will be peace."

> Mubari Jamal Tsurani, PLO executive
> committee member
> *Al-Qabas*, Kuwait, Oct. 27, 1986

"...We are speaking of the normalization of the West Bank, and even if we have strayed and begun to say only 'the West Bank' and we have seemingly forgotten Palestine, we must talk of Palestine and nothing less, for Palestine is our occupied homeland ... It is our right that we should have a state, and not just on paper, because this state will be an independent Palestinian state and will function as a base from which to liberate Jaffa, Akko, and all of Palestine, after which we will take Palestine and turn it into a part of the greater Arab nation."

> Salah Khalaf (Abu Iyad) number two in the PLO leadership,
> *Al-Sachrah*, Kuwait, Jan. 6, 1987

"O heroic sons of the Gaza Strip, O proud sons of the [West] Bank, O heroic sons of the Galilee, O steadfast sons of the Negev: ... the fires of revolution against these Zionist invaders will not fade out ... until our land—all our land—has been liberated from these usurping invaders."

> PLO Chairman Yasir Arafat
> PLO Radio, Baghdad, Dec. 10, 1987
> (After riots in Gaza following a fatal traffic
> accident sparked the uprising.)

"The establishment of an independent Palestinian state on the West Bank and the Gaza Strip does not contradict our ultimate strategic aim, which is the establishment of a democratic state in the entire territory of Palestine, but rather is a step in that direction."

> Salah Khalaf (Abu Iyad)
> interview with *Al-Safir*, Lebanon, Jan. 25, 1988

The Arabic press often reflects fundamental anti-Israel, even anti-Semitic attitudes—even in countries considered "moderate" toward Israel. For example, when Kurt Waldheim was elected president of Austria—after revelations of his World War II service with a Nazi army unit which committed atrocities in the Balkans and deported Jews to concentration camps—papers in Jordan and Egypt had this to say:

"Waldheim's election to the presidency is not only a personal victory for him . . . but also a festive occasion for all those who have been subjected to the Zionist travesty of justice, especially in this area of the world which has been more exposed than others to Zionist schemes." (*Al-Dustur*, Amman, July 7, 1986);

"Even the lies that Israel has waved for the past 40 years with regard to the extermination of Jews in Germany, in order to blackmail the international community, have now been exposed. The truth is that not one single Jew was killed in the gas chambers, and the latter were simply used for disinfection of the inmates' clothes. The gas could not kill people anyway, and the chambers could have never handled the amounts of people that Israel is talking about. The international community must stop Israel and hold her responsible for all her crimes so as not to allow her to grow into as destructive an entity as Naziism" (*Sawt-al-Arab*, Cairo, July 14, 1986).

During the Palestinian Arab uprising, Palestinian Arab writer Mahmoud Darwish, "cultural affairs" chief for the PLO executive committee and described by some as a moderate, published the poem "Those Who Pass Between Fleeting Words." Ten times in its 52 lines the poem told Israelis to "get out"—and take their dead with them.

Although Darwish later said he was referring only to the West Bank and Gaza Strip, Israeli poet Haim Guri responded that "the poem returns us to the true demons. It speaks truth, poems do not lie . . ." A second Israeli writer, Amos Keinan, also attacked Darwish's work: "What is so terrible is that all those thousands of Israelis, who were asleep until now and only because of the uprising started wondering if the time hadn't come to start talking with you, now may decide there is nothing to discuss with you, except through the barrel of a gun."

The uncompromising hostility reflected in the forty years' worth of Arab quotations cited above rests at least in part on a millenarian view of politics and religion. This view has been overtaken in much of the West by the Reformation and Enlightenment. But for many in the Arab-Islamic Middle East, especially during the current cycle of Islamic revivalism, Israel remains both a religious and historical crime.

For legalistic Islamic states like Saudi Arabia, Israel cannot be accepted since territory that was once controlled by Moslems must revert to Moslem rule. And for more secular Arab nationalists, like those leading the PLO, Israel's creation and growth represents an illegitimate imperialist conquest. While most Israelis grant at least some legitimacy to Palestinian Arab claims, even moderate Arabs face cultural-religious-political obstacles in acknowledging legitimate Jews claims to any part of what was Palestine.

Appendix

The PLO Covenant Against Israel

Terrorist organizations had at least 47 representatives in the 100-member Palestine National Council which rewrote the Palestine National Covenant in Cairo in 1968. The use of the word "covenant" rather than "charter" reflects the supposed national sanctity of the document. Following is the text of the covenant, interspersed with comments on various articles:

Article 1: *Palestine is the homeland of the Palestinian Arab people and an integral part of the great Arab homeland, and the people of Palestine is a part of the Arab nation.*

Article 2: *Palestine with its boundaries that existed at the time of the British Mandate is an indivisible territorial unit.*

Comment: This suggests that Palestine should not be separated into a Jewish and an Arab state, but rather should be one regional unit, including the West Bank, Gaza, and the states of Jordan and Israel.

Article 3: *The Palestinian Arab people possesses the legal right to its homeland, and, when the liberation of its homeland is completed, it will exercise self-determination solely according to its own will and choice.*

Comment: This may explain why the PLO has not yet declared a government-in-exile—it will wait until "liberation." The article claims that only the Palestinian Arabs possess a legal right to self-determination, not the Jews.

Article 4: *The Palestinian identity is an innate, persistent characteristic that does not disappear, and it is transferred from fathers to sons. The Zionist occupation, and the dispersal of the Palestinian Arab people as a result of the disasters which befell them, do not deprive it of its Palestinian identity and affiliation and do not nullify them.*

Article 5: *The Palestinians are the Arab nationals who were living permanently in Palestine until 1947, whether they were expelled from there or remained. Anyone born to a Palestinian Arab father after that, within Palestine or outside it, is a Palestinian.*

283

Article 6: *Jews who were living permanently in Palestine until the beginning of the Zionist invasion will be considered Palestinians.*

Comment: This is a crucial article. Arab literature marks the "Zionist invasion" as the year of the Balfour Declaration—1917. It is, therefore, unclear whether Jews born in Israel after 1917 would be allowed to remain. Jews who arrived in Israel after 1917, including the survivors of Hitler's tortures, and those who fled persecution in Arab lands, would certainly have to go—one way or another.

Article 7: *The Palestinian affiliation and the material, spiritual and historical tie with Palestine are indisputable realities. The upbringing of the Palestinian individual in an Arab and revolutionary fashion, the undertaking of all means of forging consciousness and training the Palestinian, in order to acquaint him profoundly with his homeland, spiritually and material, and preparing him for the conflict and the armed struggle, as well as for the sacrifice of his wealth and his life to restore his homeland, until the liberation—all this is a national duty.*
Article 8: *The phase in their history, through which the Palestinian people are now living, is that of national struggle for the liberation of Palestine. Thus, the conflicts among the Palestinian national forces are secondary, and should be ended for the sake of the basic conflict that exists between the forces of Zionism and of imperialism on the one hand, and the Palestinian Arab people on the other. On this basis the Palestinian masses, regardless of whether they are residing in the national homeland or in diaspora constitute—both their organization and the individuals—one national front working for the retrieval of Palestine and its liberation through armed struggle.*
Article 9: *Armed struggle is the only way to liberate Palestine and is therefore a strategy and not tactics. The Palestinian Arab people affirms its absolute resolution and abiding determination to pursue the armed struggle and to work for an armed popular revolution, to liberate its homeland and return to it to maintain its right to a natural life in it, and to exercise its right of self-determination in it and sovereignty over it.*

Comment: This precludes any negotiated peace or compromise with Israel. There is only one way to "liberate" Palestine—armed struggle to eliminate Israel.

Article 10: *Fedayeen action forms the nucleus of the popular Palestinian war of liberation. This demands its promotion, extension and protection, and the mobilization of all the mass and scientific capacities of the Palestinians, their organization and involvement in the armed Palestinian revolution, and cohesion in the national struggle among the various groups of the people of Palestine, and between them and the Arab masses, to guarantee the continuation of the revolution, its advancement and victory.*

Article 11: *The Palestinians will have three mottoes: national unity, national mobilization and liberation.*

Article 12: *The Palestinian people believe in Arab unity. In order to contribute their share toward the attainment of that objective, however, they must, at the present stage of their struggle, safeguard their Palestinian identity and develop their consciousness of that identity, and oppose any plan that may dissolve or impair it.*

Comment: Although article one proclaims that Palestinian Arab nationality is part of the whole Arab nation, article 12 contradictorily warns against any absorption of Palestinian Arab refugees by their Arab brethren.

Article 13: *Arab unity and the liberation of Palestine are two complementary aims. Each one paves the way for realization of the other. Arab unity leads to the liberation of Palestine, and the liberation of Palestine leads to Arab unity. Working for both goes hand in hand.*

Article 14: *The destiny of the Arab nation, indeed Arab existence, depends upon the destiny of the Palestinian cause. The endeavor and effort of the Arab nation to liberate Palestine follows from this connection. The people of Palestine assumes its vanguard role in realizing this sacred national aim.*

Article 15: *The liberation of Palestine, from an Arab viewpoint, is a national duty to repulse the Zionist, imperialist invasion from the great Arab homeland and to eliminate the Zionist presence from Palestine. Its full responsibilities fall upon the Arab nation, peoples and governments, with the Palestinian Arab people at their head.*

For this purpose, the Arab nation must mobilize all its military, human, material and spiritual capacities to participate actively with the people of Palestine in the liberation of Palestine. They must, especially in the present stage of armed Palestinian revolution, grant and offer the people of Palestine all possible help and every material and human support, and afford it every sure means and opportunity enabling it to continue to assume its vanguard role in pursuing its armed revolution until the liberation of its homeland.

Article 16: *The liberation of Palestine, from a spiritual viewpoint, will provide an atmosphere of tranquility and peace for the Holy Land, in the shade of which all the holy places will be safeguarded, and freedom of worship and visitation to all will be guaranteed, without distinction or discrimination of race, color, language or religion. For this reason, the people of Palestine looks to the support of all the spiritual forces in the world.*

Comment: This sets forth the goal of a "democratic Palestinian state" with freedom for all religions. The Sixth Congress of the Palestine National Council, meeting in Cairo in 1965, adopted this slogan for propaganda purposes only because it "met with remarkable world response." The council dropped the slogan of "throwing the Jews into the sea" which has done "grave damage to the Arab position in the past" (*minutes from the Congress*).

Article 17: *The liberation of Palestine, from a human viewpoint, will restore to the Palestinian his dignity, glory and freedom. For this, the Palestinian Arab people looks to the support of those in the world who believe in the dignity and freedom of man.*

Comment: According to Arab literature, the very existence of Israel flaws the Palestinian Arab personality and cosmically prevents the Arabs from achieving their national destiny.

Article 18: *The liberation of Palestine, from an international point of view, is a defensive action necessitated by the demands of self-defense. Accordingly, the Palestinian people, desirous as they are of the friendship of all people, looks to freedom-loving, justice-loving and peace-loving states for support in order to restore their legitimate rights in Palestine, to reestablish peace and security in the country, and to enable its people to exercise national sovereignty and freedom.*

Article 19: *The partitioning of Palestine in 1947 and the establishment of Israel are fundamentally null and void, whatever time has elapsed, because they were contrary to the wish of the people of Palestine and its natural right to its homeland, and contradict the principles embodied in the Charter of the United Nations, the first of which is the right of self-determination.*

Comment: This reiterates rejection of Jewish self-determination. In truth, the Arab armies voided the United Nations partition when they invaded the Palestinian Jewish state, Israel, in 1948.

Article 20: *The Balfour Declaration, the Mandate Document, and everything based upon them are deemed null and void. The claim of historical or religious ties between Jews and Palestine does not tally with historical realities nor with the constituents of statehood in their true sense. Judaism, in its character as a religion, is not a nationality with an independent existence. Likewise, the Jews are not one people with an independent identity. They are rather citizens of the states to which they belong.*

Comment: Palestinian Arab chauvinism denies the very right of self-determination of Jews in what was Palestine that Arabs there claim for themselves. The PLO claims that Jews are not a people, but only members of a religion.

Article 21: *The Palestinian Arab people, in expressing itself through the armed Palestinian revolution, rejects every solution that is a substitute for a complete liberation of Palestine, and rejects all plans that aim at the settlement of the Palestine issue or its internationalization.*

Comment: The PLO, through intimidation and murder, has largely silenced moderate Palestinian Arabs who might negotiate a peaceful resolution of the conflict. Here it seeks to foreclose any settlement based on compromise.

Article 22: *Zionism is a political movement organically related to world imperialism and hostile to all movements of liberation and progress in the world. It is a racist and fanatical movement in its formation; aggressive, expansionist and colonialist in its aims, and fascist and Nazi in its methods. Israel is the tool of the Zionist movement and a human and geographical base for world imperialism. It is a concentration and jumping-off point for imperialism in the heart of the Arab homeland, to strike at the hopes of the Arab nation for liberation, unity and progress.*

Israel is a constant threat to peace in the Middle East and the entire world. Since the liberation of Palestine will destroy the Zionist and imperialist presence and bring about the stabilization of peace in the Middle East, the people of Palestine looks to the support of all liberal men of the world and all the forces of good, progress and peace; and implores all of them, regardless of their different leanings and orientations, to offer all help and

287

support to the people of Palestine in its just and legal struggle to liberate its homeland.

Comment: Zionism here is castigated as an enemy of the world, not just of the Arabs or the Palestinians. Arab literature portrays Israel as a member of an imperialist plot to subjugate the Third World, and Israelis as followers of the czarist forgery, *The Protocols of the Elders of Zion*.

Article 23: *The demands of security and peace and the requirements of truth and justice oblige all states that preserve friendly relations among peoples and maintain the loyalty of citizens to their homelands to consider Zionism an illegitimate movement and to prohibit its existence and activity.*

Comment: This calls on Third World nations to support the Palestinian battle against "illegitimate" Israel. The PLO has received support, in one form or another, from the Soviet Union, Libya, China, Vietnam, Cuba and terrorist groups such as the Baader-Meinhof gang and the Japanese Red Army.

Article 24: *The Palestinian Arab people believes in the principles of justice, freedom, sovereignty, self-determination, human dignity and the right of peoples to exercise them.*

Comment: Yet, the PLO would deny these rights to the Jews in Israel. By its primary reliance on terror, it has long denied them to Palestinian Arabs.

Article 25: *For the realization of the goals of this Charter and its principles, the Palestine Liberation Organization will perform its role in the liberation of Palestine in accordance with the Constitution of this Organization.*

Article 26: *The Palestine Liberation Organization, which represents the forces of the Palestinian revolution, is responsible for the movement of the Palestinian Arab people in its struggle to restore its homeland, liberate it, return to it and exercise the right of self-determination in it. This responsibility extends to all military, political and financial matters, and all else that the Palestine issue requires in the Arab and international spheres.*

Comment: The PLO assumes leadership as the umbrella organization for all Palestinian terrorist groups engaged in the struggle against Israel.

Article 27: *The Palestine Liberation Organization will cooperate with all Arab states, each according to its capacities, and* *will maintain neutrality in their mutal relations in the light of, and on the basis of, requirements of the battle of liberation, and will not interfere in the internal affairs of any Arab state.*

Comment: PLO subversion in Jordan and Lebanon wrought chaos, and in the case of Lebanon was responsible for national disintegration.

Article 28: *The Palestinian Arab people insists upon the originality and independence of its national revolution and rejects every manner of interference, trusteeship and subordination.*

Comment: The Palestinian Arab liberation movement claims that it does not serve as a tool for Arab governments, but the PLO was called into being by Arab governments and it has not refused their largesse in the form of arms, money and logistical support.

Article 29: *The Palestinian Arab people possesses the fundamental and genuine right in liberating and restoring its homeland and will define its position with reference to all states and powers on the basis of their positions with reference to the issue of Palestine and the extent of their support for the Palestinian Arab people in its revolution to realize its aims.*

Comment: This legitimizes Palestinian terror attacks on countries friendly to Israel. Surrendering to this blatant threat, European governments have freed virtually all Arab terrorists caught in their countries.

Article 30: *The fighters and bearers of arms in the battle of liberation are the nucleus of the popular army, which will be the protecting arm of the gains of the Palestinian Arab people.*

Article 31: *The organization shall have a flag, an oath of allegiance and an anthem. All this shall be decided upon in accordance with special regulation.*

Article 32: *To this covenant is attached a law known as the fundamental law of the Palestine Liberation Organization, in which is determined the manner of the organization's formation, its committees, its institutions, the special functions of every one of them and all the requisite duties associated with them in accordance with this covenant.*

Article 33: *This Chapter shall not be amended save by [vote of] two-thirds of the total membership of the National Congress of the Palestine Liberation Organization [taken] at a special session convened for that purpose.*

MYTH

"The Palestine National Covenant of 1968 has been superseded by resolutions passed by recent Palestine National Councils. These resolutions show that the PLO has moved away from the extreme ideas of the Covenant toward genuine moderation."

FACT

This is a classic example of Palestinian dissimulation for Western consumption. Every program adopted by the PNC since 1968 has made a reaffirmation of the Covenant its first order of business. As the texts of the Ten Point Program (1974) and Fifteen Point Program (1977) show, PNC programs derive directly from the Covenant and are sanctioned by it.

This practice has not changed. The resolutions of the 18th PNC (April 26, 1987) have been characterized by the PLO's defenders as moderate. Yet the very first lines of the 18th PNC resolutions read:

"Proceeding from the Palestinian National Covenant and in harmony with the PNC resolutions, we emphasize the following principles as a basis for the Palestinian national action within the framework of the PLO, the sole legitimate representative of the Palestinian Arab people."

Ten Points for War

On June 8, 1974, the Palestine National Council met in Cairo to draft principles to guide the PLO's diplomacy. this resolution, known as the Ten Point Program, is often presented as evidence of PLO moderation. As the text shows (interpersed with comments in bold print), the Ten Point Program is both deceptive and militant.

Preamble

Proceeding from the Palestinian National Charter and the PLO's political program which was approved during the 11th session of the PNC held from 3 to 12 January 1973, believing in the impossibility of the establishment of a durable and just peace in the area without the restoration to our Palestinian people of all their national rights, foremost of which is their right to return to and determine their fate on all their national soil, and in the light of the study of the political circumstances which arose during the period between the Council's previous and current sessions, the Council decides the following:

Comment: The first words of the Ten Points reaffirm the PLO's adherence to the extremist Palestine National Covenant that calls for Israel's destruction. The preamble clearly defines what "all the national rights" of the Palestinian people means to the PLO: the right of Palestinian refugees to return to Israel, to overwhelm it by their numbers and to establish an Arab state in Gaza, the West Bank and Israel. This directly contradicts the putative moderation of Point 2 (below).

The Ten Points

1. The assertion of the PLO position regarding Resolution 242 is that it obliterates the patriotic and national rights of our people and deals with our people's cause as a refugee problem. Therefore, dealing with this resolution on this basis is rejected on any level of Arab and international dealings, including the Geneva conference.

Comment: The PLO has always rejected Security Council Resolution 242, which is the recognized basis for Arab-Israel peace. This rejection remains in effect to this day. It is this clause that determines the PLO's official position on Resolution 242. So long as this clause remains unamended, statements by Palestinian leaders claiming acceptance of 242 have no validity.

2. The PLO will struggle by all means, foremost of which is armed struggle, to liberate Palestinian land and to establish the people's national, independent and fighting authority on every part of Palestinian land to be liberated. This necessitates making more changes in the balance of power in favor of our people and their struggle.

Comment: This clause is often presented as evidence of the PLO's moderation because it suggests that the PLO would accept a state in less than all of Palestine. But the dishonesty of this claim is apparent. This point reaffirms the PLO's commitment to guerrilla war and to terrorism and its rejection of diplomacy. It defines the state to be achieved as a "fighting authority." The PLO later changed its original English translation of this term to the more

ambiguous "militant authority." The original Arabic and its unambiguous meaning remain the same. In the context of Points 3 and 8 (below), this clause cannot be interpreted as being moderate.

3. The PLO will struggle against any plan for the establishment of a Palestinian entity, the price of which is recognition, conciliation, secure borders, renunciation of the national right and our people's deprivation of their right to return and their right to determine their fate on their national soil.

Comment: The word "entity" in this context has the connotation of a truncated state. It refers specifically to a West Bank and Gaza state permanently confined within those borders. As points 2 and 3 make clear, the PLO would accept the tactical advantage of having a West Bank and Gaza state, but the organization would use that state as a base for further attack on Israel. The PLO rejects the idea that acceptance of a West Bank and Gaza state would mean "recognition, conciliation, secure borders" with Israel. It reasserts again its commitment to the Palestinian national right to an Arab state in all of Palestine.

4. Any liberation step that is achieved constitutes a step for continuing to achieve the PLO strategy for the establishment of the Palestinian democratic state that is stipulated in the resolution of the previous councils.

Comment: Certain Palestinian terrorist organizations, such as the Popular Front for the Liberation of Palestine, have always opposed the idea of any interim steps before the total destruction of Israel. For this reason, they objected to the idea of a West Bank and Gaza fighting authority. They continue to oppose a Palestinian government-in-exile for the same reason. In this clause, Arafat assures the PFLP and the Arab governments that any West Bank and Gaza state will not mean a departure from the goals established in previous PNC resolutions, i.e., the destruction of the Jewish state as demanded in the Palestine National Covenant.

5. To struggle with the Jordanian national forces for the establishment of a Jordanian-Palestinian national front whose aim is the establishment of a national democratic government in Jordan—a government that will cohere with the Palestinian entity to be established as a result of the struggle.

Comment: This clause makes clear that the West Bank and Gaza state would be used as a base of attack on the Hashemites and King Hussein, as well as Israel. The PLO asserts that once the Jordanian monarchy is overthrown, Jordan's resources will be enlisted for an enlarged assault upon Israel.

6. The PLO will strive to establish a unity of struggle between the two peoples [Palestinian and Jordanian] and among all the Arab liberation movement forces that agree on this program.

7. In light of this program, the PLO will struggle to strengthen national unity and elevate it to a level that will enable it to carry out its duties and its patriotic and national tasks.

8. The Palestinian national authority, after its establishment, will struggle for the unity of the confrontation state for the sake of completing the liberation of all Palestinian soil and as a step on the path of comprehensive Arab unity.

Comment: This point disproves the claim that the PLO would be satisfied with a West Bank and Gaza state. As the PLO sees it, the West Bank and Gaza state would be a nucleus around which a renewed pan-Arab attack on Israel would coalesce. The objective of this attack would be the fulfillment of the PLO's platform, the completion of the conquest of all of former Palestine, and the dismantling of the Jewish state.

9. The PLO will struggle to strengthen its solidarity with the socialist countries and the world forces of liberation and progress to foil all Zionist, reactionary and imperialist schemes.

Comment: This point is more than a simple appeal to the Soviet bloc and the Third World for assistance. It also sheds light on the PLO's view of the world, a paranoid and violent environment teeming with conspiracies. In this revealing psychological context, the PLO does not appear quite so moderate.

10. In light of this program, the revolutionary command will work out the tactics that will serve and lead to the achievement of these aims.

A recommendation has been added to the political program. The recommendation stipulates that the Executive Committee implement this program. Should a fateful situation connected with the future of the Palestinian people arise, the Council will be called to hold a special session to decide on it.

Comment: Article 10 and its attached addendum almost destroyed the Council meetings. Arafat tried to change his own wording, seeking to add a mandate for "the leadership of the revolution to use the necessary tactic" for "the liberation of Palestine." The PFLP, PFLP-GC and ALF revolted against what they perceived as Arafat's attempt to secure freedom of action and total executive power.

TEXT OF SECURITY COUNCIL RESOLUTION 242, NOV. 22, 1967

The Security Council,

Expressing its continuing concern with the grave situation in the Middle East,

Emphasizing the inadmissibility of the acquisition of territory by war and the need to work for a just and lasting peace in which every State in the area can live in security,

Emphasizing further that all Member States in their acceptance of the Charter of the United Nations have undertaken a commitment to act in accordance with Article 2 of the Charter,

1. *Affirms* that the fulfillment of Charter principles requires the establishment of a just and lasting peace in the Middle East which should include the application of both the following principles:

(i)   Withdrawal of Israeli armed forces from territories occupied in the recent conflict;

(ii)   Termination of all claims or states of belligerency and respect for and acknowledgement of the sovereignty, territorial integrity and political independence of every State in the area and their right to live in peace within secure and recognized boundaries free from threats or acts of force;

2. *Affirms further* the necessity

(a)   For guarateeing freedom of navigation through international waterways in the area;

(b)   For achieving a just settlement of the refugee problem;

(c)   For guaranteeing the territorial inviolability and political independence of every State in the area, through measures including the establishment of demilitarized zones;

3. *Requests* the Secretary General to designate a Special Representative to proceed to the Middle East to establish and maintain contacts with the states concerned in order to promote agreement and assist efforts to achieve a peaceful and accepted settlement in accordance with the provisions and principles in this resolution;

4. *Requests* the Secretary-General to report to the Security Council on the progress of the efforts of the Special Representative as soon as possible.

TEXT OF SECURITY COUNCIL RESOLUTION 338, OCT. 22, 1973

The Security Council,

1. *Calls upon* all parties to present fighting to cease all firing and terminate all military activity immediately, no later than 12 hours after the moment of the adoption of this decision, in the positions they now occupy;

2. *Calls upon* all parties concerned to start immediately after the cease-fire the implementation of Security Council Resolution 242 (1967) in all of its parts;

3. *Decides* that, immediately and concurrently with the cease-fire, negotiations start between the parties concerned under appropriate auspices aimed at establishing a just and durable peace in the Middle East.

SEPTEMBER 1975 U.S. COMMITMENT ON THE PLO

As part of the 1975 Sinai Disengagement Agreement, the United States and Israel signed a six-point Memorandum of Agreement. The document dealt with procedures on negotiations and the Geneva peace conference. Point two, reprinted here, states U.S. policy on negotiations with the PLO.

The United States will continue to adhere to its present policy with respect to the Palestine Liberation Organization, whereby it will not recognize or negotiate with the Palestine Liberation Organization so long as the Palestine Liberation Organization does not recognize Israel's right to exist and does not accept Security Council Resolutions 242 and 338. The United States Government will consult fully and seek to concert its position and strategy at the Geneva peace conference on this issue with the Government of Israel. Similarly, the United States will consult fully and seek to concert its position and strategy with Israel with regard to the participation of any other additional states. It is understood that the participation at a subsequent phase of the conference of any possible additional state, group or organization will require the agreement of all the initial participants.

THE CAMP DAVID FRAMEWORKS

Following are the texts of the two agreements signed by President Sadat of Egypt and Prime Minister Begin of Israel—and witnessed by President Carter—at the White House on September 17, 1978.

A FRAMEWORK FOR PEACE IN THE MIDDLE EAST
AGREED AT CAMP DAVID

Muhammad Anwar al-Sadat, President of the Arab Republic of Egypt, and Menachem Begin, Prime Minister of Israel, met with Jimmy Carter, President of the United States of America, at Camp David from September 5 to September 17, 1978, and have agreed on the following framework for peace in the Middle East. They invite other parties to the Arab-Israel conflict to adhere to it.

Preamble

The search for peace in the Middle East must be guided by the following:

● The agreed basis for a peaceful settlement of the conflict between Israel and its neighbors is United Nations Security Council Resolution 242, in all its parts.

● After four wars during 30 years, despite intensive human efforts, the Middle East, which is the cradle of civilization and the birthplace of three great religions, does not enjoy the blessings of peace. The people of the Middle East yearn for peace so that the vast human and natural resources of the region can be turned to the pursuits of peace and so that this area can become a model for coexistence and cooperation among nations.

● The historic initiative of President Sadat in visiting Jerusalem and the reception accorded to him by the parliament, government and people of Israel, and the reciprocal visit of Prime Minister Begin to Ismailia, the peace proposals made by both leaders, as well as the warm reception of these missions by the peoples of both countries, have created an unprecedented opportunity for peace which must not be lost if this generation and future generations are to be spared the tragedies of war.

● The provisions of the Charter of the United Nations and the other accepted norms of international law and legitimacy now provide accepted standards for the conduct of relations among all states.

● To achieve a relationship of peace, in the spirit of Article 2 of the United Nations Charter, future negotiations between Israel and any neighbor prepared to negotiate peace and security with it are necessary for the purpose of carrying out all the provisions and principles of Resolutions 242 and 338.

● Peace requires respect for the sovereignty, territorial integrity and political independence of every state in the area and their right to live in peace within secure and recognized boundaries free from threats or acts of force. Progress toward that goal can accelerate movement toward a new era of reconciliation in the Middle East marked by cooperation in promoting economic development, in maintaining stability and in assuring security.

● Security is enhanced by a relationship of peace and by cooperation between nations which enjoy normal relations. In addition, under the terms of peace treaties, the parties can, on the basis of reciprocity, agree to special security arrangements such as demilitarized zones, limited armaments areas, early warning stations, the presence of international forces, liaison, agreed measures for monitoring and other arrangements that they agree are useful.

Framework

Taking these factors into account, the parties are determined to reach a just, comprehensive, and durable settlement of the Middle East conflict through the conclusion of peace treaties based on Security Council Resolutions 242 and 338 in all their parts. Their purpose is to achieve peace and good neighborly relations. They recognize that for peace to endure, it must involve all those who have been most deeply affected by the conflict. They therefore agree that this framework, as appropriate, is intended by them to constitute a basis for peace not only between Egypt and Israel, but also between Israel and each of its other neighbors which is prepared to negotiate peace with Israel on this basis. With that objective in mind, they have agreed to proceed as follows:

A. West Bank and Gaza

1. Egypt, Israel, Jordan and the representatives of the Palestinian people should participate in negotiations on the resolution of the Palestinian problem in all its aspects. To achieve that objective, negotiations relating to the West Bank and Gaza should proceed in three stages:

(a) Egypt and Israel agree that, in order to ensure a peaceful and orderly transfer of authority, and taking into account the security concerns of all the parties, there should be transitional arrangements for the West Bank and Gaza for a period not exceeding five years. In order to provide full autonomy to the inhabitants, under these arrangements the Israeli military government and its civilian administration will be withdrawn as soon as a self-governing authority has been freely elected by the inhabitants of these areas to replace the existing military government. To negotiate the details of a transitional arrangement, Jordan will be invited to join the negotiations on the basis of this framework. These new arrangements should give due consideration both to the principle of self-government by the inhabitants of these territories and to the legitimate security concerns of the parties involved.

(b) Egypt, Israel, and Jordan will agree on the modalities for establishing elected self-governing authority in the West Bank and Gaza. The delegations of Egypt and Jordan may include Palestinians from the West Bank and Gaza or other Palestinians as mutually agreed. The parties will negotiate an agreement which will define the powers and responsibilities of the self-governing authority to be exercised in the West Bank and Gaza. A withdrawal of Israeli armed forces will take place and there will be a redeployment of the remaining Israeli forces into specified security locations. The agreement will also include arrangements for assuring internal and external security and public order. A strong local police force will be established, which may include Jordanian citizens. In addition, Israeli and Jordanian forces will participate in joint patrols and in the manning of control posts to assure the security of the borders.

(c) When the self-governing authority (administrative council) in the West Bank and Gaza is established and inaugurated, the transitional period of five years will begin. As soon as possible, but not later than the third year after the beginning of the transitional period, negotiations will take place to determine the final status of the West Bank and Gaza and its relationship with its neighbors, and to conclude a peace treaty between Israel and Jordan by the end of the transitional period. These negotiations will be conducted among Egypt, Israel, Jordan, and the elected representatives of the inhabitants of the West Bank and Gaza. Two separate but related committees will be convened, one committee, consisting of representatives of the four parties which will negotiate and agree on the final status of the West Bank and Gaza, and its relationship with its neighbors, and the second committee, consisting of representatives of Israel and representatives of Jordan to be joined by the elected representatives of the inhabitants of the West Bank and Gaza, to negotiate the peace treaty between Israel and Jordan, taking into account the agreement reached on the final status of the West Bank and Gaza. The negotiations shall be based on all the provisions and principlpes of UN Security Council Resolution 242. The negotiations will resolve, among other mattters, the location of the boundaries and the nature of the security arrangements. The solution from the negotiations must also recognize the legitimate rights of the Palestinian peoples and their just requirements. In this way, the Palestinians will participate in the determination of their own future through:

1) The negotiations among Egypt, Israel, Jordan and the representatives of the inhabitants of the West Bank and Gaza to agree on the final status of the West Bank and Gaza and other outstanding issues by the end of the transitional period.

2) Submitting their agreement to a vote by the elected representatives of the inhabitants of the West Bank and Gaza.

3) Providing for the elected representatives of the inhabitants of the West Bank and Gaza to decide how they shall govern themselves consistent with the provisions of their agreement.

4) Participating as stated above in the work of the committee negotiating the peace treaty between Israel and Jordan.

2. All necessary measures will be taken and provisions made to assure the security of Israel and its neighbors during the transitional period and beyond. To assist in providing such security, a strong local police force will be constituted by the self-governing authority. It will be composed of inhabitants of the West Bank and Gaza. The police will maintain liaison on internal security matters with the

designated Israeli, Jordanian, and Egyptian officers.

3. During the transitional period, representatives of Egypt, Israel, Jordan, and the self-governing authority will constitute a continuing committee to decide by agreement on the modalities of admission of persons displaced from the West Bank and Gaza in 1967, together with necessary measures to prevent disruption and disorder. Other matters of common concern may also be dealt with by this committee.

4. Egypt and Israel will work with each other and with other interested parties to establish agreed procedures for a prompt, just and permanent implementation of the resolution of the refugee problem.

B. Egypt-Israel

1. Egypt and Israel undertake not to resort to the threat or the use of force to settle disputes. Any disputes shall be settled by peaceful means in accordance with the provisions of Article 33 of the UN Charter.

2. In order to achieve peace between them, the parties agree to negotiate in good faith with a goal of concluding within three months from the signing of the Framework a peace treaty between them while inviting the other parties to the conflict to proceed simultaneously to negotiate and conclude similar peace treaties with a view to achieving a comprehensive peace in the area. The Framework for the Conclusion of a Peace Treaty between Egypt and Israel will govern the peace negotiations between them. The parties will agree on the modalities and the timetable for the implementation of their obligations under the treaty.

C. Associated Principles

1. Egypt and Israel state that the principles and provisions described below should apply to peace treaties between Israel and each of its neighbors—Egypt, Jordan, Syria and Lebanon.

2. Signatories shall establish among themselves relationships normal to states at peace with one another. To this end, they should undertake to abide by all the provisions of the UN Charter. Steps to be taken in this respect include:

(a) full recognition;

(b) abolishing economic boycotts;

(c) guaranteeing that under their jurisdiction the citizens of the other parties shall enjoy the protection of the due process of law.

3. Signatories should explore possibilities for economic development in the context of final peace treaties, with the objective of contributing to the atmosphere of peace, cooperation and friendship which is their common goal.

4. Claims commissions may be established for the mutual settlement of all financial claims.

5. The United States shall be invited to participate in the talks on matters related to the modalities of the implementation of the agreements and working out the timetable for the carrying out of the obligations of the parties.

6. The United Nations Security Council shall be requested to endorse the peace treaties and ensure that their provisions shall not be violated. The permanent members of the Security Council shall be requested to underwrite the peace treaties and ensure respect for the provisions. They shall be requested to conform their policies and actions with the undertaking contained in this Framework.

For the Government of the
Arab Republic of Egypt:
Muhammad Anwar al-Sadat

For the Government
of Israel:
Menachem Begin

Witnessed by:
Jimmy Carter, President of the United States of America

THE ARAB WORLD VERSUS ISRAEL

Country	Leaders	Land Area (sq. miles)	Population (Millions)	Literacy Percent	Life Expectancy (years)	Estimated GNP/GDP (billions)	Annual Defense Expenditure	Combat Aircraft	Tanks	Armed Forces
Algeria	Pres. Chedli Benjedid	919,590	20.9	52	60	1985 GDP $57b	$ 1.24b	391	910	169,000
Bahrain	Amir Isa bin Sulman al Khalifa	240	0.4	40	67.4	1984 GDP $ 4.6b	137.5m	17	60	2,800
Djibouti	Pres. Hassan Gouled Aptidon	8,800	0.3	20	50	1986 GDP $344	30m			4,230
Iraq	Pres. Saddam Hussein	167,900	15.0	50	56.1	1986 GNP $35b	11.5b	600	5,000	1,000,000
Jordan	King Hussein Crown Prince Hassan	37,800	3.3	71	61.7	1984 GNP $ 4.9b	830.1m	133	986	80,300
Kuwait	Amir Jabir al Ahmed al Sabah	6,900	1.7	71	72	1986 GDP $19.7b	1.42b	61	266	15,000
Libya	Pres. Muammar Qaddafi	680,000	3.4	55	57.5	1986 GDP $20b	1.29b	596	3,000	76,500
Mauritania	Pres. Col. Maaculya Ould Sid Ahmed Ould Tayá	398,000	1.8	17	45.5	1985 GNP $800m	47m			14,800
Morocco	King Hassan II	270,000	21.6	28	54	1985 GDP $11.9b	848.6m	141	220	203,500
Oman	Sultan Qabus Hon Said	120,000	1.1	20	62.5	1985 GDP $ 9.0b	1.5b	53	75	22,000
Qatar	Amir Khalifa bin Hamad Al Thani	4,247	.25	40	72	1987 GNP $ 6.4b	2.3b	26	24	7,000
Saudi Arabia	King Fahd Crown Prince Abdullah	830,000	10.4	52	54	1985 GDP $133.6b	17.5b	226	550	73,500

Country	Leader	Area	Population	% Urban	Literacy	GDP/GNP	Defense Budget			Armed Forces
Somalia	Pres. Mohammed Siad Barre	246,000	5.4	60	43.9	1982 GDP $ 1.4b	134.2m	71	273	65,000
Sudan	P.M. Sadiq al-Mahdi	967,000	20.9	20	47	1984 GDP $ 7.31b	740m	43	135	58,500
Syria	Pres. Hafez Assad	71,600	9.9	47	66.2	1985 GDP $21.46b	4.0b	650	4,100	407,500
Tunisia	Pres. Zine el Abidine Benali	63,000	7.0	62	61.5	1985 GNP $ 9.0b	525m	31	173	42,100
United Arab Emirates	Pres. Emir Zaid bin Sultan al Nuhayyan	22,300	1.6	68	70.5	1986 GDP $24b	1.8b	72	216	45,000
Yemen Arab Republic (North)	Pres. Ali Abdullah Saleh	75,290	7.0	15	38	1984 GDP $ 3.1b	413.7m	73	683	36,800
People's Dem. Rep. of Yemen (South)	Pres. Haydar Abu Bakr al-Atlas	130,000	2.2	25	41.5	1985 GNP $ 1.1b	194m	70	470	27,500
Arab League Total		5,022,782	134.15	43	57	370b	42.5b	3,254	17,141	2,351,030
Egypt	Pres. Hosni Mubarak	387,000	51.9	40	60	1985 GDP $21.2b	5.2b	587	2,300	453,000
Lebanon	Pres. Amin Gemayel	4,015	2.6	75	65	1983 GDP $ 5.3b	229m	5	150	30,000
Israel	Pres. Chaim Herzog P.M. Yitzhak Shamir	8,290	4.2	79	72.1	1986 GNP $27b	5.1b	676	3,900	170,000
West Bank		5,860 km	.969			1983 GNP $ 1.1b				
Gaza Strip		380 km	.56			1983 GNP $ 5.5b				

Sources: *The Military Balance, 1987-1988,* The International Institute for Strategic Studies
Country Reports on Human Rights Practices for 1987 U.S. Department of State
The World Factbook, 1987 U.S. Central Intelligence Agency
The Middle East & North Africa 1987, Europe
The Middle East Review, 1987

Index to
Myths & Facts, 1989

East Policy, 216-235; Saudi Arabia, relations with, 248-258; Strategic Petroleum Reserve, 251

United Nations Relief and Works Administration (UNWRA) (see also United Nations Agencies and Programs) 115; contributions, chart, 117; 1986 report, 120; refugee, definition of, 8

Uruguay, 21, 215

V

Vance, Cyrus, 76

Vanly, Ismet Cheriff, 161

Vatikiotis, P.J., *The History of Egypt*, 157

Venezuela, 102, 215, 248-249

Vietnam, 116, 135, 275, North Vietnam, 60, 81

Voice of Palestine, 275, 276, 277

Voice of the Arabs (Egypt), 37

W

Waldheim, Kurt, 55, 99, 281

Wall Street Journal, 49, 135, 258

Walters, Vernon, 102

Washington Post, 49, 67, 102, 134, 158, 180, 199, 210, 232, 237, 245, 283, 269, 274

Washington Jewish Week, 241

Washington Star, 160

Wau, Sudan, 163

Weinberger, Casper, 235

Weir, Rev. Benjamin, 235

Weizmann, Dr. Chaim, 4

West Bank, 23, 66, 67, 70, 72, 75-79, 124, 132, 214; infant mortality, 188; Israeli occupation, 177-202;

seizure by Transjordan, 1948, 15; strategic importance, 82-83

Western Wall, 204, 207, 211

White Paper, restricting Jewish immigration, 8

Will, George, 215

Wilson, Woodrow, 217, 218

World Organization of Jews from Arab Countries (WOJAC), 50

World Health Organization (*Who*), 187, 188

World Refugees, 116

World War I, 4, 7, 8, 13, 74, 79, 219

World War II, 7, 8, 21, 27, 81, 116, 122, 218

Y

Yamani, Sheik Ahmed Zaki, 253, 258

Yavne, 12

Ye'or, Bat, *The Dhimmi: Jews and Christians Under Islam*, 141

Yediot Acharonot, 149

Yemen, 3, 36, 140, 149, 150, 163, 164; Jews in, 149, 150

Yiftach, 109

Young, Andrew, 17

Yugoslavia, 21, 48, 116, 135, 186

Z

Zahrani River, 91

Zaire, 20, 162, 163

Zarzis, 150

Zayyad, Tawfik, 172, 242

The Zionist Revolution, Harold Fisch, 11

Zionism, 4, 5, 12, 18, 19, 217; defined, 2, 3; UN Resolution, 100, 101